P9-DEH-848

Building Custodian
Building Superintendent
Custodian Engineer

Edited by

*Hy Hammer, Chief of
Examining Service Division
New York City Department
of Personnel, (Ret.)*

and

*Robert Padula
Supervising Building Superintendent*

Prentice Hall
New York • London • Toronto • Sydney • Tokyo • Singapore

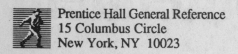

Prentice Hall General Reference
15 Columbus Circle
New York, NY 10023

An Arco Book

Arco, Prentice Hall, and colophons are
registered trademarks of Simon & Schuster, Inc.

Library of Congress Cataloging-in-Publication Data

Building custodian, building superintendent, custodian engineer /
    edited by Hy Hammer and Robert Padula.—8th ed.
        p.   cm.
ISBN 0-671-86851-9
    1. Janitors—Examinations, questions, etc. 2. Civil service—
United States—Examinations. I. Hammer, Hy. II. Padula, Robert.
III. Arco Publishing.
TX339.B85   1990
648'.076—dc20   89-48919
                                                           CIP

Manufactured in the United States of America

3   4   5   6   7   8   9   10

CONTENTS

WHAT THIS BOOK WILL DO FOR YOU

ARCO has followed testing trends and methods ever since the firm was founded in 1937. We specialize in books that prepare people for tests. Based on this experience, we have prepared the best possible book to help *you* score high.

To write this book we carefully analyzed every detail surrounding the forthcoming examination:

- the job itself

- official and unofficial announcements concerning the examination

- all the previous examinations, many not available to the public

- related examinations

- technical literature that explains and forecasts the examination

Can You Prepare Yourself For Your Test?

You want to pass this test. That's why you bought this book. Used correctly, your "self-tutor" will show you what to expect and will give you a speedy brush-up on the subjects tested in your exam. Some of these are subjects not taught in schools at all. Even if your study time is very limited, you should:

- Become familiar with the type of examination you will have.

- Improve your general examination-taking skill.

- Improve your skill in analyzing and answering questions involving reasoning, judgment, comparison, and evaluation.

- Improve your speed and skill in reading and understanding what you read—an important part of your ability to learn and an important part of most tests.

This book will tell you exactly what to study by presenting in full every type of question you will get on the actual test.

This book will help you find your weaknesses. Once you know what subjects you're weak in, you can get right to work and concentrate on those areas. This kind of selective study yields maximum test results.

This book will give you the *feel* of the exam. Almost all our sample and practice questions are taken from actual previous exams. On the day of the exam you'll see how closely this book follows the format of the real test.

This book will give you confidence *now*, while you are preparing for the test. It will build your self-confidence as you proceed and will prevent the kind of test anxiety that causes low test scores.

This book stresses the multiple-choice type of question because that's the kind you'll have on your test. You must not be satisfied with merely knowing the correct answer for each question. You must find out why the other choices are incorrect. This will help you remember a lot you thought you had forgotten.

After testing yourself, you may find that you are weak in a particular area. You should concentrate on improving your skills by using the specific practice sections in this book that apply to you.

How to Use This Book

Buying this book was a good first step toward landing your custodial job. Now you must use it well so as to score near the top of the list and get your new job as soon as possible.

Make a point of setting aside some time every day for your preparation. It is best to study at the same time each day to develop good study habits, but if that is impossible, at least be sure to study every day. Clear a well-lighted work space for yourself in a place where you will not be distracted by family affairs. Leave the television off.

You do not have to work through this book from page one to the end, but do begin at the beginning. Read the information about the work that custodians do and study the job announcements. Get yourself "psyched" so that you will want to study and do well. Learn how to take a multiple-choice, machine-scored exam. Then you can try the exams and quizzes in any order.

You will note that the time allotted to the full-length exams is 3½ hours. In order to get practice in answering the exam under "battle conditions" you should try to do one whole exam at one sitting. On days when your time is limited, work on quizzers and read the instructional material. On days when you can devote the longer stretches of time, tackle the actual exams. If you must divide an exam into two sittings, be sure the total time does not exceed the time allowed. You are not being scored on these practice exams. They are strictly for your own benefit, so you want to get the greatest possible value from them.

Time yourself accurately. Do not peek at the answers until you have completed an entire exam. Then check your answers against the correct answers we have provided. Go on to study the answer explanations. Do not limit yourself to explanations for the answers you got wrong. Read through all the explanations. You can learn from the thinking behind the correct answers even when you got the answer right. Work on pacing yourself so that you have time to read and think about every question. While there is no harm in guessing to answer all the questions at the end, your chances of getting more answers right increase as you think about and answer the questions intelligently.

By the time you have read the text, taken all the quizzers, and answered all seven exams, you should be ready for the actual exam. You should understand the procedures and should be able to pace yourself to use the time effectively. On exam day, be confident. You are well prepared. You will do well.

THE KIND OF WORK YOU WILL BE DOING

Building Custodians

NATURE OF THE WORK

Building custodians—sometimes called janitors or cleaners—maintain schools, hospitals, office buildings, apartment houses, and government buildings.

Custodial workers see that heating and ventilating equipment work properly, keep the building clean and orderly, and do other tasks that keep a building in good condition. On a typical day, a custodian may wet- or dry-mop floors, vacuum carpets, clean furniture and other equipment, make minor repairs, and exterminate insects and rodents.

Custodians use many different tools and cleaning materials. For one job, they may need only a simple mop; for another, they may use an electric polishing machine and a special cleaning compound. Chemical cleaners and power equipment have reduced the effort needed for cleaning jobs. Custodians must be familiar with cleaning equipment and materials designed for specific tasks because improper use of a chemical cleaner or machine may harm surfaces.

Some custodians supervise the cleaning and maintenance of an entire building or section of a building, and see that jobs, such as floor waxing or furniture polishing, are done well.

PLACES OF EMPLOYMENT

About 2.7 million people work as building custodians. Although jobs for custodians are found in cities and towns throughout the nation, the majority work in the more populated areas of the country.

Many building custodians are employed by hospitals, hotels, factories, and retail stores. Large numbers also work in apartment houses and office buildings; some are employed by contract firms that provide building maintenance service for a fee.

TRAINING, OTHER QUALIFICATIONS, AND ADVANCEMENT

No special education is required for most custodial jobs, but the beginner should know simple arithmetic and be able to follow instructions. High school shop courses are helpful to the building service worker who does various handyman tasks, such as minor plumbing or carpentry.

Most building custodians learn their skills on the job. Usually, beginners do routine cleaning. As workers gain experience, they are given more complicated duties.

In some cities, unions and government agencies have programs to teach necessary skills to building custodians. Students learn about the different kinds of surfaces in modern buildings and ways to clean them. They learn to operate and maintain machines, such as wet and dry vacuums, buffers, and polishers. They also receive instructions concerning minor electrical, plumbing, and other repairs. Students learn to plan their work, to deal with the public, and to work independently without supervision. A few training programs offer remedial courses in reading, writing, and arithmetic.

Advancement opportunities for custodial workers may be limited because the custodian often is the only maintenance worker in a building. Where there is a large maintenance staff, however, custodians can be promoted to supervisory jobs. For advancement to supervisor, a high school diploma is necessary. Some custodians become self-employed and maintain buildings for clients on a fee basis, after becoming thoroughly familiar with the work.

Building custodians usually find work by answering newspaper advertisements or by applying directly to a company. They also get jobs through state employment offices. For federal government positions, an employment application must be filled out and the civil service personnel headquarters contacted.

EMPLOYMENT OUTLOOK

Employment of building custodians is expected to rise moderately in the next few years as the construction of buildings that use custodial services expands.

In addition to the large number of new jobs that will be created, thousands of workers will be needed each year to replace experienced custodians who retire, die, or leave for other reasons.

EARNINGS AND WORKING CONDITIONS

In government service, building custodial workers' pay rates are similar to those paid by private industries.

Most building service workers receive paid holidays and vacations, and health insurance.

Although custodians usually work inside heated, well-lighted buildings, sometimes they work outdoors sweeping walkways, mowing lawns, or shoveling snow. Those who maintain machinery and heating systems may work in noise and grease. Custodial workers often suffer from minor cuts, bruises, and burns caused by machines, hand tools, and chemicals. An additional hazard of custodial work is heavy lifting.

Building custodians stand up most of the time at work. Many tasks, such as dusting or sweeping, require constant bending, stooping, and stretching. Some must clean buildings after the regular staff has left for the day. To provide 24-hour maintenance, custodians may be assigned shift work.

SOURCES OF ADDITIONAL INFORMATION

General information on job opportunities and wage rates in local areas may be obtained for this occupation from:

Service Employees International Union, 1313 L St. NW, Washington, D.C. 20005

PREPARING YOURSELF FOR THE CIVIL SERVICE EXAMINATION

Most federal, state, and municipal units have recruitment procedures for filling civil service positions. They have developed a number of methods to make job opportunities known. Places where such information may be obtained include:

1. The offices of the State Employment Services. There are almost two thousand throughout the country. These offices are administered by the state in which they are located, with the financial assistance of the federal government. You will find the address of the one nearest you in your telephone book.

2. Your state Civil Service Commission. Address your inquiry to the capital city of your state.

3. Your city Civil Service Commission—if you live in a large city. It is sometimes called by another name, such as the Department of Personnel, but you will be able to identify it in your telephone directory under the listing of city departments.

4. Your municipal building and your local library.

5. Complete listings are carried by such newspapers as *The Chief-Leader* (published in New York City), as well as by other city and state-wide publications devoted to civil service employees. Many local newspapers run a section on regional civil service news.

6. State and local agencies looking for competent employees will contact schools, professional societies, veterans organizations, unions, and trade associations.

7. School Boards and Boards of Education, which employ the greatest proportion of all state and local personnel, should be asked directly for information about job openings.

The Format of the Job Announcement

When a position is open and a civil service examination is to be given for it, a job announcement is drawn up. This generally contains everything an applicant has to know about the job.

The announcement begins with the job title. A typical announcement then describes the work, the location of the position, the education and experience requirements, the kind of examination to be given, and the system of rating. It may also have something to say about veteran preference and the age limit. It tells which application form is to be filled out, where to get the form, and where and when to file it. You will find sample announcements in the next chapter.

Study the job announcement carefully. It will answer many of your questions and help you decide whether you like the position and are qualified for it.

There is no point in applying for a position and taking the examination if you do not want to work where the job is. The job may be in your community or hundreds of miles away at the other end of the state. If you are not willing to work where the job is, study other announcements that will give you an opportunity to work in a place of your choice. A civil service job close to your home has an additional advantage since local residents usually receive preference in appointments.

Most job requirements give a **deadline for filing** an application. Others bear the words *No Closing Date* at the top of the first page; this means that applications will be accepted until the needs of the agency are met. In some cases a public notice is issued when a certain number of applications has been received. No application mailed past the deadline date will be considered.

Every announcement has a detailed section on **education and experience requirements** for the particular job and for the optional fields. Make sure that in both education and experience you meet the minimum qualifications. If you do not meet the given standards for one job, there may be others open where you stand a better chance of making the grade.

If the job announcement does not mention **veteran preference**, it would be wise to inquire if there is such a provision in your state or municipality. There may be none or it may be limited to disabled veterans. In some jurisdictions surviving spouses of disabled veterans are given preference. All such information can be obtained through the agency that issues the job announcement.

Applicants may be denied examinations and eligible candidates may be denied appointments for any of the following reasons:

- intentional false statements

- deception or fraud in examination or appointment

- use of intoxicating beverages to the extent that ability to perform the duties of the position is impaired

- criminal, infamous, dishonest, immoral, or notoriously disgraceful conduct

The announcement describes **the kind of test** given for the particular position. Please pay special attention to this section. It tells what areas are to be covered in the written test and lists the specific subjects on which questions will be asked. Sometimes sample questions are given.

In the competitive examination all applicants for a position compete with each other; the better the mark, the better the chance of being appointed. Also, competitive examinations are given to determine desirability for promotion among employees.

Civil service written tests are rated on a scale of 100, with 70 usually as the passing mark.

OFFICIAL ANNOUNCEMENTS

Assistant Building Custodian

FILING DATES: From September 4 through September 24. Application forms may be filed in person or by mail. Either way, properly completed application forms MUST BE *RECEIVED* BY THE LAST DATE FOR FILING. Date of receipt, rather than date of postmark, will be controlling.

PROMOTION OPPORTUNITIES: Employees in the title of Assistant Building Custodian are accorded promotion opportunities, when eligible, to the title of Building Custodian.

MINIMUM REQUIREMENTS: Three years of full-time paid experience in cleaning and maintaining a building.

DUTIES AND RESPONSIBILITIES: Under general supervision, performs work of ordinary difficulty and responsibility in supervising the cleaning, maintaining, and enforcing of safety requirements in one or more moderately sized public buildings (other than schools and colleges) and the immediate grounds, or in a larger building in supervising custodial employees on an assigned shift; performs related work.

EXAMPLES OF TYPICAL TASKS: Is responsible for the cleanliness and maintenance of moderately sized public buildings entailing supervision of a number of custodial employees performing such tasks as sweeping, dusting, mopping, polishing, waxing, gathering and disposing of refuse; operating elevators; cleaning walks and snow removal; and maintaining lawns and shrubs. Provides heat by means of a low pressure heating system. Inspects buildings and grounds to note general condition and necessity for repairs; checks work performance and proper use, cleanliness, and storage of tools. May make minor repairs and report conditions requiring services of mechanics. Arranges for the moving of furniture and equipment. May clean, adjust, and lubricate oil burners, pumps, fans, booklifts, ash lifts, and other equipment. Enforces safety requirements and protects the building and grounds from vandalism. Aids in the training of newly appointed custodial employees and in the preparation of work schedules; investigates and adjusts complaints about service and personnel. Requisitions fuel; requisitions, stores, and issues janitorial supplies. Keeps inventories, time sheets, and other records; prepares reports on work activities, accidents, and unusual conditions.

TESTS: Written, weight 100, 70% required; practical-oral, qualifying, 70% required. The written test will be of the multiple-choice type and may include questions on building and grounds cleaning and maintenance, heating and ventilation, minor plumbing, electrical, mechanical and carpentry repairs, safety, supervision, reading comprehension of reports and record keeping, and related areas. The qualifying practical-oral test will be held in a public building and may include questions on cleaning and operating boilers, safety and related maintenance of buildings and grounds.

Eligibles will be required to pass a qualifying medical test and a qualifying physical test prior to appointment. Eligibles will be required to meet the medical and physical standards posted on the bulletin board of the New York City Department of Personnel.

The pertinent sections of the General Examination Regulations and the General Provisions of the Notice of Examination are also part of this notice.

Building Custodian

PROMOTION OPPORTUNITIES: Employees in the title of Building Custodian are accorded promotion opportunities, when eligible, to Senior Building Custodian.

MINIMUM REQUIREMENTS: Four years of full-time paid experience in cleaning and maintaining a moderately-sized building, one year of which must have been in a supervisory capacity.

DUTIES AND RESPONSIBILITIES: Under general supervision, performs work of moderate difficulty and responsibility in supervising the cleaning, maintaining, and enforcing of safety requirements in large public buildings (other than schools and colleges) and the immediate grounds, or in supervising a considerable force of custodial employees on an assigned shift; performs related work.

EXAMPLES OF TYPICAL TASKS: Is responsible for the cleanliness and maintenance of large public buildings entailing supervision of a considerable force of custodial employees performing such tasks as sweeping, dusting, mopping, polishing, waxing, gathering and disposing of refuse; operating elevators; cleaning walks and snow removal; and maintaining lawns and shrubs. Oversees operation of a low pressure heating system. Inspects building and grounds to note general condition and necessity for repairs; checks work performance, and proper use, cleanliness and storage of tools. May participate in or supervise the making of minor repairs and report conditions requiring services of mechanics. Arranges for, and supervises the moving of, furniture and equipment. May make acceptability reports on the work performed by maintenance staff and outside constractors. Enforces safety requirements and protects the building and grounds from vandalism. Trains personnel in safe work methods and use of equipment and materials; prepares work schedules; investigates and adjusts complaints about service and personnel. Requisitions fuel; requisitions, stores, issues, and may make estimates of janitorial supplies. Keeps inventories, time sheets, and other records; prepares reports on work activities, accidents, and unusual conditions.

TESTS: Written, weight 100, 70% required; practical-oral, qualifying, 70% required. The written test will be of the multiple-choice type and may include questions on building and grounds cleaning and maintenance, heating and ventilating, electricity, plumbing and carpentry, supervision and training, safety and security, tenant and public relations, and other related areas. The practical-oral will be held in a public building and may include questions on boiler cleaning and operation, safety, supervision, and related maintenance of buildings and grounds.

Eligibles will be required to pass a qualifying medical test and a qualifying physical test prior to appointment. Eligibles will be required to meet the medical and physical standards posted on the bulletin board of the Department of Personnel.

In evaluating the medical qualifications of eligibles as defined in the General Provisions of the Notice of Examination, special emphasis will be given to the following: vision of less than 20/50 both eyes together, rejects (eyeglasses allowed); inability to hear a conversational voice, rejects (hearing aid allowed); hernia, rejects; varicose veins, rejects; heart condition, lung condition, hypertension, back condition, paralysis, history of mental or nervous ailment may reject. Any disease, injury, or abnormality which, in the opinion of the medical examiner, would prevent performance of duties will reject.

Medical evidence to allow participation in the physical test may be required, and the Department of Personnel reserves the right to exclude from the physical test any eligible who, upon examination of such evidence, is apparently medically unfit. Eligibles will take the physical test at their own risk of injury, although every effort will be made to safeguard them.

The physical test will consist of two subtests. In one subtest, eligibles will be required to lift a 25 pound barbell from floor to shoulder level, using both hands, carry it in that position for a distance of 20 feet and return it to the floor under control. In another subtest, eligibles will be required to walk down and up a flight of 20 steps without the assistance of the handrails within 50 seconds.

The pertinent sections of the General Examination Regulations and the General Provisions of the Notice of Examination are also part of this notice.

Senior Building Custodian

PROMOTION OPPORTUNITIES: Employees in the title of Senior Building Custodian are accorded promotion opportunities, when eligible, to the title of Supervisor of Building Custodians.

MINIMUM REQUIREMENTS: Six years of full-time paid experience in the cleaning and maintaining of a large building having more than 100,000 square feet of floor area, two years of which shall have been in a supervisory capacity.

DUTIES AND RESPONSIBILITIES: Under general supervision, performs work of a highly difficult and responsible nature in the supervision of the cleaning and maintaining of public buildings, other than schools and colleges, and their immediate grounds and in the enforcement of safety requirements. Performs related work.

EXAMPLES OF TYPICAL TASKS: In public buildings, other than public schools and colleges, is responsible for the cleanliness and maintenance of buildings having more than 100,000 square feet of floor area, entailing supervision of a large group of subordinate employees, such as building custodians, assistant building custodians, elevator operators, cleaners, watchmen, window cleaners, etc., engaged in sweeping, dusting, scrubbing, mopping, polishing, gathering and disposing of refuse, mowing and caring for lawns, and operating elevators, or may be assistant to the Supervisor of Building Custodians. May supervise the operation of heating plants. Inspects buildings to note general condition and necessity for repairs. Inspects work of subordinates to insure maximum efficiency, economy, and quality of work. Organizes tenants in Civil Defense for air raid protection. Requisitions stock and issues supplies. Trains and arranges for training of new employees. Prepares work schedules. Maintains records and prepares required reports.

TESTS: Written, weight 50, 70% required; practical-oral, weight 50, 70% required. The written test will be of the multiple-choice type and may include questions on inspection, cleaning, and maintenance of public buildings and grounds, including the operation of heating plants; supervision and training; safety; reports, record keeping, and inventory control; and other related areas. The practical-oral test will be held in a public building; candidates may be asked questions on inspection, cleaning, and maintenance of public buildings and grounds; operation of heating plants; safety and other related areas.

School Custodian

PROMOTION OPPORTUNITIES: Employees in the title of School Custodian are accorded promotion opportunities, when eligible, to the title of School Custodian Engineer.

MINIMUM REQUIREMENTS:

1. One year of full-time experience in responsible charge of cleaning, operating, and maintaining building structures and grounds, and their mechanical and electrical equipment. Such experience must have been in a building comparable to school buildings supervised by custodians in big city school districts; and either

2. Two years of full-time practical experience in cleaning, operating, and maintaining building structures and grounds and their related mechanical and electrical equipment; or

3. Two years of shipboard engineering experience; or

4. Two years of education in an accredited college which is leading to a baccalaureate degree in engineering or engineering technology; or

5. A combination of education and/or experience equivalent to (2), (3), or (4) above can be substituted up to two years. However, all candidates must have the experience shown in (1) above.

The minimum requirements must be met by the last date for the receipt of applications.

Experience Paper Form A must be filled out completely and in detail and filed with your application.

JOB DESCRIPTION

DUTIES AND RESPONSIBILITIES: Under general supervision, supervises and is responsible for the physical operation, maintenance, repair, and custodial upkeep and care of a public school building and its immediate grounds; performs related work.

TEST INFORMATION

TESTS: Your score will be determined by two tests, a written test, weight 100, and a qualifying practical-oral test. A score of at least 70% is needed in each test in order to pass.

The multiple-choice written test may include questions on supervisory techniques and procedures as related to building custodial work; building cleaning, maintenance, and repair practices; the operation of building heating and ventilation systems; building inspection requirements, safety requirements, and related practices and procedures; budget and payroll techniques; preparing forms and reports; public relations; and other related areas. A grade of at least 70% is required on the written test. Candidates who do not receive a grade of at least 70% on this part will not be called for the practical test.

The qualifying practical-oral test will be held in a Board of Education School building and may include questions on school heating and ventilating systems; sewage disposal systems; electrical distribution systems; plant maintenance; safety; and other related areas.

All candidates must be able to understand and be understood in English. A qualifying English oral examination will be given by the Department of Personnel to all candidates who, in the opinion of the appointing officer, do not meet this requirement.

School Custodian Engineer

SALARY AND VACANCIES: This is an ungraded position. School Custodian Engineers are paid various amounts depending upon the size of the building to which the assignment is made. These amounts are lump sums for the care of the respective buildings and the salaries of required help are to be paid therefrom.

PROMOTION OPPORTUNITIES: Employees in the title of School Custodian Engineers are accorded promotion opportunities, when eligible, to the title of District Supervisor of Custodians.

MINIMUM REQUIREMENTS: At least five (5) years of full-time, paid experience in the supervision of cleaning, operating, heating, and maintaining building structures and grounds, and their related mechanical and electrical equipment; or a satisfactory equivalent.

LICENSE AND CERTIFICATE REQUIREMENTS: At the time of appointment, eligibles must possess:

(1) A valid High Pressure Boiler Operating Engineer's License issued by the Department of Buildings and a valid Certificate of Equivalent Instructions isued by the Department of Environmental Protection.

(2) In addition, for certain schools, a valid Certificate of Qualification for Refrigerating Machine Operator (Unlimited Capacity) issued by the Fire Department may be required.

Experience Paper Form A must be filled out completely and in detail and filed with your application. All candidates who file an application will be summoned for the written tests prior to the determination of whether they meet the above requirements. Only the experience papers of passing candidates will be examined with respect to meeting these requirements.

JOB DESCRIPTION

DUTIES AND RESPONSIBILITIES: Under general supervision, supervises and is responsible for the physical operation, maintenance, repair, and custodial upkeep and care of a public school building and its immediate grounds; performs related work.

EXAMPLES OF TYPICAL TASKS: Supervises, plans, and is responsible for the work of the custodial and maintenance staff. Operates and is responsible for all electrical and mechanical equipment and systems including air conditioning, heating, ventilation, refrigeration, water supply and sewage systems, electric elevators and elevator equipment, automatic signal systems, electrical generating plants, filtration plants, and cleaning equipment. Makes minor repairs. Supervises cleaning of the building and grounds. Is responsible for maintaining the building and grounds in a safe, secure, and sanitary condition. Conducts inspection of building to determine needed repairs. Consults with and advises officials on problems of operation, maintenance, and repairs. Sets up the work schedules to insure maximum efficiency and minimum interference with classroom activities. Requisitions and accounts for custodial and maintenance materials, tools, and supplies. Maintains records and prepares required reports of plant operations. Hires appropriate personnel; trains or arranges for their training. For hired personnel, prepares payrolls and personnel forms; pays wages; deducts payroll taxes, State Disability Insurance, court ordered garnishees, and union dues. Provides for Workers' Compensation Insurance. Collects fees for the use of the school building by community organizations and other groups.

TEST INFORMATION

TESTS: Your score will be determined by a written test consisting of two parts, to be given in one session on the same day. You must attain a score of at least 70% in each part in order to pass.

Part I (weight 80) of the written test will be of the multiple-choice type and may include questions on maintenance and minor repairs of school buildings and equipment; cleaning techniques, materials, and equipment; athletic field maintenance; operation and maintenance of HVAC, mechanical, electrical, and automatic signal systems; proper supervisory practices including training, motivation, work scheduling, and performance evaluation; human relations; safety; preparing reports; maintaining records and performing job related arithmetic; and other related areas.

Part II (weight 20) of the written test will be of the essay type and may include questions on preparation of reports, supervision of custodial and maintenance staff, and technical areas as related to maintenance and repair of school buildings; and other related areas.

Part II (essay part) will not be rated if the candidate does not attain a score of 70% or better in Part I.

THE APPLICATION FORM

Having studied the job announcement and having decided that you want the position and are qualified for it, your next step is to get an application form. The job announcement tells you where to send for it.

On the whole, civil service application forms differ little from state to state and locality to locality. The questions, which have been worked out after years of experimentation, are simple and direct, designed to elicit a maximum of information about you.

Many prospective civil service employees have failed to get a job because of slipshod, erroneous, incomplete, misleading, or untruthful answers. Give the application serious attention, for it is the first important step toward getting the job you want.

Here, along with some helpful comments, are the questions usually asked on the average application form, although not necessarily in this order.

Name of examination or kind of position applied for. This information appears in large type on the first page of the job announcement.

Primary place of employment applied for. The location of the position was probably contained in the announcement. You must consider whether you want to work there. The announcement may list more than one location where the job is open. If you would accept employment in any of the places, list them all; otherwise list the specific place or places where you would be willing to work.

Name and address. Give in full, including your middle name if you have one, and your maiden name as well if you are a married woman.

Home and office phones. If none, write *None*.

Legal or voting residence. The state in which you vote is the one you list here.

Will you accept temporary employment if offered you for (a) one month or less, (b) one to four months, (c) four to twelve months? Temporary positions come up frequently and it is important to know whether you are available.

Will you accept less than full-time employment? Part-time work comes up now and then. Consider whether you want to accept such a position while waiting for a full-time appointment.

Were you in active military service in the Armed Forces of the United States? Veterans' preference, if given, is usually limited to active service during the following periods: 12/7/41 - 12/31/46; 6/27/50 - 1/31/55; 6/1/63 - 5/7/75; 6/1/83 - 12/1/87; 10/23/83 - 11/21/83; 12/20/89 - 1/3/90; 8/2/90 to end of Persian Gulf hostilities.

Do you claim disabled veterans credit? If you do, you have to show proof of a war-incurred disability compensable by at least 10%. This is done through certification by the Veterans Administration.

Education. List your entire educational history, including all diplomas, degrees, and special courses taken in any accredited or Armed Forces school. Also give your credits toward a college degree.

References. The names of people who can give information about you, including their occupations, and business and home addresses, are often requested.

Your health. Questions are asked concerning your medical record. You are expected to have the physical and psychological capacity to perform the job for which you are applying. Standards vary, of course, depending on the requirements of the position. A physical handicap usually will not bar an applicant from a job he can perform adequately unless the safety of the public is involved.

Work history. Considerable space is allotted on the form for the applicant to tell about all his past employment. Examiners check all such answers closely. Do not embroider or falsify your record. If you were ever fired, say so. It is better for you to state this openly than for the examiners to find out the truth from your former employer.

The application form which you must file may be as simple as the New York City application form reproduced on the next page or may be considerably more complex and more detailed than the Experience Paper which follows it.

APPLICATION FOR OPEN COMPETITIVE EXAMINATION
(See Instructions on Reverse Side)

CITY OF NEW YORK
DEPARTMENT OF PERSONNEL,
APPLICATION SECTION
49 THOMAS STREET
NEW YORK, NEW YORK 10013

EXAM NO.

YOUR FIRST NAME

YOUR STREET ADDRESS (INCLUDE APT. NO., BLDG. NO., OR CARE OF)

CITY OR TOWN

EXAM TITLE

YOUR SOCIAL SECURITY NO. (check your card before entering your number)

FEE (See Item 3 on reverse)

$

Middle Initial

YOUR LAST NAME

STATE

ZIP CODE

IF YOU LIVE IN
N.Y.C., CHECK THE
BOROUGH THAT YOU
LIVE IN.

MANHATTAN
M

BRONX
X

BROOKLYN
K

QUEENS
Q

STATEN ISLAND
R

CHECK ALL BOXES
THAT APPLY TO
YOU.

I CLAIM VETERANS'
CREDIT. (SEE ITEM
7 ON REVERSE.)
V

I CLAIM DISABLED VETERANS'
CREDIT. (MINIMUM 10% DISA-
BILITY) (SEE ITEM 7 ON REVERSE.)
D

I AM A SABBATH
OBSERVER. (SEE
ITEM 4 ON RE-
VERSE.)
S

I HAVE A HANDICAP
REQUIRING SPECIAL
TESTING ACCOMMODATIONS.
(SEE ITEM 5 ON REVERSE.)
H

DECLARATION: I declare that the statements on this form are true. I further declare that if I have made a claim for Veterans' or Disabled Veterans' credit that I meet the requirements for such credits as described on the reverse side. I am aware that I must prove that I am entitled to the credit I claim or my employment may be terminated.

Your Signature

REMINDER

- DID YOU ENCLOSE THE CORRECT FEE?
- DID YOU FILL OUT COMPLETELY AND ATTACH ALL
  OTHER FORMS REQUIRED BY NOTICE OF EXAMINATION?
- IS YOUR SOCIAL SECURITY NUMBER CORRECT?

- DID YOU SIGN YOUR NAME?
- DID YOU ANSWER EVERY QUESTION?
- DID YOU GIVE YOUR COMPLETE ADDRESS?
- DID YOU INCLUDE YOUR CORRECT ZIP CODE?

AN INCOMPLETE APPLICATION MAY NOT BE PROCESSED. BE SURE TO INDICATE YOUR FULL NAME, SOCIAL SECURITY NUMBER, ADDRESS AND ZIP CODE.

BE SURE TO READ THE INSTRUCTIONS ON THE REVERSE SIDE.

DP-848C (R. 1/86)

18

INSTRUCTIONS FOR FILLING OUT THIS APPLICATION FORM

Be sure to read the Notice of Examination carefully before completing this form.

1. **FORMS**
If the Notice of Examination calls for Experience Form A and/or other forms, these forms must be included with your application, or your application cannot be accepted.

2. **ADDRESS**
Give your full mailing address, including building, apartment number, or "in care of" information where needed. (If you change your address after applying, write to the Examining Service Division of the Department of Personnel, Room 216, 220 Church Street, New York, N.Y. 10013, with your new address, plus your Social Security Number and the number and title of the examination for which you applied.)

3. **FEE**
Enclose the correct fee made out to the N.Y.C. Department of Personnel. The amount of the fee is stated in the Notice of Examination for this examination. DO NOT MAIL CASH. If paying by check: write your name, social security number, home address, and the examination number on the front of the check. A fee is not charged if you are a N.Y.C. resident receiving public assistance from the N.Y.C. Department of Social Services. To have the fee waived you must present or enclose a clear photocopy of your current Medicaid Card. The photocopy must accompany the application, even if it is filed in person.

4. **SABBATH OBSERVER**
If because of religious belief you cannot take a test on the scheduled date, you must come or write to: Examining Service Division (Room 216): N.Y.C. Department of Personnel, 220 Church Street, New York, N.Y. 10013 no later than five work days prior to the test date to request an alternate date. All requests must be accompanied by a signed statement on letterhead from your religious leader certifying to your religious observance.

5. **HANDICAP**
If you have a handicap which will interfere with your ability to take this test without special accommodations, amanuensis, or other assistance, you must submit a written request for specific special accommodations to the Examining Service Division (Room 216): N.Y.C. Department of Personnel, 220 Church Street, New York, N.Y. 10013. The request must be received no later than 15 work days prior to the test date. A physician or agency authorized for this purpose must corroborate the specific nature of your handicap and must justify the need for the special accommodations you request. For more details, consult Regulation E.8 of the General Examination Regulations, which is available from the Application Section of the Department of Personnel.

6. **MAIL**
Check the Notice of Examination to see if applications are accepted by mail. If you mail your application, use a 4¼" x 9½" (legal size) envelope, and address to:

N.Y.C. Department of Personnel
Application Section
49 Thomas Street
New York, New York 10013

Your application MUST BE RECEIVED IN THIS DEPARTMENT BY THE LAST DAY OF FILING.

7. **VETERANS' CREDIT**
FOR VETERANS' OR DISABLED VETERANS' CREDIT YOU MUST:

a. Have served on active duty, other than for training purpose, in the Armed Forces of the United States during:
- December 7, 1941 - September 2, 1945; or
- June 26, 1950 - January 31, 1955; or
- January 1, 1963 - May 7, 1975; and

b. Be a resident of New York State at the time of list establishment; and

c. Have an honorable discharge or have been released under honorable conditions.

d. For Disabled Veterans' Credit, in addition to a, b, and c above, at the time the examination list is established you must receive or be entitled to receive at least 10% compensation from the V.A. for a disability incurred in time of war. The V.A. must also certify that the disability is permanent. If it is not permanent, you must have been examined by the V.A. within one year of the establishment of the examination list.

NOTES

1. You may use Veterans' or Disabled Veterans' Credit only once after January 1, 1951 for appointment or promotion from a City, State or County civil service list.

2. The above is only a summary of necessary conditions. The complete provisions are contained in statutory and/or decisional law.

19

DEPARTMENT OF PERSONNEL

EXPERIENCE PAPER

SOCIAL SECURITY NO.

___ / ___ / _____

FORM A

EXAMINATION NO.

_____

Exact Title of Examination

DO NOT WRITE IN THIS SPACE

Not qualified under terms of advertisement	QUALIFIED: Admitted for further examination pending final determination of qualifications.	RATING
_____	_____	_____

To Investigator: Verify items checked and also data mentioned here

....

☐ If this box is checked, submit a report with full details to

....

....

FOLLOW THESE INSTRUCTIONS CAREFULLY:

a. Type, print or write (in blue or black ink) the information requested.

b. Be COMPLETE, CONCISE AND ACCURATE. The information you enter below will be used to determine your rating on training and experience. If statements of material facts are found to be false, exaggerated or misleading, you may be disqualified.

c. DO NOT REVEAL YOUR IDENTITY in any way on this experience paper. If you are or have been in business for yourself or have been employed by a relative of the same name, write "self" or the relationship of the relative in the space headed "Name of Employer".

1. LICENSE OR REGISTRATION: If a license or registration is required, answer the following.

a. Title of lic. or reg. you possess which is valid in this State .... License or Registration No. ....

b. Name of issuing agency ....

c. Date of original issue.................. Date last renewed or registered........................... Renewal number............................ Date of expiration ....

2. EDUCATION:

3. DATE OF BIRTH* ....

Give Name and Locations of Schools Below	Day or Night	From Mo. Yr.	To Mo. Yr.	Were you Graduated (Yes or No)	Degree Received	Total Credits Completed	Major Subject	No. of Credits in Major
High School or Trade School								
College or other School								

4. List below any courses which you have passed which: (a) are necessary to meet the minimum requirements for the position; (b) provide training appropriate to the position; (c) are in related fields.

NAME OF COLLEGE OR INSTITUTION	Course Number	EXACT TITLE OF COURSE (Place "G" after graduate courses)	No. of Credits	Date Completed

*The Human Rights Law prohibits discrimination on the basis of age, creed, color, national origin, sex, disability or marital status of any individual. The law allows certain age or sex specifications if based upon a bona fide occupational qualification or statutory authorization.

QUALIFYING EMPLOYMENT. List in chronological order those positions you have held which tend to qualify you for the position sought. Begin with the present or most recent position. Use a separate block for each position. List as a separate employment every material change of duties although with the same employer. Include pertinent experience or training in the armed forces.

1

Dates of Employment (give month and year)	Length of Employment	Exact Title of Your Position	Starting Salary _____ per
From _____ To _____	Yrs. _____ Mos. _____		Last Salary _____ per

Name and Address of Employer	Nature of Employer's Business
	Title (not name) of your Immediate Superior
Number and Titles of Employees You Supervise	If with the City or State was this a provisional appointment? Yes ☐ No ☐ / No. of Hours Worked per Week

Describe Your Duties

2

Dates of Employment (give month and year)	Length of Employment	Exact Title of Your Position	Starting Salary _____ per
From _____ To _____	Yrs. _____ Mos. _____		Last Salary _____ per

Name and Address of Employer	Nature of Employer's Business
	Title (not name) of your Immediate Superior
Number and Titles of Employees You Supervise	If with the City or State was this a provisional appointment? Yes ☐ No ☐ / No. of Hours Worked per Week

Describe Your Duties

3

Dates of Employment (give month and year)	Length of Employment	Exact Title of Your Position	Starting Salary _____ per
From _____ To _____	Yrs. _____ Mos. _____		Last Salary _____ per

Name and Address of Employer	Nature of Employer's Business
	Title (not name) of your Immediate Superior
Number and Titles of Employees You Supervise	If with the City or State was this a provisional appointment? Yes ☐ No ☐ / No. of Hours Worked per Week

Describe Your Duties

4

Dates of Employment (give month and year)	Length of Employment	Exact Title of Your Position	Starting Salary _____ per
From _____ To _____	Yrs. _____ Mos. _____		Last Salary _____ per

Name and Address of Employer	Nature of Employer's Business
	Title (not name) of your Immediate Superior
Number and Titles of Employees You Supervise	If with the City or State was this a provisional appointment? Yes ☐ No ☐ / No. of Hours Worked per Week

Describe Your Duties

OTHER EXPERIENCE: List here only the other employments you have had which were not included before.

Dates of Employment		Name and Address of Employer	Business of Employer	Title of Your Position and Highest Salary	Brief Description of Duties You Performed
From	To				

Any additional qualifications you have for the position may be listed here; for example: field work in connection with training, authorship or co-authorship of books or of articles in recognized journals, special certification from professional boards, other professional attainments, etc. (Caution: Do not mention your name.) Additional courses or experience may also be listed here.

IF YOU HAVE ADDITIONAL QUALIFYING EXPERIENCE, ATTACH SEPARATE PAPER USING THE SAME FORMAT

TEST-TAKING MADE SIMPLE

Before the exam day find out how to get to the test location. Be sure you know where it is, how to get there, and how long it takes to get there. You might want to make a "dry run" to check out the transportation and time involved. You do not want to be late on test day, and you do not want to be nervous about being late.

The day before the exam, review any subject areas in which you are weak. Then reread this chapter. Sharpen your pencils and put them with your admission blank, identification papers, watch, and whatever other materials you will need to take with you to the test. Get a good night's sleep. Set your alarm for a time that will allow you to eat a good breakfast (if you are scheduled for a morning exam) and to get to the test site on time.

On test day allow ample time for getting to the examination center. Upon entering the exam room, choose a seat with good lighting, good ventilation, and a view of the clock, if possible. If you cannot see the clock, you can always rely on your watch.

A test monitor will hand out papers and will give instructions. Listen closely and follow all of the instructions. If you have any questions, *ask*. There is no penalty for asking questions, even questions that might appear to be foolish. The penalty for misunderstanding instructions might be a low score.

The monitor will give you a test booklet and will tell you the time limits. The booklet may look large, but do not panic. There is plenty of time. Most civil service exams allow thirty minutes for every fifteen questions. You will be able to answer many of the questions in only a few seconds, which will leave you enough time to answer such questions as reading comprehension or arithmetic questions that, by their nature, take longer to read and understand. If you are having trouble answering a particular question, mark that question, go on, and come back to it later.

Once the signal is given to begin the exam, you should:

- READ all the directions carefully. Skipping over the directions or misunderstanding them can lead to your marking a whole series of questions incorrectly.

- READ every word of every question. Be alert for exclusionary words that might affect your answer—words like "not," "most," "all," "every," "least," "except."

- READ all of the choices before you mark your answer. The greatest number of errors are made when the correct answer is the last choice given. Too many people mark the first answer that seems correct without reading through all the choices to find out which answer is *best*.

The following list consists of important suggestions for taking a civil service exam. Read these suggestions before you go on to the exercises in this book. Read them again before you take the exam. You will find them all useful.

1. Mark your answers by completely blackening the space for the answer you selected.

2. Mark only ONE answer for each question, even if you think that more than one answer is correct. You must choose the best answer. If you mark more than one answer, the scoring machine will give you no credit for that question.

3. If you change your mind, erase completely. Leave no doubt as to which answer you mean.

4. If you do any figuring calculations in your test booklet or on scrap paper, remember to mark your answer on the answer sheet as well. Only the answer sheet is scored.

5. You must mark your answer to every question in the right place. Check often to be sure that the answer number corresponds to the question number. If you find that you have slipped "out of line," you must take the time to find where you went awry and change your answers accordingly.

6. Do not dwell too long on any question. Although you have plenty of time, your time is not unlimited. If you are unsure of your answer, make a mark next to the question in the test booklet so that you may return to the question when you have completed the rest of the exam; but mark your best guess for each question in order.

7. Answer EVERY question. Most civil service exams do not penalize you for wrong answers, and so there is no harm in guessing. If you do not know the answer, eliminate any choices you know are wrong and guess from among the remaining choices. Even a wild guess gives you a chance to get credit for a correct answer. If you have skipped a difficult question to save time during the test, make sure you go back and fill in the answer space, even if you are still not sure of the answer. Do not leave any answers blank on your answer sheet. Even wild guesses are better than no answers at all.

8. Stay alert. Be careful not to mark a wrong answer because you were not concentrating. An example of this type of error might be: The correct answer to a question is choice B, *Dallas*, and you mark choice D instead of B.

9. Check and recheck. There is no bonus for leaving early, and if you finish before the time is up, stay until the end of the exam. Check your answer sheet to be certain that every question has been answered and that every answer has been marked in the right place. Check to be certain that only one answer is marked for each question. Then look back into the question booklet for the questions that you marked as guesses only. This is your opportunity to give any difficult questions more thought and to improve your chances by changing a wild guess into a calculated guess.

GOOD LUCK!

Answer Sheet
Sample Examination I

1. Ⓐ Ⓑ Ⓒ Ⓓ	21. Ⓐ Ⓑ Ⓒ Ⓓ	41. Ⓐ Ⓑ Ⓒ Ⓓ	61. Ⓐ Ⓑ Ⓒ Ⓓ
2. Ⓐ Ⓑ Ⓒ Ⓓ	22. Ⓐ Ⓑ Ⓒ Ⓓ	42. Ⓐ Ⓑ Ⓒ Ⓓ	62. Ⓐ Ⓑ Ⓒ Ⓓ
3. Ⓐ Ⓑ Ⓒ Ⓓ	23. Ⓐ Ⓑ Ⓒ Ⓓ	43. Ⓐ Ⓑ Ⓒ Ⓓ	63. Ⓐ Ⓑ Ⓒ Ⓓ
4. Ⓐ Ⓑ Ⓒ Ⓓ	24. Ⓐ Ⓑ Ⓒ Ⓓ	44. Ⓐ Ⓑ Ⓒ Ⓓ	64. Ⓐ Ⓑ Ⓒ Ⓓ
5. Ⓐ Ⓑ Ⓒ Ⓓ	25. Ⓐ Ⓑ Ⓒ Ⓓ	45. Ⓐ Ⓑ Ⓒ Ⓓ	65. Ⓐ Ⓑ Ⓒ Ⓓ
6. Ⓐ Ⓑ Ⓒ Ⓓ	26. Ⓐ Ⓑ Ⓒ Ⓓ	46. Ⓐ Ⓑ Ⓒ Ⓓ	66. Ⓐ Ⓑ Ⓒ Ⓓ
7. Ⓐ Ⓑ Ⓒ Ⓓ	27. Ⓐ Ⓑ Ⓒ Ⓓ	47. Ⓐ Ⓑ Ⓒ Ⓓ	67. Ⓐ Ⓑ Ⓒ Ⓓ
8. Ⓐ Ⓑ Ⓒ Ⓓ	28. Ⓐ Ⓑ Ⓒ Ⓓ	48. Ⓐ Ⓑ Ⓒ Ⓓ	68. Ⓐ Ⓑ Ⓒ Ⓓ
9. Ⓐ Ⓑ Ⓒ Ⓓ	29. Ⓐ Ⓑ Ⓒ Ⓓ	49. Ⓐ Ⓑ Ⓒ Ⓓ	69. Ⓐ Ⓑ Ⓒ Ⓓ
10. Ⓐ Ⓑ Ⓒ Ⓓ	30. Ⓐ Ⓑ Ⓒ Ⓓ	50. Ⓐ Ⓑ Ⓒ Ⓓ	70. Ⓐ Ⓑ Ⓒ Ⓓ
11. Ⓐ Ⓑ Ⓒ Ⓓ	31. Ⓐ Ⓑ Ⓒ Ⓓ	51. Ⓐ Ⓑ Ⓒ Ⓓ	71. Ⓐ Ⓑ Ⓒ Ⓓ
12. Ⓐ Ⓑ Ⓒ Ⓓ	32. Ⓐ Ⓑ Ⓒ Ⓓ	52. Ⓐ Ⓑ Ⓒ Ⓓ	72. Ⓐ Ⓑ Ⓒ Ⓓ
13. Ⓐ Ⓑ Ⓒ Ⓓ	33. Ⓐ Ⓑ Ⓒ Ⓓ	53. Ⓐ Ⓑ Ⓒ Ⓓ	73. Ⓐ Ⓑ Ⓒ Ⓓ
14. Ⓐ Ⓑ Ⓒ Ⓓ	34. Ⓐ Ⓑ Ⓒ Ⓓ	54. Ⓐ Ⓑ Ⓒ Ⓓ	74. Ⓐ Ⓑ Ⓒ Ⓓ
15. Ⓐ Ⓑ Ⓒ Ⓓ	35. Ⓐ Ⓑ Ⓒ Ⓓ	55. Ⓐ Ⓑ Ⓒ Ⓓ	75. Ⓐ Ⓑ Ⓒ Ⓓ
16. Ⓐ Ⓑ Ⓒ Ⓓ	36. Ⓐ Ⓑ Ⓒ Ⓓ	56. Ⓐ Ⓑ Ⓒ Ⓓ	76. Ⓐ Ⓑ Ⓒ Ⓓ
17. Ⓐ Ⓑ Ⓒ Ⓓ	37. Ⓐ Ⓑ Ⓒ Ⓓ	57. Ⓐ Ⓑ Ⓒ Ⓓ	77. Ⓐ Ⓑ Ⓒ Ⓓ
18. Ⓐ Ⓑ Ⓒ Ⓓ	38. Ⓐ Ⓑ Ⓒ Ⓓ	58. Ⓐ Ⓑ Ⓒ Ⓓ	78. Ⓐ Ⓑ Ⓒ Ⓓ
19. Ⓐ Ⓑ Ⓒ Ⓓ	39. Ⓐ Ⓑ Ⓒ Ⓓ	59. Ⓐ Ⓑ Ⓒ Ⓓ	79. Ⓐ Ⓑ Ⓒ Ⓓ
20. Ⓐ Ⓑ Ⓒ Ⓓ	40. Ⓐ Ⓑ Ⓒ Ⓓ	60. Ⓐ Ⓑ Ⓒ Ⓓ	

SAMPLE EXAMINATION I

THE TIME ALLOWED FOR THE ENTIRE EXAMINATION IS 3½ HOURS.

DIRECTIONS: Each question has four suggested answers lettered (A), (B), (C), and (D). Decide which one is the best answer and, on your answer sheet, darken the space for that letter.

1. Of the following, the one action which will most likely prolong the useful life of a hair broom is to

   (A) store it after use by hanging it by the handle
   (B) keep the bristles moist at all times
   (C) use the wooden back of the broom to hammer down any nails which protrude from the floor surface
   (D) lean heavily on the broom when sweeping so that all the dirt is moved with one stroke.

2. Sweep cloths are often chemically treated with

   (A) water
   (B) scouring powder
   (C) corn starch
   (D) mineral oil

3. In the event of a temporary shortage of custodial help at a college, first priority should be given to cleaning the

   (A) Dean's office
   (B) general office
   (C) medical office
   (D) Superintendent's office

4. Of the following, the one which should be used to remove chewing gum from an asphalt tile floor is

   (A) coarse sandpaper
   (B) a putty knife
   (C) lemon oil
   (D) gasoline

5. The best cleaning tool to use to dust the tops of radiator covers is a

   (A) wet sponge
   (B) bowl brush
   (C) counter brush
   (D) corn broom

6. The best cleaning tool to use to clean a slate blackboard is a

   (A) wet sponge
   (B) bowl brush
   (C) counter brush
   (D) corn broom

7. The best cleaning tool to use to clean a commode is a

   (A) wet sponge
   (B) bowl brush
   (C) counter brush
   (D) corn broom

8. The best cleaning tool to use to sweep a rough concrete floor is a

(A) wet sponge   (C) counter brush
(B) bowl brush   (D) corn broom

9. For wet mopping the floor of a corridor by hand, the minimum number of pails needed is

(A) one   (B) two   (C) three   (D) four

10. A comparison of wet mopping by hand with scrubbing by hand indicates that mopping

(A) needs more cleaning solution   (C) requires twice as much water
(B) is more time consuming   (D) is less effective on hardened soil

11. Of the following, the most important consideration when choosing a cleaning agent for use in a college building is the

(A) high cost of cleaning agents when compared to labor costs
(B) effect it has on the amount of labor required
(C) kind of odor it gives off
(D) quantity on hand

12. Of the following, the best way that a custodial supervisor can reduce waste in the use of cleaning supplies is to

(A) dole out the supplies at the beginning of the shift and collect the remainder at the end of the shift
(B) issue a storeroom key to each cleaner so that supplies can be obtained anytime
(C) train the cleaners to use the supplies and equipment properly
(D) have cleaners sign a receipt for all supplies issued

13. A detergent manufacturer recommends mixing 8 ounces of detergent in one gallon of water to prepare a cleaning solution. The amount of the same detergent which should be mixed with thirty gallons of water to obtain the same strength cleaning solution is

(A) 24 ounces   (B) 30 ounces   (C) 240 ounces   (D) 380 ounces

14. The floor area of a corridor 8 feet wide and 72 feet long is most nearly

(A) 80 square feet   (C) 580 square feet
(B) 420 square feet   (D) 870 square feet

15. Of the following types of flooring, the one which does *not* require waxing to preserve its finish is

(A) rubber tile   (C) linoleum
(B) cork tile   (D) terrazzo

16. Of the following, the one cleaning task which must be done most frequently is to

(A) damp mop the floor   (C) dust the venetian blinds
(B) empty the waste baskets   (D) simonize the furniture

17. The total area in square feet of the following rooms:

    Room 201   1,196 square feet
    Room 202   1,196 "   "
    Room 203   827 "   "
    Room 204   827 "   "

    is most nearly

    (A) 3,000   (B) 4,000   (C) 5,000   (D) 6,000

18. The average area of the rooms listed in question 17 above is

    (A) ¼ of the total   (C) ½ of the total
    (B) ⅓ of the total   (D) ¾ of the total

19. Of the following terms, the one which best describes the size of a floor mop is

    (A) 10 quart   (B) 32 ounces   (C) 24 inch O.D.   (D) 10 square foot

20. Of the following terms, the one which best describes the size of a water pail is

    (A) 10 quart   (B) 32 ounce   (C) 24 inch O.D.   (D) 10 square foot

21. Of the following terms, the one which best describes the size of a floor-scrubber brush is

    (A) 10 quart   (B) 32 ounce   (C) 24 inch O.D.   (D) 10 square foot

22. Of the following items, the one which is best to use when dusting a mahogany table is a

    (A) feather duster   (C) crocus cloth
    (B) treated cotton cloth   (D) wet sponge

23. Of the following tasks, the one which should be a two-person assignment is

    (A) vacuum cleaning a rug   (C) washing blackboards in a classroom
    (B) sweeping a classroom   (D) washing fluorescent light fixtures

24. The grease filters in a kitchen range exhaust system are usually found

    (A) in the hood   (C) on the roof
    (B) after the first bend in the duct   (D) in the base of the range

25. The greatest benefit which can result from a custodial supervisor's daily inspection program occurs when the inspections are used to indicate to the employees

    (A) how they can improve the work they are doing
    (B) that they are being watched
    (C) that the supervisor is worried about losing his job
    (D) that becoming a supervisor will release them from manual labor

26. Of the following, the one which takes up more of a custodial supervisor's time than any of the others is

    (A) work planning and job analysis   (C) safety and training
    (B) personnel problems   (D) supervision and inspection

27. Neat's-foot oil is usually used on

(A) sore feet
(B) asphalt tile floors
(C) wood furniture
(D) leather

28. Of the following tasks which are usually performed each day, when a full staff of cleaners is present, which one should the custodial supervisor select to have done only twice a week if his staff is temporarily reduced by one-half?

(A) Toilet cleaning
(B) Sweeping corridors
(C) Trash collection
(D) Elevator cleaning

29. Of the following, the one which can be used both as a disinfectant and as a bleach is

(A) chlorine solution
(B) powdered whiting
(C) pine oil
(D) boric acid

30. The word <u>abrasive</u> means most nearly the same as

(A) smooth   (B) powdered   (C) scratchy   (D) sticky

31. The word <u>vandalism</u> means most nearly the same as

(A) destruction   (B) security   (C) safety   (D) juvenile

32. Of the following, the one which is *not* considered to be a hard floor is

(A) concrete   (B) marble   (C) terrazzo   (D) asphalt title

33. A custodial supervisor in charge of an adequately staffed college building observes that the standard of cleanliness in the building is very poor. Of the following, the best thing she can do to raise the standard is to

(A) start a training program for the cleaners
(B) fire half of the cleaners and hire new ones
(C) reprimand the cleaner who is doing the best job, in the presence of the other cleaners
(D) clean the lobby herself so that visitors will believe the whole building is clean

34. A supervisor's first step toward correcting the problem of a worker who is often late for work should be to

(A) check to see whether the worker completes her assigned work
(B) report her to higher authority
(C) talk to her to find out why she is late
(D) ignore the problem

35. One of the best ways for supervisors to gain the cooperation of their employees is to

(A) encourage employees to make suggestions
(B) favor certain employees
(C) avoid complimenting good work performance
(D) find fault with everything they do

36. A night cleaner reports to the custodial supervisor that he has accidentally damaged a piece of office equipment while cleaning an office. The custodial supervisor should

(A) tell him to stop cleaning the office and leave things where he found them so that no one will know he was in the office
(B) explain what happened to the occupant of the office and arrange to have the damage repaired or the equipment replaced, if possible
(C) tell the cleaner to finish cleaning the office and to deny any knowledge of the damage if anyone asks
(D) tell the cleaner he will have to pay for the damage with his own money

37. When it is necessary for a supervisor to reprimand an employee, he or she should do so

(A) in private
(B) only in writing
(C) in the presence of all the employees
(D) by first apologizing for the reprimand

38. When no one in a group of subordinates has ever made any complaints or ever reported having difficulty in carrying out assignments, the supervisor should realize that

(A) the group has no interest in the work
(B) his performance as a supervisor is perfect
(C) he may be making it too difficult for them to make a complaint
(D) their work is too easy

39. The one of the following for which a custodial supervisor is *not* responsible is

(A) cleaning methods
(B) cleaning equipment utilization
(C) lunch time activity
(D) women's lavatory supplies

40. Of the following, the best way for custodial supervisors to keep their subordinates informed of new rules and regulations is to

(A) ask the union to take care of it
(B) post them on the bulletin board
(C) wait until a subordinate breaks a rule and then reprimand all of them
(D) hold meetings periodically to explain the rules

41. In order to assist his subordinates to advance in the civil service system, a custodial supervisor should

(A) teach them as much as he can about their jobs
(B) put them in charge of a group and let them sink or swim
(C) tell them to read "The Chief"
(D) reduce their assigned work load by 50 percent so that they can study for a promotion exam

42. A custodial supervisor scheduled the thorough cleaning of the college swimming pool to take place during the last week of the students' summer vacation period. This planning was

(A) good, because the pool will be clean when the students return for the fall semester
(B) good, because the pool can be cleaned in an hour or two at any time
(C) bad, because if for some reason the job cannot be done on schedule, there is no time left in which to do it before the fall semester starts
(D) bad, because the pool should not be cleaned during summer vacation

43. Of the following, the most important reason for giving each cleaner a written schedule of the routine daily tasks he or she is to perform is that it

(A) relieves the supervisor of responsibility for the routine work
(B) tells the cleaner in detail how to do the work
(C) relieves the supervisor of the job of inspecting the building each day
(D) tells the cleaner what he or she is expected to do each day

44. Poor planning is indicated by failure to clean several rooms one night because

(A) several cleaners were sick
(B) of a blackout
(C) the water main burst
(D) delivery of the cleaning supplies was delayed two days

45. The *least* probable benefit to be derived from a good training program for custodial workers is that

(A) a higher standard of cleanliness will be attained
(B) productivity will increase
(C) materials will be saved
(D) the poorest worker will be equal to the most highly skilled worker

46. Of the following, the main advantage of training groups of people rather than giving individual instruction is that

(A) everyone will obtain the same benefit from the training
(B) no one will feel "left out"
(C) everyone will be given the same information at the same time
(D) no further individual instruction will be necessary

47. Plans for a training session for a group of custodial workers should include requests for training films and training aids which are obtainable free of charge from the

(A) cleaning material manufacturer   (C) Department of Personnel
(B) Museum of Art   (D) Budget Bureau

48. The first step in the procedure for instructing an employee is to prepare the worker to receive the instruction. This preparation should *not* include

(A) putting the employee at ease
(B) asking her what she already knows about the job
(C) placing her in the right location to see your demonstration
(D) having her do the job first and then showing her what she did wrong

49. A cleaner was injured while attempting to carry a floor scrubbing machine up a short stairway. In order to prevent this type accident, a custodial supervisor should order her cleaners to

(A) keep the scrubbing machines on the ground floor
(B) stop using the machines until he can buy lightweight models
(C) get another cleaner to help lift the machines when necessary
(D) continue lifting the machines without help, since no one was ever previously hurt

50. Before lifting a heavy box from the floor to a table, an employee should

(A) raise one side of the box slightly to determine whether he can lift it alone
(B) get a scale and weigh the box to determine whether he can lift it alone or not
(C) ask the foreman whether it is too heavy to lift alone
(D) get someone to help lift it no matter how heavy it is

51. A custodial supervisor in charge of a small group of employees must not only direct the work of the employees assigned to him, but he may also have to do a portion of the manual work himself. The tasks he should do are those which

(A) are the simplest
(B) are the most disagreeable
(C) require the most physical strength
(D) require the most skill and experience

52. Of the following statements concerning accidental injury to people at work, the one which is *false* is

(A) some degree of hazard is associated with every form of activity
(B) people generally have an interest in accident prevention
(C) only the City suffers a loss from accidental injury
(D) every uncontrolled hazard will, in time, produce its share of accidents and injuries

53. The type of fire extinguisher which should *not* be used on an oil fire is the

(A) soda-acid type
(B) carbon-dioxide type
(C) foam type
(D) dry-chemical type

54. An extension ladder has been placed with its top resting against a wall and its base resting on a concrete floor. The horizontal distance from the wall to the base of the ladder should be

(A) one-tenth of the length of the ladder
(B) one-quarter of the length of the ladder
(C) one-half of the length of the ladder
(D) three-quarters of the length of the ladder

55. The following cleaning task which is also an important step in fire prevention is

(A) dusting furniture
(B) waxing floors
(C) washing walls
(D) clearing away rubbish

56. The two types of fire extinguishers which should be placed in a boiler room which has automatically controlled rotary cup oil burners are

(A) foam and soda acid
(B) carbon dioxide and loaded stream
(C) carbon dioxide and foam
(D) foam and loaded stream

57. A cleaner tells his supervisor, Mr. Green, that the supervisor in another building, Mr. Brown, is teaching a different method of performing a certain cleaning operation and the cleaner thinks Mr. Brown's method is much better. Mr. Green should

(A) order the cleaner to do it his way or request a transfer
(B) order the cleaner to mind his own business
(C) discuss the operation with Mr. Brown and try to come to an agreement on the best method
(D) tell his own superior that Mr. Brown must be doing something wrong

58. The head of the biology department tells the custodial supervisor that one of the laboratories was not cleaned properly the night before. In response, the custodial supervisor should tell the department head

(A) to report the incident to the Superintendent of Buildings and Grounds
(B) that she will investigate and report back to him promptly
(C) that her cleaners do not like to clean the laboratories
(D) that she cannot get the cleaners to do what she tells them

59. A student complains to a custodial supervisor that a cleaner while mopping the floor in the men's lavatory splashed water on the student's shoes. The best thing for the custodial supervisor to do is to

(A) tell the student the lavatory is closed while it is being mopped and that he had no right to be there
(B) tell the student he will speak to the cleaner and that he is very sorry that it happened
(C) call the cleaner into the office and let the student and the cleaner argue
(D) smile and ask the student why he is complaining about an old pair of shoes

60. A passerby suggested a different way of doing a job to a custodial supervisor who was supervising a group working on the college grounds. The custodial supervisor already had tried the suggested method and found it to be too time-consuming. She should tell the passerby that

(A) experienced supervisors have decided on the best way
(B) if he knows so much, he should take the test for custodial supervisor
(C) she will discuss the suggestion with her superior
(D) she has no time to waste listening to half-baked ideas

Questions 61 to 68 are to be answered only in accordance with the following paragraph:

"Many custodial supervisors have discovered through experience that there are economies to be <u>realized</u> by using discretion when ordering items which are similar to each other. For example, it may be cheaper to order a Sponge block, cellulose, <u>wet size</u>: 6 in. x 4¾ in. x <u>approximately</u> 34 inches long <u>at</u> $7.00 than it is to order separate Sponges, cellulose, wet size: 2 in. × 4 in. × 6 in. at 60¢. It does not pay to 'over-<u>order</u>' on floor wax which may turn sour if not used soon enough. An average size college building cannot afford to have extra 30 inch floor brooms costing $19.75 each stored 'on the shelf' for a couple of years or to let moths destroy the hair in such brooms if proper safeguards are not used."

61. According to the above paragraph, the items mentioned which are similar are

(A) floor brooms   (B) sponges   (C) floor waxes   (D) moths

62. As used in the above paragraph, the term "<u>over-order</u>" means to

(A) order again
(B) back order
(C) order too little
(D) order too much

63. Of the items for which prices are given in the above paragraph, the most expensive one is the

(A) 30 inch floor broom   (C) 2″ × 4″ × 6″ sponge
(B) 6 in. × 4¾ in. × 34 in. sponge block   (D) floor wax

64. As used in the above paragraph, the word <u>realized</u> means most nearly

(A) obtained   (B) lost   (C) equalized   (D) cheapened

65. According to the above paragraph, the one of the following which may be damaged by moths is the

(A) floor broom   (B) sponge   (C) cellulose   (D) wool cloth

66. As used in the above paragraph the term <u>wet size</u> means

(A) the chemical treatment given to sponges
(B) the amount of water the sponge can hold
(C) that the sponges must be kept moist at all times
(D) that the measurements given were taken when the sponges were wet

67. As used in the above paragraph the word <u>at</u> means

(A) near   (B) arrived   (C) each   (D) new

68. As used in the above paragraph, the word <u>approximately</u> means

(A) exactly   (B) about   (C) economical   (D) tan

69. A <u>ballast</u> is a part of

(A) a fluorescent light fixture   (C) a door bell circuit
(B) an electric motor   (D) an incandescent light fixture

70. An ordinary wall switch which is called a "silent switch" contains a liquid called

(A) water   (B) mercury   (C) oil   (D) naphtha

71. The rating of the circuit breaker in a lighting circuit is determined by the

(A) load connected to the circuit
(B) current carrying capacity of the wire
(C) ambient temperature
(D) length of the wire

72. Faucet seats are usually made of

(A) brass   (C) lead
(B) silver   (D) rubber

73. The best way to stop a faucet drip is to

(A) replace the washer   (C) replace the faucet
(B) tighten the faucet handle with a wrench   (D) clean the trap

74. Of the following, the most important step to be taken before starting to operate a steam boiler is to see that the

    (A) water is at the proper level
    (B) fuel is heated
    (C) steam pressure is above 2 psi
    (D) vacuum pump is off

75. Of the following hand saws, the one best suited for general use when sawing wood is the

    (A) band-saw   (B) jig-saw   (C) cross-cut saw   (D) rip-saw

76. The wood most generally used for classroom floors is

    (A) balsa   (B) teak   (C) mahogany   (D) hard maple

77. The nails usually used to attach wooden molding are known as

    (A) cut nails   (B) finishing nails   (C) common nails   (D) flat-head nails

78. Of the following, the best tool to use to remove a chrome-plated bonnet from a faucet is a

    (A) a vise-grip plier   (C) a stillson wrench
    (B) an open-end wrench   (D) a chisel

79. A short piece of pipe which is externally threaded at both ends is known as a

    (A) nipple   (B) spacer   (C) coupling   (D) union

Answer Key

1. A	11. B	21. C	31. A	41. A	51. D	61. B	71. B
2. D	12. C	22. B	32. D	42. C	52. C	62. D	72. A
3. C	13. C	23. D	33. A	43. D	53. A	63. A	73. A
4. B	14. C	24. A	34. C	44. D	54. B	64. A	74. A
5. C	15. D	25. A	35. A	45. D	55. D	65. A	75. C
6. A	16. B	26. D	36. B	46. C	56. C	66. D	76. D
7. B	17. B	27. D	37. A	47. A	57. C	67. C	77. B
8. D	18. A	28. D	38. C	48. D	58. B	68. B	78. B
9. B	19. B	29. A	39. C	49. C	59. B	69. A	79. A
10. D	20. A	30. C	40. D	50. A	60. A	70. B	

Explanatory Answers
Sample Examination I

1. **(A)** Brooms will keep their shape longer if their weight is kept off them.

2. **(D)** Dust clings to oil.

3. **(C)** It is imperative that a medical office where patients are being treated be kept sanitary at all times. The other offices can wait. Health and safety come first.

4. **(B)** Sandpaper and gasoline would damage the surface. Lemon oil would be ineffective and make the floor dangerously slippery. Therefore a putty knife is the best tool to remove chewing gum from a tile floor.

5. **(C)** A counter brush is a good tool for dusting radiator covers.

6. **(A)** A wet sponge is the best way to remove chalk residue completely.

7. **(B)** A bowl brush has the correct shape and density to clean a commode.

8. **(D)** A broom is the only tool hard enough to sweep a concrete floor.

9. **(B)** Wet mopping requires at least one pail for the soapy water and one for the rinse.

10. **(D)** A wet mop will not always do the job that hard scrubbing will. Here is where you might hear the phrase "use a little elbow grease."

11. **(B)** The cost of labor is always an important consideration in the maintenance of a public building.

12. **(C)** Proper training will eliminate waste.

13. **(C)** $30 \times 8 = 240$

$$\frac{1 \text{ gal.}}{8 \text{ oz.}} = \frac{30 \text{ gal.}}{240 \text{ oz.}}$$

14. **(C)** $8' \times 72' = 576$ sq. ft. (closest to 590)

15. **(D)** Terrazzo flooring is more expensive to install, but it never needs waxing, just periodic mopping.

16. **(B)** Waste baskets should be emptied on a daily basis.

17. **(B)** The total is 4046 (closest to 4000).

18. **(A)** To get the average of a set of numbers, add them together and divide the total by the number of items added together. In this case there are four rooms, so the total should be divided by 4 for ¼ of the total.

19. **(B)** Mops are designated by weight, measured in ounces.

20. **(A)** Water pails are measured in quarts and gallons.

21. **(C)** A brush is measured from one outside end to the other. O.D. stands for "outside diameter."

22. **(B)** A crocus cloth and a wet sponge will damage the surface of a mahogany table, while a feather duster will not pick up all the dust. Cotton cloth is soft enough that it will not scratch the furniture, and, when, treated with a mineral oil, will pick up the dust easily.

23. **(D)** One person should hand the parts down to the second from the step ladder. Also, when using water around electricity, there is always the possibility of electrical shock, so it is safer to have another person assist you when washing light fixtures.

24. **(A)** Grease filters catch the splatter of grease from a frying pan. They are located in the hood for easy cleaning without disassembling many parts.

25. **(A)** Work improvement is a continuous project.

26. **(D)** A custodial supervisor should spend most of his time inspecting (observing) the work of subordinates and in all the phases of supervision (planning, training, safety, etc.).

27. **(D)** Neat's-foot oil softens and preserves leather.

28. **(D)** Elevator cleaning can stand a less intensive effort; other jobs like toilet cleaning should be performed daily.

29. **(A)** Chlorine is used widely to purify water, as a disinfectant, and as a bleaching agent. It can also be combined with nearly all other elements, whereas some other agents, such as boric acid, cannot.

30. **(C)** If something is abrasive, it is not smooth; it causes friction.

31. **(A)** Vandals destroy property, often for no good reason.

32. **(D)** Concrete, marble, and terrazzo are hard; asphalt tile is not.

33. **(A)** Proper training will always improve work performance.

34. **(C)** If a worker is late, try to discover the reason. You may be able to solve the problem easily.

35. **(A)** The workers will feel that their suggestions for work improvement are wanted and needed if they are encouraged to suggest improvements. The suggestions of those closest to the work are always valuable.

36. **(B)** Telling the occupant of an office about equipment that has been damaged by night cleaners is the only acceptable course of action. Damage should not be hidden.

37. **(A)** Praise in public; reprimand in private.

38. **(C)** If there are no complaints, the supervisor must not be encouraging communication from his subordinates. No working conditions are so perfect that there are no complaints or criticisms.

39. **(C)** Lunch time is the worker's time; it should not be monitored by the supervisor.

40. **(D)** Periodic meetings are the only way to keep subordinates informed about new rules. Everyone does not read bulletin boards, announcing new rules is not the job of the union, and reprimanding a subordinate for breaking a rule he did not know about would be bad for morale.

41. **(A)** Knowing how to do one job is the best preparation for promotion to the next higher job.

42. **(C)** Always leave room for unforeseen occurrences when scheduling.

43. **(D)** The cleaner can refer to the written schedule if necessary; it indicates exactly what the cleaner will be held responsible for.

44. **(D)** If late delivery of supplies occurred because of late ordering of supplies, this would indicate poor planning. The absence of one cleaner should be planned for, but of several cleaners is beyond planning.

45. **(D)** All workers have different skills and abilities. There is no way all people can be equal in these areas.

46. **(C)** Training groups rather than individuals is the most economical. Training is expensive.

47. **(A)** Cleaning material manufacturers often provide free training films.

48. **(D)** The worst way to begin training is to have the employee perform for you so you can criticize her. You are just making the trainee feel inadequate.

49. **(C)** If something is too heavy, seek help. This advice should be instilled in the workers.

50. **(A)** By lifting one corner of a box, a worker can discover whether he can lift it alone or must seek help.

51. **(D)** The custodial supervisor should be able to do those tasks requiring skill and experience better than his subordinates.

52. **(C)** Every worker involved suffers when an accident occurs in the work place.

53. **(A)** If water, the extinguishing agent in a soda-acid type extinguisher, is used on a Class B fire (oil), it can cause the fire to spread.

54. **(B)** The base of a ladder should be placed a distance ¼ of its height away from the wall. Larger or smaller distances will be dangerous.

55. **(D)** Accumulated rubbish is often the cause of fires. It must be cleared. The other choices, while fine activities, will not prevent fires.

56. **(C)** Carbon dioxide is an incombustible gas. Foam, a thick chemical froth, is also incombustible and will smother a fire.

57. **(C)** If subordinates feel that one supervisor's cleaning methods are better than another's, the supervisors should come to an agreement between themselves on the best method.

58. **(B)** Always listen to the complaints of building occupants and investigate them.

59. **(B)** Treat complaints from personnel using the building with courtesy, no matter how trivial the complaints.

60. **(A)** Be polite to passersby.

61. **(B)** See the second sentence.

62. **(D)** "Over-ordering," or ordering too much of something, is wasteful. Under-ordering, or ordering too little of something, means that supplies may not be on hand when they are needed.

63. **(A)** See the last sentence.

64. **(A)** "Realized" can mean *obtained* or *achieved*.

65. **(A)** See the last sentence.

66. **(D)** "Wet size" is the size of a sponge when wet.

67. **(C)** "Sponges *at* $7.00" indicates the price of each individual item.

68. **(B)** "Approximately" means *about the same*.

69. **(A)** A ballast is a choke used in a fluorescent light fixture.

70. **(B)** Liquid mercury eliminates the clicking sound in ordinary light fixtures.

71. **(B)** If circuit breakers were not rated according to the current-carrying capacity of the wire, an overloaded wire might overheat, causing a fire.

72. **(A)** Brass is commonly used for parts which come into contact with water because it resists rusting.

73. **(A)** A washer is made of rubber which tends to wear down or lose its shape after extensive use. Worn washers are therefore the most common cause of dripping faucets.

74. **(A)** A low water level can lead to a burned-out boiler or a boiler explosion and can cause damage to the boiler tubes. A high water level can cause "carry-over," which means that water is in the steam lines. This can cause "water hammer" and possibly line ruptures.

75. **(C)** The alternate teeth on a cross-cut saw are cut so that the teeth go in opposite directions. The edges of the teeth can cut wood fibers like a knife.

76. **(D)** Hard maple flooring resists wear-and-tear very effectively.

77. **(B)** Finishing nails have no heads, so they do not show.

78. **(B)** An open-end wrench should not do any damage to the surface of a bonnet if it is the proper size.

79. **(A)** A nipple is used to connect two pieces of pipe.

Answer Sheet
Sample Examination II

PART 1: BUILDING CUSTODIAN AND ASSISTANT BUILDING CUSTODIAN

1. Ⓐ Ⓑ Ⓒ Ⓓ
2. Ⓐ Ⓑ Ⓒ Ⓓ
3. Ⓐ Ⓑ Ⓒ Ⓓ
4. Ⓐ Ⓑ Ⓒ Ⓓ
5. Ⓐ Ⓑ Ⓒ Ⓓ
6. Ⓐ Ⓑ Ⓒ Ⓓ
7. Ⓐ Ⓑ Ⓒ Ⓓ
8. Ⓐ Ⓑ Ⓒ Ⓓ
9. Ⓐ Ⓑ Ⓒ Ⓓ
10. Ⓐ Ⓑ Ⓒ Ⓓ
11. Ⓐ Ⓑ Ⓒ Ⓓ

12. Ⓐ Ⓑ Ⓒ Ⓓ
13. Ⓐ Ⓑ Ⓒ Ⓓ
14. Ⓐ Ⓑ Ⓒ Ⓓ
15. Ⓐ Ⓑ Ⓒ Ⓓ
16. Ⓐ Ⓑ Ⓒ Ⓓ
17. Ⓐ Ⓑ Ⓒ Ⓓ
18. Ⓐ Ⓑ Ⓒ Ⓓ
19. Ⓐ Ⓑ Ⓒ Ⓓ
20. Ⓐ Ⓑ Ⓒ Ⓓ
21. Ⓐ Ⓑ Ⓒ Ⓓ
22. Ⓐ Ⓑ Ⓒ Ⓓ

23. Ⓐ Ⓑ Ⓒ Ⓓ
24. Ⓐ Ⓑ Ⓒ Ⓓ
25. Ⓐ Ⓑ Ⓒ Ⓓ
26. Ⓐ Ⓑ Ⓒ Ⓓ
27. Ⓐ Ⓑ Ⓒ Ⓓ
28. Ⓐ Ⓑ Ⓒ Ⓓ
29. Ⓐ Ⓑ Ⓒ Ⓓ
30. Ⓐ Ⓑ Ⓒ Ⓓ
31. Ⓐ Ⓑ Ⓒ Ⓓ
32. Ⓐ Ⓑ Ⓒ Ⓓ

33. Ⓐ Ⓑ Ⓒ Ⓓ
34. Ⓐ Ⓑ Ⓒ Ⓓ
35. Ⓐ Ⓑ Ⓒ Ⓓ
36. Ⓐ Ⓑ Ⓒ Ⓓ
37. Ⓐ Ⓑ Ⓒ Ⓓ
38. Ⓐ Ⓑ Ⓒ Ⓓ
39. Ⓐ Ⓑ Ⓒ Ⓓ
40. Ⓐ Ⓑ Ⓒ Ⓓ
41. Ⓐ Ⓑ Ⓒ Ⓓ
42. Ⓐ Ⓑ Ⓒ Ⓓ

43. Ⓐ Ⓑ Ⓒ Ⓓ
44. Ⓐ Ⓑ Ⓒ Ⓓ
45. Ⓐ Ⓑ Ⓒ Ⓓ
46. Ⓐ Ⓑ Ⓒ Ⓓ
47. Ⓐ Ⓑ Ⓒ Ⓓ
48. Ⓐ Ⓑ Ⓒ Ⓓ
49. Ⓐ Ⓑ Ⓒ Ⓓ
50. Ⓐ Ⓑ Ⓒ Ⓓ
51. Ⓐ Ⓑ Ⓒ Ⓓ
52. Ⓐ Ⓑ Ⓒ Ⓓ

PART 2: BUILDING CUSTODIAN

53. Ⓐ Ⓑ Ⓒ Ⓓ
54. Ⓐ Ⓑ Ⓒ Ⓓ
55. Ⓐ Ⓑ Ⓒ Ⓓ
56. Ⓐ Ⓑ Ⓒ Ⓓ
57. Ⓐ Ⓑ Ⓒ Ⓓ
58. Ⓐ Ⓑ Ⓒ Ⓓ
59. Ⓐ Ⓑ Ⓒ Ⓓ

60. Ⓐ Ⓑ Ⓒ Ⓓ
61. Ⓐ Ⓑ Ⓒ Ⓓ
62. Ⓐ Ⓑ Ⓒ Ⓓ
63. Ⓐ Ⓑ Ⓒ Ⓓ
64. Ⓐ Ⓑ Ⓒ Ⓓ
65. Ⓐ Ⓑ Ⓒ Ⓓ
66. Ⓐ Ⓑ Ⓒ Ⓓ

67. Ⓐ Ⓑ Ⓒ Ⓓ
68. Ⓐ Ⓑ Ⓒ Ⓓ
69. Ⓐ Ⓑ Ⓒ Ⓓ
70. Ⓐ Ⓑ Ⓒ Ⓓ
71. Ⓐ Ⓑ Ⓒ Ⓓ
72. Ⓐ Ⓑ Ⓒ Ⓓ
73. Ⓐ Ⓑ Ⓒ Ⓓ

74. Ⓐ Ⓑ Ⓒ Ⓓ
75. Ⓐ Ⓑ Ⓒ Ⓓ
76. Ⓐ Ⓑ Ⓒ Ⓓ
77. Ⓐ Ⓑ Ⓒ Ⓓ
78. Ⓐ Ⓑ Ⓒ Ⓓ
79. Ⓐ Ⓑ Ⓒ Ⓓ
80. Ⓐ Ⓑ Ⓒ Ⓓ

PART 2: ASSISTANT BUILDING CUSTODIAN

53. Ⓐ Ⓑ Ⓒ Ⓓ
54. Ⓐ Ⓑ Ⓒ Ⓓ
55. Ⓐ Ⓑ Ⓒ Ⓓ
56. Ⓐ Ⓑ Ⓒ Ⓓ
57. Ⓐ Ⓑ Ⓒ Ⓓ
58. Ⓐ Ⓑ Ⓒ Ⓓ
59. Ⓐ Ⓑ Ⓒ Ⓓ

60. Ⓐ Ⓑ Ⓒ Ⓓ
61. Ⓐ Ⓑ Ⓒ Ⓓ
62. Ⓐ Ⓑ Ⓒ Ⓓ
63. Ⓐ Ⓑ Ⓒ Ⓓ
64. Ⓐ Ⓑ Ⓒ Ⓓ
65. Ⓐ Ⓑ Ⓒ Ⓓ
66. Ⓐ Ⓑ Ⓒ Ⓓ

67. Ⓐ Ⓑ Ⓒ Ⓓ
68. Ⓐ Ⓑ Ⓒ Ⓓ
69. Ⓐ Ⓑ Ⓒ Ⓓ
70. Ⓐ Ⓑ Ⓒ Ⓓ
71. Ⓐ Ⓑ Ⓒ Ⓓ
72. Ⓐ Ⓑ Ⓒ Ⓓ
73. Ⓐ Ⓑ Ⓒ Ⓓ

74. Ⓐ Ⓑ Ⓒ Ⓓ
75. Ⓐ Ⓑ Ⓒ Ⓓ
76. Ⓐ Ⓑ Ⓒ Ⓓ
77. Ⓐ Ⓑ Ⓒ Ⓓ
78. Ⓐ Ⓑ Ⓒ Ⓓ
79. Ⓐ Ⓑ Ⓒ Ⓓ
80. Ⓐ Ⓑ Ⓒ Ⓓ

TEAR HERE

SAMPLE EXAMINATION II

THE TIME ALLOWED FOR THE ENTIRE EXAMINATION IS 3½ HOURS.

DIRECTIONS: Each question has four suggested answers lettered (A), (B), (C), and (D). Decide which one is the best answer and, on your answer sheet, darken the space for that letter.

Building Custodian and Assistant Building Custodian

Part 1 (Questions 1 to 52) is for all candidates for the positions of both Building Custodian and Assistant Building Custodian.

Part 2 (Questions 53 to 80) is different for each position.

PART 1: BUILDING CUSTODIAN—ASSISTANT BUILDING CUSTODIAN

1. Linseed oil is most commonly used to

   (A) seal wooden floors
   (B) polish brass fixtures
   (C) thin exterior oil base paints
   (D) lubricate fan bearings

2. The approximate number of square feet of unobstructed corridor floor space that one cleaner can sweep in an hour is

   (A) 1200
   (B) 2400
   (C) 4000
   (D) 6000

3. Of the following materials, the one most effective in dusting office furniture is a

   (A) silk cloth
   (B) chamois
   (C) soft cotton cloth
   (D) counter brush

4. Of the following materials, the one that should be used to produce the most resilient flooring is

   (A) concrete
   (B) terrazzo
   (C) ceramic tile
   (D) asphalt tile

5. Sweeping compound is used on concrete floors mainly to

(A) keep the dust down
(B) polish the floor
(C) harden the floor surface
(D) indicate which part of the floor has not been swept

6. The type of floor finish or wax that will produce an anti-slip surface on resilient floor coverings is

(A) resin-based floor finish
(B) water emulsion wax
(C) paste wax
(D) paraffin

7. High sheen and good wearing qualities can be obtained when polishing a waxed floor by using an electric scrubbing machine equipped with

(A) nylon disks
(B) soft brushes
(C) steel wool pads
(D) pumice wheels

8. Spalling of the surface of a marble floor may result if the floor is washed with

(A) a solution of trisodium phosphate
(B) a soft soap solution
(C) a neutral liquid detergent solution
(D) cold water

9. When not in use, a broom should be stored

(A) resting on the floor with the handle end down
(B) resting on the floor with the bristle end down
(C) hanging by the handle from a hook
(D) lying flat on the floor

10. The one of the following items which ordinarily requires the most time to wash is a (an)

(A) 5 ft. x 10 ft. venetian blind
(B) 4 foot fluorescent fixture
(C) incandescent fixture
(D) 5 ft. x 10 ft. ceramic tile floor

11. A broom that has been properly used should generally be replaced after

(A) it has been used for one month
(B) its bristles have been worn down by more than one-third of their original length
(C) it has been used for two months
(D) its bristles have been worn down by more than two-thirds of their original length

12. The floor area of a room which measures 10 feet long x 10 feet wide is

(A) 20 sq. feet
(B) 40 sq. feet
(C) 100 sq. feet
(D) 1000 sq. feet

13. The first thing that should be checked before an oil-fired, low-pressure steam boiler is started up in the morning is the

(A) boiler water level
(B) stack temperature
(C) aquastat
(D) vaporstat

14. The main reason for preheating number 6 fuel oil before allowing it to enter an oil burner is to

(A) increase its viscosity
(B) decrease its viscosity
(C) increase its heating value
(D) decrease its flash point

15. A house pump is used to

(A) drain basements that become flooded
(B) pump sewage from the basement to the sewer
(C) pump city water to a roof storage tank
(D) circulate domestic hot water

16. The device which shuts down an automatic rotary cup oil burner when the steam pressure reaches a preset high limit is a

(A) pressure gauge
(B) pressuretrol
(C) safety valve
(D) low water cutoff

17. A pressure gauge connected to a compressed air tank usually reads in

(A) pounds
(B) pounds per square inch
(C) inches of mercury
(D) feet of water

18. The device which shuts off the oil burner when the water level in the boiler is too low is the

(A) feedwater regulator
(B) low water cutoff
(C) high water alarm
(D) programmer

19. The device which shuts down an oil burner when there is a flame failure is the

(A) stack switch
(B) thermostat
(C) manometer
(D) modutrol motor

20. The switch which is used to shut off the oil burner in case of a fire in the boiler room is located

(A) on the programmer cover
(B) near the boiler room entrance
(C) on the burner motor
(D) in the custodian's office

21. The most likely reason for a cold water faucet to continue to drip after its washer has been replaced is a defective

(A) handle
(B) stem
(C) seat
(D) bib

22. In water lines, the type of valve which should always be either fully open or fully closed is the

(A) needle valve
(B) gate valve
(C) globe valve
(D) mixing valve

23. The best tool to use on a 1″ galvanized iron pipe nipple when unscrewing the nipple from a coupling is a

(A) crescent wrench
(B) stillson wrench
(C) monkey wrench
(D) spad wrench

24. The best way to locate a leak in a natural gas pipe line is to

(A) hold a lighted match under the pipe and move it along the length of the pipe slowly
(B) hold a lighted match about two inches above the pipe and move it along the length of the pipe slowly
(C) coat the pipe with a soapy solution and watch for bubbles
(D) shut off the gas at the meter and then coat the pipe with a soapy solution and watch for bubbles

25. When comparing a 60 watt yellow bulb with a 60 watt clear bulb it can be said that they both

(A) give the same amount of light
(B) use the same amount of power
(C) will burn for at least 60 hours
(D) will burn for at least 60 days

26. The output capacity of an electric motor is usually rated in

(A) kilowatts
(B) horsepower
(C) percent
(D) cubic feet

27. A fuse will burn out whenever it is subjected to excessive

(A) resistance
(B) voltage
(C) current
(D) capacitance

28. Of the following, the device which uses the greatest amount of electric power is the

(A) electric typewriter
(B) ¼ inch electric drill
(C) floor scrubbing machine
(D) oil burner ignition transformer

29. Meters which indicate the electric power consumed in a public building are read in

(A) kilowatt-hours
(B) bolts
(C) cubic feet
(D) degree days

30. Tongue and groove lumber is used for

(A) desk drawers
(B) hardwood floors
(C) picture frames
(D) cabinet doors

31. When hand sawing a 1 inch x 4 inch board parallel to the grain of the wood the best saw to use is the

(A) cross-cut saw
(B) back saw
(C) hack saw
(D) rip saw

32. The best tool to use to make a recess for the head of a flat-head wood screw is a (an)

(A) counterbore
(B) countersink
(C) auger
(D) nail set

33. In attaching two pieces of wood with a nut and bolt, the holes drilled should be

(A) slightly undersize in one piece, slightly oversize in the other
(B) slightly oversize in both pieces
(C) slightly undersize in both pieces
(D) drilled from opposite sides of the joint

34. The one of the following transmission devices which should be oiled most often is the

(A) V-belt
(B) roller chain
(C) rigid coupling
(D) clutch plate

35. A motor-generator set is usually part of a (an)

(A) steam boiler
(B) hydraulic elevator
(C) electric elevator
(D) incinerator

36. The one of the following devices which most frequently contains hydraulic fluid is a

(A) door closer
(B) worm gear reducer
(C) foam fire extinguisher
(D) hand winch

37. A breakdown of the causes of accidental injuries by percent would show that such injuries are most nearly caused

(A) 100 percent by unsafe physical working conditions
(B) 100 percent by unsafe acts of people
(C) 50 percent by unsafe physical working conditions and 50 percent by unsafe acts of people
(D) 20 percent by unsafe physical working conditions and 80 percent by unsafe acts of people

38. When using an eight-foot step ladder, a worker should climb up not more than

(A) 4 rungs
(B) 5 rungs
(C) 6 rungs
(D) 7 rungs

39. A supervisor interested in the safety of his subordinates would *not* permit

(A) using a wooden rule to take measurements near electrical apparatus
(B) using a machinist's hammer to strike a chisel
(C) removing metal chips from a machine with a rag
(D) testing the heat of a soldering iron with a piece of solder

40. If a worker feels an electric shock while using a portable electric drill, she should immediately

(A) stand on a piece of scrap lumber
(B) reverse the plug in the receptacle
(C) hold onto a grounded pipe or piece of metal
(D) take the drill out of service

41. An electric motor fire should be put out with an extinguisher that uses

(A) carbon dioxide
(B) soda-acid
(C) foam
(D) a pump tank

42. The charge in a soda-acid fire extinguisher should be replaced

(A) once a month
(B) once every three months
(C) once every six months
(D) once a year

43. An elevator machinery room should have a fire extinguisher of the

(A) soda-acid type
(B) foam type
(C) carbon dioxide type
(D) sand pail type

44. The one of the following subjects of a fire prevention training program which is most readily applied on the job is the

(A) elimination of fire hazards
(B) use of portable fire extinguishers
(C) knowledge of types of fires
(D) method of reporting fires

45. A good supervisor will *not*

(A) tell his men what their jobs are and why they are important
(B) show his men how their jobs are to be done in the right way
(C) require some of the men to do their jobs in the presence of the supervisor demonstrating that they understand the job
(D) leave his men alone because they will always do their jobs correctly once they have received their instructions

46. When a supervisor sees a worker doing her job incorrectly he should

(A) tell the worker to be more careful
(B) suspend the worker until she learns to do the job correctly
(C) tell the worker specifically how the job should be done
(D) scold the person

47. An office worker complains to a custodian that one of the cleaners broke off a branch of a plant which she kept on her desk and that she can identify the cleaner. The best thing for the custodian to do is to

(A) convince her that the plant will grow another branch eventually
(B) make the cleaner apologize and pay for a new plant out of his own pocket
(C) sympathize with the office worker and assure her that he will speak to the cleaner about it
(D) tell her not to bother him about her personal property

48. An employee who is a good worker but is often late for work

(A) is lazy and should be dismissed
(B) cannot tell time
(C) can have no excuse for being late more than once a month
(D) should be questioned by his supervisor to try to find out why he is late

49. When starting any disciplinary action, a good supervisor should

(A) show his annoyance by losing his temper
(B) be apologetic
(C) be sarcastic
(D) be firm and positive

50. Good public relations can be damaged by a custodian who treats tenants, fellow workers, friends, relatives, and the public with

(A) courtesy   (C) contempt
(B) consideration   (D) respect

51. The best way for a supervisor to maintain good employee morale is to

(A) avoid praising any one employee
(B) always have an alibi for her own mistakes
(C) encourage cliques by giving them information before giving it to other workers
(D) give adequate credit and praise when due

52. When a new employee reports to a custodian on his first day on the job, the custodian should

(A) extend a hearty welcome and make the new employee feel welcome
(B) have the man sit and wait for a while before seeing him so that the employee realizes how busy the custodian is
(C) warn him of stern disciplinary action if he is late or absent excessively
(D) tell him he probably will have difficulty doing the work so that he doesn't become overconfident

PART 2: BUILDING CUSTODIAN

53. During a shortage of custodial help in a public building, the cleaning task which will probably receive *least* attention is

(A) picking up sweepings   (C) washing walls
(B) emptying ashtrays   (D) dust-mopping offices

54. Of the following substances commonly used on floors, the most flammable is

(A) resin-based floor finish   (C) water emulsion wax
(B) floor sealer   (D) trisodium phosphate

55. The most effective method for cleaning badly soiled carpeting is

(A) wet shampooing   (C) dry shampooing
(B) vacuum cleaning   (D) wire brushing

56. Before repainting becomes necessary, a painted wall can usually be washed completely

(A) only once   (C) eight to ten times
(B) two or three times   (D) sixteen to twenty times

57. The first step in routine cleaning of offices at night should be

(A) sweeping floors   (C) dusting furniture
(B) emptying ash trays   (D) damp mopping the floors

58. Among the factors pertaining to the maintenance and cleaning of a building, the one most likely to be under the control of the building custodian is the

(A) size of the area   (C) type of occupancy
(B) density of occupancy   (D) standards to be maintained

59. "Treated" or "dustless" sweeping of resilient-type floors requires

(A) spraying the floors with water to keep the dust down
(B) spreading sweeping compound on the floor
(C) sweeping cloths that are chemically treated with mineral oil
(D) spraying the sweeping tool with neat's-foot oil

60. A modern central vacuum cleaner system

(A) is cheaper to operate than one portable machine
(B) generally produces less suction than a portable machine
(C) conveys the dirt directly to a basement tank
(D) must be operated only in the daytime

61. Oxalic acid can be used to

(A) remove ink spots from wood
(B) clear floor drains
(C) solder copper flashing
(D) polish brass

62. The best material for sealing a terrazzo floor is

(A) varnish
(B) a penetrating seal
(C) shellac
(D) a surface seal

63. The most troublesome feature in cleaning public washrooms is

(A) cleaning and deodorizing urinals
(B) washing the toilet bowls
(C) mopping the tile floors
(D) removing chewing gum from the floors

64. In order to improve its appearance, extend its life, and reduce the labor involved in dusting, wood furniture should be polished with a (an)

(A) oil polish
(B) water emulsion wax
(C) silicone and spirit chemical spray
(D) clear water

65. Ringelmann charts are useful in determining

(A) interest rates
(B) smoke density
(C) standard times for cleaning operations
(D) fuel consumption

66. A fusible plug is usually found in a

(A) lighting panel
(B) fire door
(C) boiler wall
(D) house tank

67. In an air conditioned office, most people would feel comfortable when the room temperature and humidity are maintained respectively at

(A) 75°F and 50%
(B) 70°F and 30%
(C) 75°F and 20%
(D) 65°F and 75%

68. The one of the following sets of conditions which will provide the most efficient combustion in an oil-fired low-pressure steam boiler is

(A) 400°F stack temperature, 12% CO_2
(B) 500°F stack temperature, 10% CO_2
(C) 600°F stack temperature, 8% CO_2
(D) 700°F stack temperature, 6% CO_2

69. The best way for a building custodian to tell if the night cleaners have done their work well is to

(A) check on how much cleaning material has been used
(B) check on how much waste paper was collected
(C) check the building for cleanliness
(D) check the floor mops to see if they are still wet

70. Of the following, the *best* reason for introducing a training program is that the

(A) quality of work is above standard
(B) employees are all experienced
(C) accident rate is too high
(D) tenant complaints are negligible

71. The first step in training an inexperienced individual in a particular job is to

(A) put him to work and watch for mistakes
(B) put him to work and tell him to call for help if he needs it
(C) put him at ease and then find out what he knows about the work
(D) tell him to watch the least experienced worker on the job because the training is still fresh in his mind

72. As used in job analysis, the term "job breakdown" means

(A) any equipment failure
(B) any failure on the part of the worker to complete the job
(C) dividing the job into a series of steps
(D) reducing the number of workers by 50 percent

73. At times when a public building is closed to the public, the building custodian should

(A) keep all doors locked and admit no one
(B) admit only custodial employees
(C) admit anyone as long as he signs the log
(D) admit only those who have business in the building

74. When a public building is equipped for security purposes with exterior lights on or around the building, the lights should be kept lit

(A) all night except for Saturdays, Sundays, and holidays
(B) twenty four hours a day on weekends
(C) throughout the night, every night of the week
(D) until midnight, every night of the week

75. Custodial workers are most liable to injury when they are engaged in

(A) sweeping floors
(B) mopping floors
(C) dusting furniture
(D) moving furniture

76. The best place to store a wooden step ladder is

(A) in a boiler room
(B) in a stairwell
(C) in a dry room
(D) outside a basement window provided that there is a locked grating overhead

77. Of the following, the best action for a building custodian to take when she notices that an office worker in her building has a hot plate connected to a heavily loaded electric circuit, is to

(A) remove the hot plate from the office when its owner is not present
(B) demand that the office worker remove the hot plate immediately
(C) write a report to the supervisor of the office requesting corrective action
(D) ignore the situation

78. In dealing with the public, a building custodian should be

(A) indulgent
(B) courteous
(C) disagreeable
(D) unavailable

79. If a building custodian sees a group of people in front of his building preparing to form a picket line, he should

(A) turn on a lawn sprinkler to spray the pickets
(B) order the pickets off the sidewalk in front of the building
(C) show the pickets he is sympathetic with their complaint against the City
(D) contact his supervisor immediately for instructions

80. When electric service in a public building is to be shut off from 10 a.m. Tuesday to 11:30 the next morning because a new electric feeder cable is being installed, the building custodian should

(A) prepare a memo to all office supervisors in the building, notifying them of the situation, and deliver a copy to each office as soon as possible
(B) prepare a notice of the impending power stoppage and post it in the lobby early Tuesday morning
(C) tell the electrical contractor to notify the tenants when she is about to shut off the power
(D) discontinue elevator service at 10 a.m. on Tuesday as an indication to the tenants that the power supply is off

PART 2: ASSISTANT BUILDING CUSTODIAN

53. The American flag should be

(A) raised slowly and lowered briskly
(B) raised briskly and lowered slowly
(C) raised briskly and lowered briskly
(D) raised slowly and lowered slowly

54. The material which is used to seal the outside edges of a pane of window glass is

(A) stellite
(B) putty
(C) plastic wood
(D) caulking compound

55. The ceiling of a room which measures 20 feet x 30 feet is to be given two coats of paint. If one gallon of paint will cover 500 square feet, the two coats of paint will require a minimum of

(A) 1.5 gallons   (C) 2.4 gallons
(B) 2 gallons   (D) 3.2 gallons

56. Rubbish, sticks, and papers on the lawn in front of a building should be collected by using a

(A) rake   (C) paper sticker
(B) broom   (D) hoe

57. Mortar stains on brick work can be scrubbed off by using a solution of

(A) benzine   (C) muriatic acid
(B) trisodium phosphate   (D) acetic acid

58. The best chemical for melting ice on sidewalks is

(A) sodium chloride   (C) hydrogen sulphide
(B) calcium carbonate   (D) calcium chloride

59. Before painting a kitchen wall

(A) a degreaser must be mixed with the paint
(B) all traces of grease must be washed off
(C) a water-based paint must be used to dissolve the grease
(D) the walls must be sanded to remove all traces of grease and old paint

60. For interior walls which must be washed very often the preferred paint is

(A) enamel   (C) exterior varnish
(B) flat   (D) calsomine

61. A type of window which is usually equipped with sash cords or chains is the

(A) hopper type   (C) casement type
(B) awning type   (D) double-hung type

62. The slats of a venetian blind are usually tilted by a device containing a

(A) worm gear   (C) hypoid gear
(B) spur gear   (D) bevil gear

63. When washing the outside of a window with a narrow inside sill, a window cleaner should place his water pail on

(A) the outside window sill
(B) the nearest desk or chair
(C) a radiator at the center of the window
(D) the floor at a convenient point toward one side of the window

64. In order to determine the carrying capacity of a passenger elevator, a custodian would have to

   (A) measure the floor area
   (B) check the diameter of the cable
   (C) read the inspection certificate
   (D) read the motor nameplate

65. Before pruning a tree, the first step should be to determine

   (A) if there is insect infestation
   (B) the general health of the tree
   (C) the desired results
   (D) amount of excess foliage

66. Tree fertilizer should have a high content of

   (A) slaked lime   (C) rose dust
   (B) chlordane   (D) nitrogen

67. A gasoline-driven snow blower should be stored for the summer with its fuel tank

   (A) filled with gasoline
   (B) and fuel lines drained
   (C) filled wtih water
   (D) half filled with number 4 fuel oil

68. A pipe that "sweats" in the summer time probably contains

   (A) hot water   (C) domestic gas
   (B) low pressure steam   (D) cold water

69. A good preventive maintenance program requires that each item of equipment

   (A) be represented by an up-to-date record card on file
   (B) be lubricated daily
   (C) be brand new at the start of the program
   (D) be painted inside and out

Questions 70 through 73 inclusive are to be answered solely on the basis of the following paragraph:

"All cleaning agents and supplies should be kept in a central storeroom which should be kept locked and only the custodian, storekeeper, and supervisor should have keys. Shelving should be provided for the smaller items while barrels containing scouring powder or other bulk material should be set on the floor or on special cradles. Each compartment in the shelves should be marked plainly and only the item indicated stored therein. Each barrel should also be marked plainly. It may also be desirable to keep special items such as electric lamps, flashlight batteries, etc., in a locked cabinet or separate room to which only the custodian and the night building supervisor have keys."

70. According to the preceding paragraph

(A) scouring powder should be kept on shelves
(B) scouring powder comes in one-pound cans
(C) scouring powder should be kept in a locked cabinet
(D) scouring powder is a bulk material

71. According to the preceding paragraph

(A) the storekeeper should not be entrusted with the safekeeping of light bulbs
(B) flashlight batteries should be stored in barrels
(C) the central storeroom should be kept locked
(D) only special items should be stored under lock and key

72. According to the preceding paragraph

(A) each shelf compartment should contain at least four different items
(B) barrels must be stored in cradles
(C) all items stored should be in marked compartments
(D) crates of light bulbs should be stored in cradles

73. As used in the preceding paragraph, the word cradle means a

(A) dolly   (C) doll's bed
(B) support   (D) hand truck

Questions 74 through 77 inclusive are to be answered solely on the basis of the following paragraph:

"There are on the market many cleaning agents for which amazing claims are made. Chemical analysis shows that the majority of them are well known chemicals slightly modified and packaged and sold under various trade names. For that reason the agents which have been selected for your use are those whose cleaning properties are well known and whose use can be standardized. It is obviously undesirable to offer too wide a selection as that would be confusing to the cleaner, but a sufficient number must be provided so that a satisfactory agent is available for each task."

74. According to the preceding paragraph

(A) there are few cleaning agents on the market
(B) there are no really good cleaning agents on the market
(C) cleaning agents are sold under several different brand names
(D) all cleaning agents are the same

75. According to the preceding paragraph

(A) all cleaning agents should be chemically analyzed before use
(B) the best cleaning agents are those for which no claims are made
(C) different cleaning agents may be needed for different tasks
(D) all cleaning agents have been standardized by the federal government

76. As used in the preceding paragraph, the word amazing means

(A) illegal   (C) astonishing
(B) untrue   (D) specific

77. As used in the preceding paragraph, the word <u>modified</u> means

(A) changed   (C) labelled
(B) refined   (D) diluted

78. The main reason for keeping an inventory of housekeeping supplies is to

(A) be sure that supplies are available when needed
(B) determine the cost of the supplies
(C) automatically prevent waste of the supplies
(D) be sure that at least two years' supplies are on hand at all times

79. Current daily records are most desirable in dealing with problems concerning

(A) accidents   (C) employee time and attendance
(B) vandalism   (D) the consumption of electricity

80. The continuous record of activities taking place in a boiler room is called a

(A) computer   (C) log book
(B) data bank   (D) time sheet

Answer Key

PART 1: BUILDING CUSTODIAN AND ASSISTANT BUILDING CUSTODIAN

1. C	8. A	15. C	22. B	29. A	35. C	41. A	47. C
2. D	9. C	16. B	23. B	30. B	36. A	42. D	48. D
3. C	10. A	17. B	24. C	31. D	37. D	43. C	49. D
4. D	11. B	18. B	25. B	32. B	38. C	44. A	50. C
5. A	12. C	19. A	26. B	33. B	39. C	45. D	51. D
6. A	13. A	20. B	27. C	34. B	40. D	46. C	52. A
7. B	14. B	21. C	28. C				

PART 2: BUILDING CUSTODIAN

53. C	57. B	61. A	65. B	69. C	72. C	75. D	78. B
54. B	58. D	62. B	66. C	70. C	73. D	76. C	79. D
55. A	59. C	63. A	67. A	71. C	74. C	77. C	80. A
56. B	60. C	64. C	68. A				

PART 2: ASSISTANT BUILDING CUSTODIAN

53. B	57. C	61. D	65. C	69. A	72. C	75. C	78. A
54. B	58. D	62. A	66. D	70. D	73. B	76. C	79. C
55. C	59. B	63. D	67. B	71. C	74. C	77. A	80. C
56. A	60. A	64. C	68. D				

Explanatory Answers
Sample Examination II

1. **(C)** Because linseed oil is also an oil, it thins out oil-based paint. It will also thicken and harden when exposed to air, thus giving a good seal.

2. **(D)** Sweeping 6000 sq. ft. is just about an hour's productive labor. However, a day's work is not 48,000 square feet (6000 multiplied by 8) because fatigue will set in.

3. **(C)** Cotton picks up dust better than silk, leather, or a brush.

4. **(D)** Asphalt tile flooring is much more resilient than concrete, terrazzo, or ceramic.

5. **(A)** Without sweeping compound the dust would fly about.

6. **(A)** Resin is a viscous substance that resists when pressure or weight is applied to it, and thus produces a no-slip surface.

7. **(B)** Soft brushes are not as abrasive as nylon, steel wool, and pumice are, so polishing a waxed floor with them results in a high sheen.

8. **(A)** Trisodium phospate reacts violently with a marble floor, especially when mixed with water, causing spalling, which is chipping or splitting.

9. **(C)** If the weight is taken off a broom it will keep its shape better.

10. **(A)** Washing Venetian blind slats individually involves a great deal of time.

11. **(B)** After a broom's bristles have been worn down more than $1/3$ of their original length, it loses its effectiveness. The length of time a broom has been in use is not a factor; what is important is how much it is used.

12. **(C)** $10' \times 10' = 100$ sq. ft.

13. **(A)** Without an appropriate amount of water, the boiler can be damaged. Too much water can cause water hammer or carry-over; too little can lead to a burned-out boiler.

14. **(B)** Number 6 fuel oil must be preheated to decrease its viscosity so it can be pumped and then further heated to burn it.

15. **(C)** A house pump pumps city water to a roof storage tank and water to the higher floors in a high-rise building.

16. **(B)** The pressuretrol is a switch that starts and stops a boiler and controls its operating range, e.g., on at 3 lbs.–off at 6 lbs.

17. **(B)** Pressure is measured in psi (pounds per square inch). A pressure gauge lets you know whether you are in a safe operating range.

18. **(B)** A low water cutoff will shut off the burner in the event of a low level of water. Lack of water can lead to a burned-out boiler or a boiler explosion.

19. **(A)** A stackswitch senses drafts and gases of combustion.

20. **(B)** The emergency shut-off switch for a boiler is located near the boiler room entrance because fire may make it impossible to enter the boiler room.

21. **(C)** If the faucet continues to drip after replacement of the washer, consider a defective seat. It may need only reaming. If reaming does not work, the seat must be replaced.

22. **(B)** You cannot throttle with a gate valve; it must be either fully open or fully closed.

23. **(B)** A stillson wrench is the only wrench you can use on a round surface. It will grip a pipe so you can remove it easily.

24. **(C)** To detect natural gas leaks, coat the pipe with a soapy solution and watch for bubbles. If you shut off the flow of gas you will never be able to find the leak. Use of a match would find the leak but cause an explosion. Do NOT use a match.

25. **(B)** Equal wattage means equal use of power. Results will differ on different bulbs.

26. **(B)** Horsepower is a measure of the strength of a motor's output.

27. **(C)** A fuse is a safety device with an assigned amperage. If this amperage is exceeded, that is, if there is too much current, the fuse will blow, opening the circuit.

28. **(C)** Floor scrubbing machines require a great deal of power, more than drills, typewriters, or other appliances.

29. **(A)** Kilowatt-hours are the measurement of the amount of electricity used.

30. **(B)** When tongue and groove lumber is used, nails are hammered in at a 45 degree angle so as to be invisible, as in hardwood floors.

31. **(D)** A rip saw's teeth are in a straight line and work like chisels, pushing out small chips of wood.

32. **(B)** A countersink accommodates the screw head by enlarging the hole.

33. **(B)** When attaching two pieces of wood with a nut and bolt, both holes should be slightly oversized for easy alignment and installation of the bolts.

34. **(B)** Oiling reduces friction. Roller chains, which experience a lot of friction, should be oiled most often.

35. **(C)** A generator is used to convert mechanical energy to electric energy, and a motor converts any form of energy into mechanical energy. Thus an elevator, because it is not used at all times, has a motor generator on standby ready to be used at the push of a button.

36. **(A)** Door closers often contain hydraulic fluid so that the door won't slam and will close easily.

37. **(D)** Careless workers are the cause of most accidents.

38. **(C)** Climbing higher than six rungs on an eight-foot step ladder makes it easy for the ladder to tip over.

39. **(C)** If the machine accidentally starts up, the rag could be caught inside, and the worker could be pulled into the machine.

40. **(D)** A drill which shocks its user is not properly grounded and needs repair.

41. **(A)** Carbon dioxide is an incombustible gas. Other fire extinguishers which contain water, such as foam extinguishers, can cause electrocution or short circuiting and start additional fires if used on an electric motor fire (Class C fire).

42. **(D)** Replace the charge in soda-acid fire extinguishers once a year. If it is left any longer than that the charge will not be as powerful.

43. **(C)** Because there is electricity in the machine room, it should have a CO_2 fire extinguisher.

44. **(A)** Learning to eliminate fire hazards is the most important part of a fire prevention training program, although not the easiest to accomplish.

45. **(D)** A good supervisor will never simply leave his men alone after they have received their instructions. Everyone may not have understood the instructions. (This is a negative question requiring you to select the *incorrect* answer.)

46. **(C)** Incorrect methods may become habitual, and should be corrected immediately.

47. **(C)** Treat office workers' complaints with courtesy and everyone will be happier.

48. **(D)** Often the cause of a worker's lateness can be easily rectified. You cannot solve a problem before it is identified.

49. **(D)** Discipline is a necessity. It must be taken without delay when needed, and must be firm and decisive to be beneficial. Essentially, discipline is a training measure used to change an individual's attitude or behavior.

50. **(C)** Courtesy, consideration, and respect will promote public relations. Showing contempt will not do so.

51. **(D)** Giving credit and praise when it is deserved will promote the morale of the group.

52. **(A)** It is important to make a new employee feel welcome on his first day. He will feel wanted and needed from the beginning.

PART 2: BUILDING CUSTODIAN

53. **(C)** Washing walls has the lowest priority. Dust mopping, emptying ashtrays, and picking up sweepings are tasks which must be done regularly to achieve acceptable working conditions.

54. **(B)** Floor sealer is oil-based and flammable. Most other substances used on floors are water-based and not flammable.

55. **(A)** Wet shampoo is the most effective way to loosen dirt on a carpet.

56. **(B)** Painted walls can be washed two or three times without discoloring or removing the paint.

57. **(B)** Clean an office doing the tasks in this order: empty ashtrays, dust furniture, sweep floors, damp mop floors.

58. **(D)** The building custodian is only concerned with maintaining the standards of cleaning in his building.

59. **(C)** Chemically treated cloths attract dust and keep it down in "dustless" sweeping.

60. **(C)** A central vacuum cleaner system conveys the dust directly into a basement tank.

61. **(A)** Oxalic acid removes ink spots from wood—very useful in a school building.

62. **(B)** A seal on a terrazzo floor must penetrate, or else it will mar the floor.

63. **(A)** The urinals are the most used feature in a public building, and they have areas which are hard to get at and are often soiled.

64. **(C)** A silicone and spirit chemical spray puts a long-lasting coat on wood furniture.

65. **(B)** The Ringelmann chart measures the density of oil burner smoke.

66. **(C)** A fusible plug is located one to two inches above the highest heating surface on a boiler wall in the direct path of the gases of combustion.

67. **(A)** Average temperatures and humidity will satisfy most people, although there will always be a few who are hard to please.

68. **(A)** At 400°F stack temperature and 12% CO_2 a steam boiler generates the lowest amount of waste heat with the highest percentage of burnt fuel.

69. **(C)** The inspection process is used as a control. Inspecting the night cleaners' work is the only way to check whether it was performed properly.

70. **(C)** When the accident rate is too high, it is an indication that working conditions are unsafe and that the workers are careless and using unsafe practices. A training program should correct these problems.

71. **(C)** A trainee must be receptive and at ease if the training is to be beneficial. The goal of training is to close the gap between what the worker already knows and what he or she needs to know to perform the job properly.

72. **(C)** A "job breakdown" is used in training so that the steps may be taught one at a time. It is also used in job analysis, work simplification, etc.

73. **(D)** Admitting only those who have business within the building is the only way to keep the number of people in the building under control at night without interfering in the work that goes on.

74. **(C)** If exterior lights were installed, evidently this type of security is needed. The lights should be on all night, every night.

75. **(D)** Moving furniture can be dangerous if the furniture is not lifted properly. Also, furniture can be broken during moving and can thus be the cause of accidents.

76. **(C)** Wooden equipment will not mold in a dry room. The heat of a boiler room could damage the wood, and storing equipment in a stairwell or outside a basement window would be dangerous.

77. **(C)** Dangerous conditions caused by office personnel must be corrected using the proper chain of command.

78. **(B)** Courtesy breeds courtesy. Courtesy on the part of the workers is a necessity in all types of buildings, but especially in public buildings.

79. **(D)** Instructions on how to deal with a picket line should be given from a higher level. The police may be brought in to preserve peace.

80. **(A)** If the power is to be shut off in a building, the sooner people can be notified, the better, so that personnel throughout the building can make necessary arrangements.

PART 2: ASSISTANT BUILDING CUSTODIAN

53. **(B)** Raising the flag briskly and lowering it slowly is a time-honored tradition.

54. **(B)** Putty is pliable, weather-resistant, and universally used.

55. **(C)** 20′ × 30′ = 600 sq. ft.
600 sq. ft. × 2 = 1200 sq. ft.
$1200 \text{ sq. ft.} \times \dfrac{1 \text{ gallon}}{500 \text{ sq. ft.}} = 2.4$ gallons of paint

56. **(A)** A rake is the proper instrument to collect rubbish on a lawn.

57. **(C)** Muriatic acid, also known as hydrochloric acid, is an aqueous solution of hydrogen chloride commonly used as a cleaning solution.

58. **(D)** Calcium chloride melts ice well, and does not damage or crack the sidewalk as rock salt does.

59. **(B)** Washing all traces of grease off a wall before painting is necessary if the paint is to take.

60. **(A)** Enamel paint's gloss will hold up well even after numerous washings.

61. **(D)** The bottom and top of a double-hung window open independently. Each half has its own sash cords or chains.

62. **(A)** A worm gear, often found in Venetian blinds, consists of a threaded shaft and a wheel with teeth that mesh into it.

63. **(D)** When washing windows, place the pail on the floor nearby so that it will not be knocked over and so that possible damage from placing it on a desk or chair will be avoided.

64. **(C)** The inspection certificate indicates an elevator's safe load and its designed capacity. Floor space area is not a valid indicator of an elevator's carrying capacity.

65. **(C)** Before pruning a tree, find out exactly what is wanted from the tree: shade, a desired image, etc.

66. **(D)** Nitrogen is the effective element of fertilizer.

67. **(B)** Drain the fuel tank and the fuel lines before storing a gasoline-driven snow blower, both for safety reasons and to make the machine easier to start the next year. If left in the machine, the gasoline will go bad and clog the lines and the carburetor.

68. **(D)** The contact between a cold pipe and warm air causes a pipe to sweat.

69. **(A)** Having an up-to-date file of all equipment means that necessary maintenance is not overlooked.

70. **(D)** See the second sentence.

71. **(C)** See the first sentence.

72. **(C)** See the third sentence.

73. **(B)** A "cradle" is any supporting base. It can be made of various designs to supply the necessary support.

74. **(C)** See the second sentence.

75. **(C)** See the last sentence.

76. **(C)** "Amazing claims" are those which will astonish the reader. However, according to the passage, the word is used just as a part of marketing.

77. **(A)** A "modification" is a change of small proportions and is usually not very significant.

78. **(A)** If you keep an inventory you are aware of when supplies are running low and therefore when they should be reordered.

79. **(C)** Keeping daily records means that work performed can be compared to time spent and then compared with work standards.

80. **(C)** The log book is very important for boiler maintenance. It assures that the required tasks are completed.

Answer Sheet
Sample Examination III

TEAR HERE

1. Ⓐ Ⓑ Ⓒ Ⓓ	21. Ⓐ Ⓑ Ⓒ Ⓓ	41. Ⓐ Ⓑ Ⓒ Ⓓ	61. Ⓐ Ⓑ Ⓒ Ⓓ
2. Ⓐ Ⓑ Ⓒ Ⓓ	22. Ⓐ Ⓑ Ⓒ Ⓓ	42. Ⓐ Ⓑ Ⓒ Ⓓ	62. Ⓐ Ⓑ Ⓒ Ⓓ
3. Ⓐ Ⓑ Ⓒ Ⓓ	23. Ⓐ Ⓑ Ⓒ Ⓓ	43. Ⓐ Ⓑ Ⓒ Ⓓ	63. Ⓐ Ⓑ Ⓒ Ⓓ
4. Ⓐ Ⓑ Ⓒ Ⓓ	24. Ⓐ Ⓑ Ⓒ Ⓓ	44. Ⓐ Ⓑ Ⓒ Ⓓ	64. Ⓐ Ⓑ Ⓒ Ⓓ
5. Ⓐ Ⓑ Ⓒ Ⓓ	25. Ⓐ Ⓑ Ⓒ Ⓓ	45. Ⓐ Ⓑ Ⓒ Ⓓ	65. Ⓐ Ⓑ Ⓒ Ⓓ
6. Ⓐ Ⓑ Ⓒ Ⓓ	26. Ⓐ Ⓑ Ⓒ Ⓓ	46. Ⓐ Ⓑ Ⓒ Ⓓ	66. Ⓐ Ⓑ Ⓒ Ⓓ
7. Ⓐ Ⓑ Ⓒ Ⓓ	27. Ⓐ Ⓑ Ⓒ Ⓓ	47. Ⓐ Ⓑ Ⓒ Ⓓ	67. Ⓐ Ⓑ Ⓒ Ⓓ
8. Ⓐ Ⓑ Ⓒ Ⓓ	28. Ⓐ Ⓑ Ⓒ Ⓓ	48. Ⓐ Ⓑ Ⓒ Ⓓ	68. Ⓐ Ⓑ Ⓒ Ⓓ
9. Ⓐ Ⓑ Ⓒ Ⓓ	29. Ⓐ Ⓑ Ⓒ Ⓓ	49. Ⓐ Ⓑ Ⓒ Ⓓ	69. Ⓐ Ⓑ Ⓒ Ⓓ
10. Ⓐ Ⓑ Ⓒ Ⓓ	30. Ⓐ Ⓑ Ⓒ Ⓓ	50. Ⓐ Ⓑ Ⓒ Ⓓ	70. Ⓐ Ⓑ Ⓒ Ⓓ
11. Ⓐ Ⓑ Ⓒ Ⓓ	31. Ⓐ Ⓑ Ⓒ Ⓓ	51. Ⓐ Ⓑ Ⓒ Ⓓ	71. Ⓐ Ⓑ Ⓒ Ⓓ
12. Ⓐ Ⓑ Ⓒ Ⓓ	32. Ⓐ Ⓑ Ⓒ Ⓓ	52. Ⓐ Ⓑ Ⓒ Ⓓ	72. Ⓐ Ⓑ Ⓒ Ⓓ
13. Ⓐ Ⓑ Ⓒ Ⓓ	33. Ⓐ Ⓑ Ⓒ Ⓓ	53. Ⓐ Ⓑ Ⓒ Ⓓ	73. Ⓐ Ⓑ Ⓒ Ⓓ
14. Ⓐ Ⓑ Ⓒ Ⓓ	34. Ⓐ Ⓑ Ⓒ Ⓓ	54. Ⓐ Ⓑ Ⓒ Ⓓ	74. Ⓐ Ⓑ Ⓒ Ⓓ
15. Ⓐ Ⓑ Ⓒ Ⓓ	35. Ⓐ Ⓑ Ⓒ Ⓓ	55. Ⓐ Ⓑ Ⓒ Ⓓ	75. Ⓐ Ⓑ Ⓒ Ⓓ
16. Ⓐ Ⓑ Ⓒ Ⓓ	36. Ⓐ Ⓑ Ⓒ Ⓓ	56. Ⓐ Ⓑ Ⓒ Ⓓ	76. Ⓐ Ⓑ Ⓒ Ⓓ
17. Ⓐ Ⓑ Ⓒ Ⓓ	37. Ⓐ Ⓑ Ⓒ Ⓓ	57. Ⓐ Ⓑ Ⓒ Ⓓ	77. Ⓐ Ⓑ Ⓒ Ⓓ
18. Ⓐ Ⓑ Ⓒ Ⓓ	38. Ⓐ Ⓑ Ⓒ Ⓓ	58. Ⓐ Ⓑ Ⓒ Ⓓ	78. Ⓐ Ⓑ Ⓒ Ⓓ
19. Ⓐ Ⓑ Ⓒ Ⓓ	39. Ⓐ Ⓑ Ⓒ Ⓓ	59. Ⓐ Ⓑ Ⓒ Ⓓ	79. Ⓐ Ⓑ Ⓒ Ⓓ
20. Ⓐ Ⓑ Ⓒ Ⓓ	40. Ⓐ Ⓑ Ⓒ Ⓓ	60. Ⓐ Ⓑ Ⓒ Ⓓ	80. Ⓐ Ⓑ Ⓒ Ⓓ

SAMPLE EXAMINATION III

THE TIME ALLOWED FOR THE ENTIRE EXAMINATION IS 3½ HOURS.

DIRECTIONS: Each question has four suggested answers lettered (A), (B), (C), and (D). Decide which one is the best answer and, on your answer sheet, darken the space for that letter.

1. Time standards for cleaning are of value only if

    (A) a bonus is promised if the time standards are beaten
    (B) the cleaners determine the methods and procedures to be used
    (C) accompanied by a completely detailed description of the methods to be used
    (D) a schematic diagram of the area is made available to the cleaners

2. Of the following, the one which is the *least* important factor in deciding that additional training is necessary for the workers you supervise is that

    (A) the quality of work is below standard
    (B) supplies are being wasted
    (C) too much time is required to do specific jobs
    (D) the absentee rate has declined

3. To promote proper safety practices in the operation of power tools and equipment, the senior building custodian should emphasize in meetings with his staff that

    (A) every accident can be prevented through proper safety regulations
    (B) proper safety practices will probably make future safety meetings unnecessary
    (C) when safety rules are followed, tools and equipment will work better
    (D) safety rules are based on past experience with the best methods of preventing accidents

4. Under normal conditions, during the growing season lawns should receive a good saturation of water with a spray

    (A) once a day   (C) once a month
    (B) once a week   (D) twice a month

5. The average temperature on a day in January was 24°F. The number of degree-days for that day was

    (A) 12   (B) 24   (C) 41   (D) 48

6. With the same outdoor winter temperature (24° F), the load on a heating boiler starting up is greater than the normal morning load mainly because of

    (A) loss of heat escaping through the stack
    (B) steam required to heat boiler water and piping to radiators
    (C) viscosity of the fuel oil
    (D) low outdoor temperatures

7. One of the important benefits to floors that wax does *not* provide is

(A) easier soil removal   (C) reduction in wear
(B) improved stain resistance   (D) resistance to fire

8. "Cascading" of raw city water when filling a cleaned boiler should be avoided because it

(A) is harmful to the mud drum
(B) adds additional free oxygen in the boiler
(C) adds considerable time to the filling procedure
(D) will stress tube and sheet joints

9. The *first* operation when starting a boiler after it has been on bank overnight should be to

(A) blow down the boiler
(B) clean the furnace
(C) check the gate valves
(D) look at the water gauge and try the gauge cocks

10. In the Ringelmann chart of smoke density, number 4 indicates

(A) the darkest smoke condition
(B) the lightest smoke condition
(C) smoke density of 80%
(D) no smoke condition

11. As senior building custodian, a good practical method to use in determining if an employee is doing her job properly is to

(A) assume that if she asks no questions she knows the work
(B) question her directly on details of the job
(C) inspect and follow-up the work which is assigned to her
(D) ask other employees how this employee is making out

12. If an employee continually asks how he should do his work, a supervisor should

(A) dismiss him immediately
(B) pretend he does not hear him unless he persists
(C) explain the work carefully but encourage him to use his own judgment
(D) tell him not to ask so many questions

13. As senior building custodian you have instructed an employee to wet-mop a certain area. To be sure that the employee understands the instructions you have told her, you should

(A) ask her to repeat the instructions to you
(B) check with her after she has done the job
(C) watch her while she is doing the job
(D) repeat the instructions to the employee

14. As senior building custodian one of your men disagrees with your evaluation of his work. Of the following, the best way to handle this situation would be to

   (A) explain that you are in a better position to evaluate his work than he is
   (B) tell him that since other workers are satisfied with your evaluation, he should accept their opinions
   (C) explain the basis of your evaluation and discuss it with him
   (D) refuse to discuss his complaint in order to maintain discipline

15. Of the following, the one which is *not* a quality of leadership desirable in a supervisor is

   (A) intelligence   (B) integrity   (C) forcefulness   (D) partiality

16. Of the following, the one which *least* characterizes the "grapevine" is that it

   (A) consists of a tremendous amount of rumor, conjecture, information, advice, prediction, and even orders
   (B) seems to rise spontaneously, is largely anonymous, spreads rapidly, and changes in unpredictable directions
   (C) can be eliminated without any great effort
   (D) commonly fills the gaps left by the regular organizational channels of communication

17. Of the following, the one which is *not* a purpose of a cleaning job breakdown is to

   (A) eliminate unnecessary steps
   (B) determine the type of floor wax to use
   (C) rearrange the sequence of operations to save time
   (D) combine steps or actions where practicable

18. Of the following, the principal function of a supervisor is to

   (A) train and instruct his subordinates in the proper methods of doing their work
   (B) eliminate all accidents
   (C) prepare reports on his activities to his supervisor
   (D) prepare a thorough job methods analysis

19. The best method of making cleaning assignments in a large building is by means of

   (A) daily rotation   (C) individual choice
   (B) specific assignment   (D) chronological order

20. When one of your new cleaning employees is making little progress after the usual training period with one of your experienced men, you should

   (A) recommend to your superior that he should be discharged
   (B) tell your superior he is not interested in the job
   (C) determine the reason for the poor results
   (D) discontinue all training

21. For a supervisor to have her cleaning employees willing to follow standardized cleaning procedures, she must be prepared to

   (A) associate with her employees
   (B) show that the procedures are reasonable
   (C) give extra time off
   (D) set up a penalty system

22. One of the employees you supervise has broken the rule against keeping liquor in his locker. You should

(A) make believe it never happened and forget the incident
(B) explain the rule to him and that a repetition may result in disciplinary action
(C) suspend him immediately
(D) fire him immediately

23. The best action for you as senior building custodian in charge of a building to take on receiving complaints of poor illumination in one of the offices is to

(A) wait until you have several complaints of this kind
(B) tell the complainant nothing can be done
(C) request that additional ceiling lights be installed
(D) check the office for the cause of poor illumination

24. The main purpose of periodic inspections and tests of mechanical equipment is to

(A) keep the workers busy during otherwise slack periods
(B) discover minor faults before they develop into major faults
(C) make the workers familiar with the equipment
(D) encourage the workers to take better care of the equipment

25. Of the following, the extinguishing agent that should be used on fires in flammable liquids is

(A) steam   (B) water   (C) foam   (D) soda and acid

26. A soda-acid fire extinguisher is recommended for use on fires consisting of

(A) wood or paper
(B) fuel oil or gasoline
(C) electrical causes or fuel oil
(D) paint or turpentine

27. Assume that you are a senior building custodian and one of your employees has been slightly injured while doing a cleaning job. After the employee has been cared for, you should next

(A) investigate the cause of the accident
(B) notify the union
(C) charge the employee with recklessness
(D) transfer the employee

28. The chief reason wooden ladders should *not* be painted is that the paint may

(A) hide defects
(B) mark up the walls
(C) make the ladder slippery
(D) damage the rungs

29. In accordance with the uniform method of identifying piping in public buildings, pipes carrying materials classified as being dangerous are colored

(A) blue
(B) red
(C) orange and yellow
(D) green and white

30. The most effective way to eliminate fire hazards in public buildings is to

(A) hold frequent fire drills
(B) have the fire department inspect the building annually
(C) promote constant self-inspection
(D) supply each building with ample fire fighting equipment

31. When a room is air conditioned in the summer, the windows should be

(A) opened at the top and bottom to improve circulation
(B) screened to keep out the dirt
(C) kept closed
(D) opened at the top only to let hot air escape

32. In order to clean an office with 20,000 square feet of space in 4 hours, using a standard of 900 square feet per hour, the number of cleaners you should assign to do the job is most nearly

(A) 4   (B) 6   (C) 8   (D) 10

33. The area of a floor 35 feet wide and 45 feet long is, in square yards, most nearly

(A) 175   (B) 262   (C) 525   (D) 1575

34. A pyrometer is an instrument used for measuring

(A) condensation and humidity   (C) noise pollution
(B) high temperatures   (D) water flow

35. It is usually desirable to assign the cleaning of an office to one employee only because

(A) the amount of time wasted through talking is decreased
(B) an employee working alone is more efficient
(C) there is no question who is responsible for the work done
(D) working alone reduces the rate and severity of accidents

36. Of each dollar spent on the cleaning of public buildings, the amount spent on cleaning supplies is usually not more than

(A) 5 cents   (B) 35 cents   (C) 55 cents   (D) 75 cents

37. Of the following solutions, the one most often used in washing exterior glass is

(A) cold water and a small quantity of turpentine
(B) cold water and a small quantity of ammonia
(C) cold water and a small quantity of soft soap
(D) warm water and a small quantity of soft soap

38. Rust stains in wash basins can best be prevented by

(A) applying wax film to the rusty surface
(B) replacing leaking faucet washers
(C) adding rust inhibitor to the domestic cold water storage tank
(D) sandpapering the rusty surfaces

39. Of the following, the one which is likely to be most harmful to asphalt tile is

(A) coffee   (B) ketchup   (C) salad oil   (D) vinegar

40. Of the following, when sweeping a corridor with a floor brush, the cleaner should

    (A) lean on the brush and walk the length of the corridor
    (B) give the brush a slight jerk after each stroke to free it of loose dirt
    (C) make certain there is no overlap on sweeping strokes
    (D) use moderately long pull strokes

41. When vacuum cleaning rugs, the suction tool should be pushed

    (A) diagonally across the lay of the nap
    (B) with the lay of the nap
    (C) across the lay of the nap
    (D) against the lay of the nap

42. Of the following, the preferred sequence of tasks to be followed in office cleaning is

    (A) dust desks, empty ash trays and waste baskets, mop floor
    (B) mop floor, dust desks, empty ash trays and waste baskets
    (C) empty ash trays and waste baskets, dust desks, mop floor
    (D) mop floor, empty ash trays and waste baskets, dust desks

43. The brownish discoloration that sometimes occurs in hot water circulating systems is usually due to

    (A) molds   (B) algae   (C) bacteria   (D) rust

44. The type of valve that does *not* have a stuffing or packing gland is a

    (A) globe valve   (C) check valve
    (B) radiator valve   (D) gate valve

45. Assuming that the hot and cold water demand of a fixture will be the same, then the normal size of the hot water pipe with respect to that of the cold water pipe should be

    (A) the same   (C) one and one-half times as great
    (B) twice as great   (D) one-half as great

46. If the pitch of a horizontal steam line is ½ inch in 10 feet, one end of a 45 foot steam line is lower than the other end by, most nearly

    (A) 2 inches   (B) 2¼ inches   (C) 3 inches   (D) 3½ inches

47. A pump that removes 30 gallons of water per minute is pumping water from a cellar 30 feet x 50 feet covered with eight inches of water. One cubic foot of water equals 7.5 gallons of water. The number of minutes it will take to remove the eight inches of water from the cellar is most nearly

    (A) 200   (B) 225   (C) 250   (D) 275

48. Oil preheaters are used to

    (A) economize on fuel oil
    (B) reduce friction in the oil blower
    (C) improve the flow of oil
    (D) reduce oil volatility

49. The first item which should be checked when a sump pit overflows because the automatic electric sump pump is not operating properly is the

(A) feedwater pressure   (C) stat switch
(B) float switch mechanism   (D) discharge line check valve

50. Chloride of lime should be used for the removal of

(A) alkali stains on wood
(B) grass stains on wood or marble
(C) indelible pencil and marking ink stains on concrete or terrazzo
(D) ink stains on wood

51. Of the following, the lack of a vapor barrier on the inside surface of a well insulated wall may eventually cause, during the winter,

(A) plugging of weep holes
(B) peeling of exterior paint
(C) lower heat losses through the wall
(D) improvement in insulation performance by plugging air spaces with the insulation

52. When cold water pipes in a room "sweat" it is usually due to the

(A) surface of the pipes being below the dew point temperature of the room air
(B) specific humidity exceeding the relative humidity
(C) air in the room exceeding 100% relative humidity
(D) surface of the pipe being below the wet bulb temperature of the room air

53. The main reason for applying floor finish to a floor surface is to

(A) protect against germs   (C) increase traction
(B) protect the floor surface   (D) waterproof the floor

54. The main reason for preventing sewer gas from entering buildings through the plumbing system is because the gas

(A) is highly flammable and explosive in nature and could result in a fire hazard
(B) has an eroding effect on plumbing fixtures and pipe lines
(C) is highly infectious and contagious in nature
(D) has a nuisance effect on occupants

55. The one of the following that is a concrete floor sealer is

(A) sodium silicate   (C) sodium hydroxide
(B) neat's-foot oil   (D) linseed oil

56. To help plants survive the shock of transplanting, in most cases it is best to

(A) spray them with insecticide every day for a week
(B) cover the foliage with burlap for a day or two
(C) shade them from the sun for a week or two
(D) prune them every day for a week or two

57. When cutting a branch off a tree it is desirable to undercut because it will

(A) prevent the weight of the branch from tearing off bark and wood below the cut
(B) make the tree grow stronger and straighter
(C) let the saw work smoother and easier
(D) make it easier to cut up the limb

58. The main reason for applying lime to soil is to control its

(A) aridity   (B) fertilization   (C) acidity   (D) porosity

59. The greatest danger to a tree from a large unprotected wound is that

(A) birds may build a nest in it
(B) the tree may bleed to death
(C) the wound may become infected
(D) it is open to the elements

60. The fertilizer that is used for the care of trees should have a high content of

(A) DDT   (B) nitrogen   (C) sulphur   (D) carbon

61. The area of the plot plan shown below is

(A) 25,300 square feet
(B) 26,700 square feet
(C) 28,100 square feet
(D) 30,500 square feet

270'
70'
150'
155'
115'

62. The best of the following combinations of instruments to use in checking the combustion efficiency of a heating boiler is

(A) anemometer, stack thermometer, and orsat apparatus
(B) draft gauge, psychrometer, and barometer
(C) draft gauge, stack thermometer, and orsat apparatus
(D) draft gauge, stack thermometer, and barometer

63. The one of the following that does *not* indicate low water in a steam boiler is the

(A) fusible plug   (B) safety valve   (C) try cocks   (D) gauge glass

64. The increase in the stack temperature toward the end of the heating system above what it was at the beginning of the season is an indication that the

(A) radiators and convectors are air bound
(B) tubes and heating surfaces of the boiler are becoming insulated with soot
(C) furnace fire brick is failing
(D) heat content of the fuel is improving

65. Of the following, the one which is *not* a general class of oil burners is the

(A) water atomizing
(B) rotary cup atomizing
(C) mechanical atomizing
(D) air atomizing

66. Of the following, the one which should be between a boiler and its safety valve is

(A) a swing check valve of a size larger than that of the safety valve
(B) a butterfly valve located in the boiler-nozzle
(C) a gate valve of the same nominal size as that of the safety valve
(D) no valve of any type

67. The term "spinner cup" refers to

(A) screw type stokers   (C) rotary type oil burners
(B) gun type oil burners   (D) chain grate stokers

68. A "gun" type burner is often used on a

(A) pot type oil burner
(B) low pressure gas boiler
(C) coal underfeed stoker boiler
(D) high pressure oil fired boiler

69. Of the following, the action that should be taken as the first step if a properly adjusted safety valve on a steam boiler "pops off" when in operation, is

(A) open the draft   (C) wire the valve shut
(B) add more water to the boiler   (D) reduce the draft

70. When the water gets below the safe level in an operating boiler, it is best to

(A) add new water up to the safe level and open up the fire so that the water will heat quickly
(B) check the fire and let the boiler cool down before new water is added
(C) add new water to the boiler immediately
(D) check the fire and empty the boiler

71. Vents on fuel oil storage tanks are used to

(A) fill the fuel tanks
(B) allow air to escape during filling
(C) check oil flash points
(D) make tank fuel soundings

72. Of the following, the most desirable way to remove carbon deposits from the atomizing cup of an oil burner is to

(A) apply a hot flame to the carbonized surfaces to burn off the carbon deposits
(B) use kerosene to loosen the deposits and wipe with a soft cloth
(C) wash the cup with a mild trisodium phosphate solution and dry with a cloth
(D) use a scraper, followed by light rubbing with emery cloth

73. Of the following, the most important precaution that should be taken when "cutting in" a boiler in a battery is to see that the

(A) water column is at least 1 inch below top row of tubes
(B) non-return valve is closed when the boiler pressure is rising
(C) safety valves function properly
(D) boiler pressure is about equal to header pressure

74. A condensate feedwater tank in a low pressure steam plant

(A) is hermetically sealed to prevent contamination of feed water
(B) contains a surface blow down line
(C) is vented to the atmosphere
(D) has a vaccum breaker exposed to the atmosphere

75. Of the following, the first action to take in the event a low pressure steam boiler gauge glass breaks is to

(A) bank the fires
(B) close the water gauge glass cocks
(C) open the safety valve
(D) blow down the boiler

76. A "barometric damper" would be used in a boiler installation fired under draft conditions that are called

(A) induced   (B) natural   (C) regenerate   (D) forced

77. The flue gas temperature, when firing oil, should be just high enough to evaporate any contained moisture in order to

(A) prevent an acid from forming and eroding the breeching
(B) decrease the amount of excess air needed
(C) prevent an air pollution condition
(D) decrease the combustion efficiency of the boiler

78. A compound gauge in a boiler room

(A) measures pressures above and below atmospheric pressure
(B) indicates the degree of compounding in a steam engine
(C) shows the quantity of boiler treatment compound on hand
(D) measures steam and water pressure

79. In the combustion of the common fuels, the principal boiler heat loss is that due to the heat

(A) carried away by the moisture in the fuel
(B) lost by radiation
(C) carried away by the flue gases
(D) lost by incomplete combustion

80. Of the following, the correct sequence of steps to use when removing a boiler from service in order to perform extensive repairs on it, is

(A) discontinue firing, drain boiler, turn off valves, cool boiler
(B) discontinue firing, drain boiler, turn off valves
(C) turn off valves, drain boiler, discontinue firing, cool boiler
(D) discontinue firing, turn off valves, cool boiler, drain boiler

Answer Key

1. C	11. C	21. B	31. C	41. B	51. B	61. C	71. B
2. D	12. C	22. B	32. B	42. C	52. A	62. C	72. B
3. D	13. A	23. D	33. A	43. D	53. B	63. B	73. D
4. B	14. C	24. B	34. B	44. C	54. D	64. B	74. C
5. C	15. D	25. C	35. C	45. A	55. A	65. A	75. B
6. B	16. C	26. A	36. A	46. B	56. C	66. D	76. B
7. D	17. B	27. A	37. B	47. C	57. A	67. C	77. A
8. B	18. A	28. A	38. B	48. C	58. C	68. D	78. A
9. D	19. B	29. C	39. C	49. B	59. C	69. D	79. C
10. C	20. C	30. C	40. B	50. C	60. B	70. B	80. D

Explanatory Answers
Sample Examination III

1. **(C)** A standard indicates the amount and quality of work to be performed in a given period of time by one worker. However, it is of little value if the method of performance is not included.

2. **(D)** There is very little correlation between absenteeism and the need for training. A worker is not usually absent from work because he or she cannot perform the job properly.

3. **(D)** An agency can profit from an accident by rectifying its cause to prevent similar accidents in the future.

4. **(B)** Watering a lawn once a day is too much; once a month is too little.

5. **(C)** Degree-day is a unit used in estimating quantities of fuel and power consumption based on a daily ratio of consumption and mean temperature below 65°F.

    65°F − 24°F = 41 degree-days.

6. **(B)** The water and pipes cool off during a period of inactivity. More power is needed to reheat the boiler at startup.

7. **(D)** This is a negative question. Floor wax does *not* affect the floor's resistance to fires. It will affect wear, soil removal, and stain resistance.

8. **(B)** Cascading or filling from the top adds free oxygen to the boiler. It is better to fill from the bottom.

9. **(D)** When first starting a boiler, look at the water gauge to check the water level, and double check with the gauge cocks.

10. **(C)** On the Ringelmann chart of smoke density, 4 is approximately 80%.

11. **(C)** A good senior building custodian should observe the employees at work, inspect the product, and make necessary corrections.

12. **(C)** Employees who continually ask how they should do their work probably lack confidence. Such workers should be encouraged to work things out on their own if they can.

13. **(A)** Asking an employee to repeat your instructions is the only way to be sure that she understood them.

14. **(C)** By explaining and discussing work evaluations you will not only pinpoint whatever difficulties exist, you will also form a basis for work improvement.

15. **(D)** Impartiality, not partiality, is a requisite for successful leadership, as are intelligence, integrity, and forcefulness.

16. **(C)** A well-established "grapevine" is extremely difficult to eliminate.

17. **(B)** The type of supplies used in an operation is not specified in a job breakdown.

18. **(A)** Training subordinates is the main function of a supervisor.

19. **(B)** Giving employees specific assignments will ensure that everything which needs to be done will be done.

20. **(C)** If a new employee seems to be having trouble, first try to identify the problem. Then you can take corrective measures.

21. **(B)** Work standards, procedures, and methods of operation must be accepted by the workers before they can be successfully implemented.

22. **(B)** Do not let rule infractions go unnoticed, but do not punish a first-time offender too harshly. Explain the rule and warn him that a repetition will result in disciplinary action.

23. **(D)** First you must determine if a complaint is valid, and if it is, the cause of it. Then take corrective measures.

24. **(B)** Periodic inspections and tests are used as "preventive maintenance."

25. **(C)** A fire in flammable liquids is a Class B fire which creates a gas when heated. Foam will smother the fire and gases.

26. **(A)** On a Class A fire of common material (wood, paper, coal rubbish, etc.) soda-acid can be used without injuring yourself or spreading the fire.

27. **(A)** Determine the cause of an accident in order to eliminate or correct it.

28. **(A)** Do not paint a ladder; a crack in the wood may be hidden by the paint.

29. **(C)** Orange and yellow are warning colors.

30. **(C)** Constant self-inspection makes the inhabitants of a buildings conscious of fire hazards and should help eliminate or reduce hazards.

31. **(C)** Opening windows will reduce the effectiveness of air-conditioning. Keep the windows closed.

32. **(B)** One cleaner will do 3600 square feet in four hours (900 × 4 = 3600). To do a 20,000 sq. ft. room, divide 20,000 by 3600 = 5⁵⁄₉, or 6 cleaners. (There is no such thing as ⁵⁄₉ cleaners!)

33. **(A)** 35′ × 45′ = 1575 square feet. To convert to square yards, divide by 9. 1575 ÷ 9 = 175 sq. yards.

34. **(B)** A pyrometer is an electrical thermometer used for measuring high temperatures.

35. **(C)** Cleaning an office should be assigned to only one person to pinpoint responsibility to the one employee involved.

36. **(A)** The cost of supplies is the smallest item in the cleaning budget of a public building: labor is the most expensive.

37. **(B)** Ammonia cleans exterior glass without leaving streaks.

38. **(B)** Continuously dripping faucets are the major cause of rust stains in wash basins.

39. **(C)** All oily substances, such as salad oil, are harmful to asphalt tile.

40. **(B)** Give the broom a slight jerk after each stroke to lessen the amount of dirt and dust clinging to the broom.

41. **(B)** The vacuuming will be more effective when done with the lay of the nap.

42. **(C)** Dusting desks and emptying trash cans and ash trays will dirty a mopped floor, so you should do these jobs first. The ash trays and waste baskets should be taken care of before the dusting because the desks will accumulate additional dust from these two operations.

43. **(D)** Where there is water there will be rust, whether it is cold or hot water. After many years, the rust in a hot water circulating system will gradually become worse.

44. **(C)** A check valve is not a valve that can be opened or closed. It allows flow in one direction and not the other. Thus preventing back flow.

45. **(A)** If the demands on two pipes are the same, they should be the same size no matter what kind of water they carry.

46. **(B)** The pitch is ½″ per 10′: on a 45′ line, 2″ for 40′ and ¼″ for 5′ more = 2¼″ lower.

47. **(C)** 8″ = ²⁄₃′; 30′ × 50′ × ²⁄₃′ = 1000 cubic feet of water.

    30 gallons × $\dfrac{1 \text{ cubic foot}}{7.5 \text{ gal.}}$ = 4; each minute 4 cubic feet of water will be eliminated.

    1000 ÷ 4 = 250 minutes.

48. **(C)** Oil preheaters are used because heated oil flows more easily.

49. **(B)** The float switch mechanism turns the pump on and off. If a sump pump causes the sump pit overflow, either the switch or the float may not be operating properly.

50. **(C)** Chloride of lime is basically chlorine, a bleaching agent capable of combining with nearly all other elements. Thus it does not damage a concrete or terrazzo surface.

51. **(B)** Moisture or "vapor" will eventually go through a wall and damage a painted surface unless a "vapor barrier" (plastic, etc.) is installed to stop it.

52. **(A)** If cold pipes are in a warmer atmosphere they will sweat.

53. **(B)** Apply floor finish to protect, not to enhance the finish.

54. **(D)** Sewer gas is not particularly harmful, but it is a great nuisance because of its foul odor.

55. **(A)** Sodium silicate is a salt silicon element that protects concrete floor.

56. **(C)** Shading a transplanted plant keeps the plant moist and helps it withstand the shock of being transplanted.

57. **(A)** Tearing off bark or wood can infect a tree.

58. **(C)** Lime neutralizes acidity in soil.

59. **(C)** If a tree wound becomes infected, the infection can spread to the rest of the tree, killing it.

60. **(B)** Tree fertilizer must have a high nitrogen content to promote growth.

61. **(C)** $150' \times 270' = 40{,}500$ sq. ft.
    $150' - 70' = 80'$
    $80' \times 155' = 12{,}400$ sq. ft.
    $40{,}500$ sq. ft. $- 12{,}400$ sq. ft. $= 28{,}100$ sq. ft.

62. **(C)** A draft gauge, stack thermometer, and orsat apparatus all measure CO_2, draft, and temperature in the stack to find the percentage of unused fuel and thus measure efficiency.

63. **(B)** The safety valve does not measure low water level because it is at the top of the boiler and there is no water up there, only steam.

64. **(B)** Fusible plugs, try cocks, and gauge glasses indicate low water level in a steam boiler. An increase in stack temperature indicates that the heating system is not transferring heat well; the heat is going up the flue because the tubes are insulated with soot. It should be cleaned twice a year.

65. **(A)** Water is not used to atomize oil.

66. **(D)** Another valve between the boiler and the safety valve will reduce its effectiveness. If someone closes the second valve, the safety valve is useless.

67. **(C)** Rotary type oil burners "spin."

68. **(D)** "Gun" type burners shoot the oil into the boiler at high pressure.

69. **(D)** By reducing the draft you reduce the pressure. A safety valve is designed to stay open until the pressure inside the boiler drops significantly.

70. **(B)** New water in a boiler will be cold and contain air, so it is best to use as little as possible. If you have to use it, add chemicals and heat slowly.

71. **(B)** Without vents, air would be trapped in a fuel storage tank, and would thus reduce the tank's capacity, pushing the oil out and causing a spill.

72. **(B)** Kerosene will loosen or break down the carbon in the atomizing cup of an oil burner, and a soft cloth will not damage the cup.

73. **(D)** If boiler pressure is not equal to header pressure when you cut in a boiler in a battery, slugs of water may be carried over into the steam line. This is called "carry-over."

74. **(C)** A condensate feedwater tank is vented to prevent the condensate from flashing or causing the condensate pump to become steam bound.

75. **(B)** If a low pressure steam boiler gauge glass breaks, first close the water gauge cock, then the steam gauge cock, then open the gauge glass blow-down valve and replace the glass with a new one.

76. **(B)** A barometric damper is controlled by atmospheric pressure. Natural draft law is that warm air rises. Natural draft is regulated by the amount of heated gases going up the chimney and by the height of the chimney and is reduced with a barometric damper.

77. **(A)** Flue gas temperature is just high enough to evaporate any moisture because moisture can cause an acid build-up and/or erosion of the breeching.

78. **(A)** A compound gauge in a pressure room reads pressure on one side and vacuum on the other.

79. **(C)** Keep the heat in the boiler and not up the chimney. Most waste heat is lost through the flue gases. Dampers and draft regulators will help.

80. **(D)** Never drain a boiler until it is reasonably cool.

Answer Sheet
Sample Examination IV

1. Ⓐ Ⓑ Ⓒ Ⓓ	21. Ⓐ Ⓑ Ⓒ Ⓓ	41. Ⓐ Ⓑ Ⓒ Ⓓ	61. Ⓐ Ⓑ Ⓒ Ⓓ
2. Ⓐ Ⓑ Ⓒ Ⓓ	22. Ⓐ Ⓑ Ⓒ Ⓓ	42. Ⓐ Ⓑ Ⓒ Ⓓ	62. Ⓐ Ⓑ Ⓒ Ⓓ
3. Ⓐ Ⓑ Ⓒ Ⓓ	23. Ⓐ Ⓑ Ⓒ Ⓓ	43. Ⓐ Ⓑ Ⓒ Ⓓ	63. Ⓐ Ⓑ Ⓒ Ⓓ
4. Ⓐ Ⓑ Ⓒ Ⓓ	24. Ⓐ Ⓑ Ⓒ Ⓓ	44. Ⓐ Ⓑ Ⓒ Ⓓ	64. Ⓐ Ⓑ Ⓒ Ⓓ
5. Ⓐ Ⓑ Ⓒ Ⓓ	25. Ⓐ Ⓑ Ⓒ Ⓓ	45. Ⓐ Ⓑ Ⓒ Ⓓ	65. Ⓐ Ⓑ Ⓒ Ⓓ
6. Ⓐ Ⓑ Ⓒ Ⓓ	26. Ⓐ Ⓑ Ⓒ Ⓓ	46. Ⓐ Ⓑ Ⓒ Ⓓ	66. Ⓐ Ⓑ Ⓒ Ⓓ
7. Ⓐ Ⓑ Ⓒ Ⓓ	27. Ⓐ Ⓑ Ⓒ Ⓓ	47. Ⓐ Ⓑ Ⓒ Ⓓ	67. Ⓐ Ⓑ Ⓒ Ⓓ
8. Ⓐ Ⓑ Ⓒ Ⓓ	28. Ⓐ Ⓑ Ⓒ Ⓓ	48. Ⓐ Ⓑ Ⓒ Ⓓ	68. Ⓐ Ⓑ Ⓒ Ⓓ
9. Ⓐ Ⓑ Ⓒ Ⓓ	29. Ⓐ Ⓑ Ⓒ Ⓓ	49. Ⓐ Ⓑ Ⓒ Ⓓ	69. Ⓐ Ⓑ Ⓒ Ⓓ
10. Ⓐ Ⓑ Ⓒ Ⓓ	30. Ⓐ Ⓑ Ⓒ Ⓓ	50. Ⓐ Ⓑ Ⓒ Ⓓ	70. Ⓐ Ⓑ Ⓒ Ⓓ
11. Ⓐ Ⓑ Ⓒ Ⓓ	31. Ⓐ Ⓑ Ⓒ Ⓓ	51. Ⓐ Ⓑ Ⓒ Ⓓ	71. Ⓐ Ⓑ Ⓒ Ⓓ
12. Ⓐ Ⓑ Ⓒ Ⓓ	32. Ⓐ Ⓑ Ⓒ Ⓓ	52. Ⓐ Ⓑ Ⓒ Ⓓ	72. Ⓐ Ⓑ Ⓒ Ⓓ
13. Ⓐ Ⓑ Ⓒ Ⓓ	33. Ⓐ Ⓑ Ⓒ Ⓓ	53. Ⓐ Ⓑ Ⓒ Ⓓ	73. Ⓐ Ⓑ Ⓒ Ⓓ
14. Ⓐ Ⓑ Ⓒ Ⓓ	34. Ⓐ Ⓑ Ⓒ Ⓓ	54. Ⓐ Ⓑ Ⓒ Ⓓ	74. Ⓐ Ⓑ Ⓒ Ⓓ
15. Ⓐ Ⓑ Ⓒ Ⓓ	35. Ⓐ Ⓑ Ⓒ Ⓓ	55. Ⓐ Ⓑ Ⓒ Ⓓ	75. Ⓐ Ⓑ Ⓒ Ⓓ
16. Ⓐ Ⓑ Ⓒ Ⓓ	36. Ⓐ Ⓑ Ⓒ Ⓓ	56. Ⓐ Ⓑ Ⓒ Ⓓ	76. Ⓐ Ⓑ Ⓒ Ⓓ
17. Ⓐ Ⓑ Ⓒ Ⓓ	37. Ⓐ Ⓑ Ⓒ Ⓓ	57. Ⓐ Ⓑ Ⓒ Ⓓ	77. Ⓐ Ⓑ Ⓒ Ⓓ
18. Ⓐ Ⓑ Ⓒ Ⓓ	38. Ⓐ Ⓑ Ⓒ Ⓓ	58. Ⓐ Ⓑ Ⓒ Ⓓ	78. Ⓐ Ⓑ Ⓒ Ⓓ
19. Ⓐ Ⓑ Ⓒ Ⓓ	39. Ⓐ Ⓑ Ⓒ Ⓓ	59. Ⓐ Ⓑ Ⓒ Ⓓ	79. Ⓐ Ⓑ Ⓒ Ⓓ
20. Ⓐ Ⓑ Ⓒ Ⓓ	40. Ⓐ Ⓑ Ⓒ Ⓓ	60. Ⓐ Ⓑ Ⓒ Ⓓ	

SAMPLE EXAMINATION IV

THE TIME ALLOWED FOR THE ENTIRE EXAMINATION IS 3½ HOURS.

DIRECTIONS: Each question has four suggested answers lettered (A), (B), (C), and (D). Decide which one is the best answer and, on your answer sheet, darken the space for that letter.

1. Of the following, the first thing a junior building custodian should do when he enters the boiler room to check on the operation of the boiler is to

   (A) check the boiler water level
   (B) blow down the boiler
   (C) check the boiler water temperature
   (D) check the fuel supply

2. A boiler test kit is used to test

   (A) boiler water   (C) pressure gauges
   (B) fuel oil   (D) steam consumption

3. A good indication of the quality of the cleaning operation in a public building is the

   (A) amount of cleaning material used each month
   (B) number of cleaners employed
   (C) number of complaints of unsanitary conditions received
   (D) number of square feet of hall space cleaned daily

4. Of the following, the one which is *not* recommended for prolonging the useful life of a hair broom is to

   (A) rotate the brush to avoid wear on one side only
   (B) wash the brush by using it as a mop once a week
   (C) comb the brush weekly
   (D) hang the brush in storage to avoid resting on the bristles

5. The most important aim of a training program in fire prevention is to train the custodial staff to

   (A) be constantly alert to fire hazards
   (B) assist the city fire department in extinguishing fires
   (C) maintain the sprinkler system
   (D) climb ladders safely

6. Spontaneous ignition is most likely to occur in a

   (A) pile of oily rags
   (B) vented fuel oil tank
   (C) metal file cabinet filled with papers in file folders
   (D) covered metal container containing clean rags

7. Cleaners will usually be motivated to do a good job by a supervisor who

(A) lets them get away with poor performance
(B) treats them fairly
(C) treats some of them more favorably than others
(D) lets them take a nap in the afternoon

8. The most common cause of a dripping faucet is a

(A) broken stem
(B) cracked bonnet
(C) worn washer
(D) loose retaining screw on the handle

9. A type of hammer which can be used to remove nails from wood is the

(A) ball-peen   (B) mallet   (C) sledge   (D) claw

10. A vacuum pump is used in a (an)

(A) steam heating system   (C) hot water heating system
(B) hot air heating system   (D) electric heating system

11. An expansion tank is used in a (an)

(A) steam heating system   (C) hot water heating system
(B) hot air heating system   (D) electric heating system

12. The thermostat in the office area of a public building should have a winter daytime setting of about

(A) 50°F   (B) 60°F   (C) 70°F   (D) 80°F

13. The fuel oil which usually requires preheating before it enters an oil burner is known as

(A) #1   (B) #2   (C) #4   (D) #6

14. The domestic hot water in a large public building is circulated by

(A) gravity flow
(B) a pump which runs continuously
(C) a pump which is controlled by water pressure
(D) a pump which is controlled by water temperature

15. The vaporstat on a rotary-cup oil burner senses

(A) oil temperature   (C) secondary air pressure
(B) primary air pressure   (D) oil pressure

16. The emergency switch for a fully automatic oil burner is usually located

(A) at the entrance to the boiler room
(B) on the burner
(C) at the electrical distribution panel in the boiler room
(D) at the electrical service meter panel

17. The try cocks on a steam boiler are used to

    (A) drain the boiler
    (B) check the operation of the safety valves
    (C) check the water level in the boiler
    (D) drain the pressure gauge

18. The draft in a natural draft furnace is usually measured in

    (A) pounds
    (B) inches of mercury
    (C) inches of water
    (D) cubic feet

19. The stack temperature in a low pressure oil-fired steam boiler installation should be about

    (A) 212°F   (B) 275°F   (C) 350°F   (D) 875°F

20. A material that transmits heat very poorly is a good

    (A) insulator   (B) conductor   (C) radiator   (D) convector

21. The one thing a junior building custodian should *not* do after his building has been broken into is to

    (A) notify the police
    (B) report the incident to his supervisor
    (C) leave the damage to doors or windows unrepaired until his supervisor can inspect them on his regularly scheduled visit
    (D) make the point of entry more secure than it was before the break-in

22. The insulation covering on steam lines

    (A) increases the flow of steam
    (B) reduces the loss of heat
    (C) increases the loss of heat
    (D) prevents leaks

23. The air in a closed room that is heated by a radiator usually

    (A) settles to the floor
    (B) rises
    (C) remains stationary
    (D) contracts

24. A gallon of water which is changed to steam at atmosphere pressure will increase in volume about

    (A) 5 times   (B) 15 times   (C) 150 times   (D) 1500 times

25. The humidity of the air means its

    (A) clarity   (B) weight   (C) dust content   (D) moisture content

26. The safety device which opens automatically to release excessive steam pressure in a boiler is the

    (A) check valve
    (B) safety valve
    (C) gate valve
    (D) quick opening valve

27. Of the following devices, the one which is *not* usually found on a natural draft coal-fired boiler is the

    (A) feedwater regulator
    (B) low-water cutout
    (C) safety valve
    (D) water column

28. The number of degree-days for two days in New York City when the temperature for these two days averages 55°F is

(A) 2   (B) 10   (C) 20   (D) 30

29. A detergent is generally used in

(A) waterproofing walls   (C) cleaning floors and walls
(B) killing crabgrass   (D) exterminating rodents

30. The main reason for using a sweeping compound is to

(A) spot-finish waxed surfaces
(B) retard dust when sweeping floors
(C) loosen accumulations of grease
(D) remove paint spots from tile flooring

31. The one of the following cleaning agents which is recommended for use on marble floors is

(A) an acid cleaner   (C) trisodium phosphate
(B) a soft soap   (D) a neutral liquid detergent

32. A cleaning solution of one cup of soap chips dissolved in a pail of warm water can be used to wash

(A) painted walls   (C) marble walls
(B) rubber tile   (D) terrazzo floors

33. Sodium fluoride is a

(A) pesticide   (B) disinfectant   (C) detergent   (D) paint thinner

34. Scratches or burns in linoleum, rubber tile, or cork floors should be removed by rubbing with

(A) crocus cloth   (B) fine steel wool   (C) sandpaper   (D) emery cloth

35. A room 12 feet wide by 25 feet long has a floor area of

(A) 37 square feet   (C) 300 square feet
(B) 200 square feet   (D) 400 square feet

36. A cleaning solution should be applied to a painted wall using a

(A) wool rag   (B) brush   (C) sponge   (D) squeegee

37. When scrubbing a wooden floor it is advisable to

(A) flood the surface with the cleaning solution in order to float the dirt out of all cracks and crevices
(B) hose off the loosened dirt before starting the scrubbing operation
(C) pick up the cleaning solution as soon as possible
(D) mix a mild acid with the cleaning solution in order to clean the surface quickly

38. How many hours will it take a worker to sweep a floor space of 2800 square feet if he sweeps at the rate of 800 square feet per hour?

(A) 8   (B) 6½   (C) 3½   (D) 2½

39. One gallon of water contains

(A) 2 quarts   (B) 4 quarts   (C) 2 pints   (D) 4 pints

40. A standard cleaning solution is prepared by mixing 4 ounces of detergent powder in 2 gallons of water. The number of ounces of detergent powder needed, for the same strength solution, in 5 gallons of water is

(A) 4   (B) 6   (C) 8   (D) 10

41. The best agent to use to remove chewing gum from fabric is

(A) ammonia   (B) chlorine bleach   (C) a degreaser   (D) water

42. Water emulsion wax should *not* be used on

(A) linoleum
(B) cork tile flooring
(C) wood furniture
(D) rubber tile flooring

43. Tops of desks, file cabinets, and book cases are best dusted with a

(A) damp cloth
(B) treated cotton cloth
(C) damp sponge
(D) feather duster

44. The one of the following which is *not* a material used in scrub brushes is

(A) tampico   (B) terrazzo   (C) palmetto   (D) bassine

45. A chamois is properly used to

(A) wash enamel surfaces
(B) wash window glass
(C) dry enamel surfaces
(D) dry window glass

46. The proper sequence of operations used in cleaning an office, when the floor is to be swept with a broom, is

(A) clean ash trays, empty wastebaskets, sweep, dust
(B) sweep, dust, clean ash trays, empty wastebaskets
(C) dust, sweep, clean ash trays, empty wastebaskets
(D) clean ashtrays, empty wastebaskets, dust, sweep

47. Of the following, the most common result of accidents occurring while using hand tools is

(A) loss of limbs
(B) loss of eyesight
(C) infection of wounds
(D) loss of life

48. A twenty-four foot long extension ladder is placed with its top resting against a vertical wall. The safest procedure would be to place the base of the ladder a distance from the wall of

(A) 3 feet   (B) 6 feet   (C) 9 feet   (D) 12 feet

49. The one of the following extinguishing agents which should *not* be used on an oil fire is

(A) foam   (B) sand   (C) water   (D) carbon dioxide

50. The extinguishing agent in a portable soda-acid fire extinguisher is

(A) sodium bicarbonate
(B) sulphuric acid
(C) carbon dioxide
(D) water

51. The information on an accident report which is most useful toward prevention of similar accidents is the

(A) name of the victim
(B) cause of the accident
(C) type of injury sustained
(D) date of the accident

52. A fusible link is used to

(A) weld two pieces of chain together
(B) solder an electric wire to a terminal
(C) attach a ground wire to a water pipe
(D) hold a fire door open

53. As a supervisor, if you want to be sure that a worker understands some difficult job instructions you just gave her, it is most important for you to

(A) ask her questions about the instructions
(B) ask her to write the instructions down and show them to you
(C) ask an experienced worker to check on her work
(D) ask her if she understands your instructions

54. A junior building custodian should know approximately how long it takes to do each job so that he can

(A) judge correctly if the person doing the job is working too slowly
(B) tell how much time to take if he has to do it himself
(C) retrain experienced employees in better work habits
(D) tell how much time to dock a worker if he skips that part of the work

55. In order to have building employees willing to follow standardized cleaning procedures the supervisor must be prepared to

(A) demonstrate the advantages of the procedures
(B) do part of the cleaning work each day until the employees learn the procedures
(C) let the employees go home early if they save time using the procedures
(D) offer incentive pay to encourage their use

56. The best way for a junior building custodian to keep control of her work assignments is to

(A) inspect the building weekly
(B) make a written schedule and check it against the work being done each day
(C) have the workers report to her at the completion of each job and then give them a new assignment
(D) leave the workers on their own until complaints are received

57. The most important thing a supervisor must do is to

(A) plan ahead
(B) keep stock records
(C) put out the lights when leaving the building
(D) answer the telephone

58. One of the ways in which a supervisor can maintain proper control of his subordinates is to

    (A) punish every minor infraction of the rules
    (B) deny making any mistakes himself
    (C) criticize his own supervisor to show his own superiority
    (D) instill the idea that he keeps an eye on everything in his department

59. You see that one of your workers is not doing a job according to the safety rules. You should

    (A) correct her so that she will know how to work
    (B) take her off the job and send her to training class
    (C) let it go and wait to see if she works this way all the time
    (D) bawl her out

60. When making up a pipe joint in the shop, between a nipple and a valve, the

    (A) valve should be held in a square-jawed vise and the pipe screwed into it
    (B) pipe should be held in a square-jawed vise and the valve screwed onto it
    (C) the valve should be held in a pipe vise and the pipe screwed into it
    (D) pipe should be held in a pipe vise and the valve screwed onto it

61. A water meter is usually read in

    (A) pounds   (B) cubic feet   (C) pounds per square inch   (D) degrees

62. The valve which automatically prevents back flow in water pipe is called a

    (A) check valve   (B) globe valve   (C) gate valve   (D) by-pass valve

63. The best wrench to use to tighten a galvanized iron pipe valve or fitting which has hexagonal ends is a

    (A) stillson wrench   (C) monkey wrench
    (B) strap wrench   (D) socket wrench

64. A flushometer would be connected to a

    (A) water meter   (B) toilet bowl   (C) garden hose   (D) fire hose

65. Electric service meters are read in

    (A) kilowatt hours   (B) electrons   (C) amperes   (D) volts

66. The device used to reduce the voltage of an electric circuit is the

    (A) voltmeter   (B) fuse   (C) circuit breaker   (D) transformer

67. Ordinary light bulbs are usually rated in

    (A) watts   (B) ohms   (C) amperes   (D) filaments

68. The electric plug on a scrubbing machine should be plugged into a

    (A) light socket   (C) fuse receptacle
    (B) wall outlet   (D) dimmer switch

69. The device which should be used to connect the output shaft of an electric motor to the input shaft of a centrifugal pump is the

(A) flexible coupling   (B) petcock   (C) alemite fitting   (D) clutch

70. The type of wood screw which is used to attach a hinge to a door jamb is the

(A) flat head screw   (C) round head screw
(B) lag screw   (D) square head screw

71. Of the following bolt sizes, the one which identifies the bolt that has the largest diameter is

(A) 4–40   (B) 6–32   (C) 8–32   (D) 10–24

72. The tool most commonly used with a mitre box to cut wooden molding is the

(A) hack saw   (B) rip saw   (C) keyhole saw   (D) back saw

73. The type of lock which can be opened only from the lock side of a door is the

(A) cylinder lock   (B) spring latch   (C) padlock   (D) mortise lock

74. A key which will open many locks of the same type is usually called a

(A) tumbler key   (B) master key   (C) magnetic key   (D) cotter key

75. Of the following, the best lubricant to use on locks is

(A) grease   (B) graphite   (C) mineral oil   (D) talc

76. A junior building custodian should tour his assigned building a short time time after the public closing time mainly to see that

(A) any office workers who are on overtime are really working
(B) no unauthorized persons are in the building
(C) all the hall lights are turned off
(D) all the typewriters have dust covers on

77. The most useful information for preventing future vandalism which should be included in a vandalism report is

(A) a list of damaged items
(B) how the vandals got into the building
(C) a list of stolen items
(D) how many hours it took to clean up the mess

78. A device which allows an exit door to be opened from the inside by pressing on a horizontal bar is known as a

(A) door pull   (C) cross bolt dead lock
(B) double bolt bar lock   (D) panic bolt

79. The best action a junior building custodian can take to promote the security of her building is to

(A) depend on the police department to constantly patrol the area
(B) turn out all outside lights so that it will be difficult for intruders to find entry at night
(C) be sure all doors and windows are locked securely before the last person leaves the building at night
(D) allow only city employees to enter the building during the day

Answer Key

1. A	11. C	21. C	31. D	41. C	51. B	61. B	71. D
2. A	12. C	22. B	32. A	42. C	52. D	62. A	72. D
3. C	13. D	23. B	33. A	43. B	53. A	63. C	73. C
4. B	14. D	24. D	34. B	44. B	54. A	64. B	74. B
5. A	15. B	25. D	35. C	45. D	55. A	65. A	75. B
6. A	16. A	26. B	36. C	46. A	56. B	66. D	76. B
7. B	17. C	27. B	37. C	47. C	57. A	67. A	77. B
8. C	18. C	28. C	38. C	48. B	58. D	68. B	78. D
9. D	19. C	29. C	39. B	49. C	59. A	69. A	79. C
10. A	20. A	30. B	40. D	50. D	60. D	70. A	

Explanatory Answers Sample Examination IV

1. **(A)** Low water can cause damage to the heating surface of a boiler. Without an adequate supply of water the boiler cannot function properly, and with no water the boiler may crack. High water, on the other hand, can cause a boiler explosion.

2. **(A)** All water contains minerals or scale which form salts. The water must be tested and treated to change the minerals and salts to non-adhering sludge, which is easier to remove from a boiler.

3. **(C)** The "complaint file" is one indication of the efficiency of an operation. Having few or no complaints is usually an indication of an efficient operation. However, the absence of complaints does not warrant the elimination of inspections by the supervisor.

4. **(B)** Using a broom as a mop will render it useless. Rotating the brush, combing it, and hanging the broom up in storage will all increase a broom's useful life.

5. **(A)** Many fires can be prevented if the staff detects fire hazards in advance. The custodial staff does not usually help the fire department put out fires or maintain the sprinkler system. Safe use of ladders would be part of other training programs.

6. **(A)** Oily rags must be disposed of properly. They should never be left lying around because they are a fire hazard.

7. **(B)** Fair and impartial treatment of subordinates creates a high level of morale in a supervisor's team, and motivates cleaners to do a good job.

8. **(C)** A dripping faucet is usually caused by a worn washer. If it is replaced and the faucet still drips, then the seat should be reamed or replaced.

9. **(D)** Claw hammers have claws that other hammers do not have. These claws remove nails from wood.

10. **(A)** A vacuum pump pumps condensate back to the vacuum tank to create a positive return of condensate.

11. **(C)** A hot water heating system uses an expansion tank to allow for the expanded volume of hot water.

12. **(C)** In the winter most people will be comfortable if the thermostat is set at around 70°F.

13. **(D)** Preheating #6 fuel oil improves its viscosity, or ability to flow, so that it can enter the burner more easily.

14. **(D)** As hot water is needed in a building, the pump will start.

15. **(B)** A vaporstat senses primary air pressure at the point at which the oil is a vapor or mist.

16. **(A)** The emergency switch is always placed at the entrance to the boiler room so that it can be reached quickly.

17. **(C)** Try cocks measure water level in a boiler.

   Top—Try cock opened, should get steam
   Middle—Try cock opened, steam and water
   Bottom—Try cock opened, water

18. **(C)** A draft gauge measures the difference in pressure between the atmosphere and the boiler fire box or breeching or stack. It is calibrated in tenths of inches of water.

19. **(C)** A stack temperature of 350°F is a very good temperature for combustion efficiency in a low pressure oil-fired steam boiler.

20. **(A)** An insulator prevents the transmission of heat.

21. **(C)** Repairs should be made as soon as possible to prevent damage from weather or further vandalism through the broken doors and windows.

22. **(B)** The heat contained by the insulation covering on steam lines is thus conserved.

23. **(B)** A basic law of physics; heat rises.

24. **(D)** The tremendous increase in volume from liquid to gas produces the power of steam.

25. **(D)** Humidity is the dampness of air.

26. **(B)** The safety valve pops open at a set pressure, usually 15 lbs. PSI.

27. **(B)** Low water level is not important in a natural draft coal-fired burner.

28. **(C)** A degree-day is the difference between the design temperature and the average temperature. 65°F − 55°F = 10°. 10° × 2 days = 20 degree days.

29. **(C)** A detergent is a soap which does not use fats and lye as its base. Like soap, detergent is used for cleaning.

30. **(B)** A sweeping compound keeps the dust from rising while sweeping.

31. **(D)** A neutral liquid detergent will clean without reducing the shine.

32. **(A)** Soap chips will not clean marble, rubber, or terrazzo adequately; they are fine for painted walls.

33. **(A)** Sodium fluoride eliminates pests.

34. **(B)** A crocus cloth is just abrasive enough to clean linoleum, rubber, or cork floors; other cloths will cause damage.

35. **(C)** $12' \times 25' = 300$ sq. ft.

36. **(C)** A sponge is the right texture to clean a painted wall; and it absorbs cleaning solution and water well.

37. **(C)** Cleaning solution should be picked up fast enough so that the water is not absorbed into a wood floor.

38. **(C)** 2800 sq. ft. divided by $\dfrac{800 \text{ sq. ft.}}{1 \text{ hr.}} = 3\frac{1}{2}$ hrs.

39. **(B)** 4 quarts to a gallon; 4 cups to a quart.

40. **(D)** 4 oz. detergent to 2 gal. water.
    2 oz. detergent to 1 gal. water.
    10 oz. detergent to 5 gal. water.

41. **(C)** Degreasers will remove chewing gum from fabric.

42. **(C)** Water should not be used on wood furniture.

43. **(B)** Dust adheres to treated cotton cloths.

44. **(B)** Terrazzo is used in flooring (not scrub brushes).

45. **(D)** Chamois dries and polishes without streaking.

46. **(A)** Dusting should be the final stage of cleaning to remove the dust caused by the other operations.

47. **(C)** Small cuts are often neglected, yet they can become infected if not promptly cleaned and covered, especially if the worker continues with his or her duties.

48. **(B)** Place the base of a ladder one fourth of its height away from the wall it is leaning on.

49. **(C)** Do not use water on an oil fire. Water is heavier than oil; water and oil will not mix. The water will sink to the bottom where the heat will cause the water to turn to steam, which may cause an explosion.

50. **(D)** A soda-acid extinguisher contains sodium bicarbonate, sulphuric acid, carbon dioxide, and water. When the first three are mixed together the reaction forces the water out to extinguish the fire.

51. **(B)** If the cause of an accident is identified it can be eliminated and similar accidents prevented in the future.

52. **(D)** A fusible link is used to hold a fire door open or closed because it is fused or melted by the heating. When heated, the door will close. When not heated, the door will stay open.

53. **(A)** If you question a worker on key points after giving some difficult instructions you can evaluate the worker's understanding of the instructions.

54. **(A)** The purpose of establishing work standards is to judge whether someone is working too slowly. If the worker is too slow perhaps more training is needed.

55. **(A)** Workers will follow preset procedures if they are convinced that they are the best way of doing the job.

56. **(B)** A written schedule is a control which, when properly implemented, will accurately indicate work completed and work to be performed.

57. **(A)** Proper planning will eliminate many problems and will help provide solutions to those which cannot be avoided.

58. **(D)** If subordinates believe their superior is aware of what is happening they will perform their assigned work. Unfortunately there are some workers who will avoid work if they think they can get away with it.

59. **(A)** Unsafe practices should be stopped immediately in order to prevent accidents which are costly to both employer and the employee.

60. **(D)** Hold the pipe in a vise and screw the valve onto the pipe so that the housing of the valve is not broken. The pipe is less expensive to replace than the valve.

61. **(B)** Water meters are read in cubic feet of water used.

62. **(A)** A check valve will permit flow one way and restrict the flow the other way.

63. **(C)** The monkey wrench is designed to grip almost any shaped fitting, so it is probably the best for a hexagonal fitting.

64. **(B)** A flushometer is used mainly in commercial or public rest rooms. By pushing the handle or button the toilet is flushed automatically to the sewer and the bowl or urinal is rinsed in a matter of seconds by a sudden pressure. No tanks are necessary.

65. **(A)** Kilowatt hours measure how many kilowatts of electricity are used in an hour. One kilowatt equals 1000 watts.

66. **(D)** A circuit breaker reduces the voltage of an electric circuit by transferring electric energy from one circuit to another.

67. **(A)** Wattage is a measure of electrical power. The more watts, the brighter the light.

68. **(B)** A electric plug is plugged into a wall outlet.

69. **(A)** A flexible coupling is usually made of rubber and is durable enough to withstand the friction created between a motor and pump shafts.

70. **(A)** A screw should fit flush into a door jamb to permit the door to close properly. It is countersunk.

71. **(D)** The first number in a bolt size indicates the diameter of the bolt. The second number indicates the number of threads per inch.

72. **(D)** A mitre box ensures a straight cut at a given angle on a wooden molding. A back saw further ensures a straight cut because it is not flexible.

73. **(C)** A padlock can only be opened from one side. Most other locks can be opened from both sides.

74. **(B)** Master keys should be tightly controlled, because they can open any lock.

75. **(B)** Lubricate locks with graphite. It will not leave a residue.

76. **(B)** When a public building is closed, the public is not authorized to be in it. The custodian must be certain that there are no unauthorized persons. The activities of authorized workers are not the concern of the custodian.

77. **(B)** A vandalism report should tell how the vandals entered the building so that preventive measures can be taken.

78. **(D)** A panic bolt allows people to leave but prevents them from entering. It is frequently prescribed as a fire safety precaution.

79. **(C)** The best action a custodian can take to prevent intruders is to lock all doors and windows securely before the last person leaves.

Answer Sheet
Sample Examination V

1. Ⓐ Ⓑ Ⓒ Ⓓ
2. Ⓐ Ⓑ Ⓒ Ⓓ
3. Ⓐ Ⓑ Ⓒ Ⓓ
4. Ⓐ Ⓑ Ⓒ Ⓓ
5. Ⓐ Ⓑ Ⓒ Ⓓ
6. Ⓐ Ⓑ Ⓒ Ⓓ
7. Ⓐ Ⓑ Ⓒ Ⓓ
8. Ⓐ Ⓑ Ⓒ Ⓓ
9. Ⓐ Ⓑ Ⓒ Ⓓ
10. Ⓐ Ⓑ Ⓒ Ⓓ
11. Ⓐ Ⓑ Ⓒ Ⓓ
12. Ⓐ Ⓑ Ⓒ Ⓓ
13. Ⓐ Ⓑ Ⓒ Ⓓ
14. Ⓐ Ⓑ Ⓒ Ⓓ
15. Ⓐ Ⓑ Ⓒ Ⓓ
16. Ⓐ Ⓑ Ⓒ Ⓓ
17. Ⓐ Ⓑ Ⓒ Ⓓ
18. Ⓐ Ⓑ Ⓒ Ⓓ
19. Ⓐ Ⓑ Ⓒ Ⓓ
20. Ⓐ Ⓑ Ⓒ Ⓓ

21. Ⓐ Ⓑ Ⓒ Ⓓ
22. Ⓐ Ⓑ Ⓒ Ⓓ
23. Ⓐ Ⓑ Ⓒ Ⓓ
24. Ⓐ Ⓑ Ⓒ Ⓓ
25. Ⓐ Ⓑ Ⓒ Ⓓ
26. Ⓐ Ⓑ Ⓒ Ⓓ
27. Ⓐ Ⓑ Ⓒ Ⓓ
28. Ⓐ Ⓑ Ⓒ Ⓓ
29. Ⓐ Ⓑ Ⓒ Ⓓ
30. Ⓐ Ⓑ Ⓒ Ⓓ
31. Ⓐ Ⓑ Ⓒ Ⓓ
32. Ⓐ Ⓑ Ⓒ Ⓓ
33. Ⓐ Ⓑ Ⓒ Ⓓ
34. Ⓐ Ⓑ Ⓒ Ⓓ
35. Ⓐ Ⓑ Ⓒ Ⓓ
36. Ⓐ Ⓑ Ⓒ Ⓓ
37. Ⓐ Ⓑ Ⓒ Ⓓ
38. Ⓐ Ⓑ Ⓒ Ⓓ
39. Ⓐ Ⓑ Ⓒ Ⓓ
40. Ⓐ Ⓑ Ⓒ Ⓓ

41. Ⓐ Ⓑ Ⓒ Ⓓ
42. Ⓐ Ⓑ Ⓒ Ⓓ
43. Ⓐ Ⓑ Ⓒ Ⓓ
44. Ⓐ Ⓑ Ⓒ Ⓓ
45. Ⓐ Ⓑ Ⓒ Ⓓ
46. Ⓐ Ⓑ Ⓒ Ⓓ
47. Ⓐ Ⓑ Ⓒ Ⓓ
48. Ⓐ Ⓑ Ⓒ Ⓓ
49. Ⓐ Ⓑ Ⓒ Ⓓ
50. Ⓐ Ⓑ Ⓒ Ⓓ
51. Ⓐ Ⓑ Ⓒ Ⓓ
52. Ⓐ Ⓑ Ⓒ Ⓓ
53. Ⓐ Ⓑ Ⓒ Ⓓ
54. Ⓐ Ⓑ Ⓒ Ⓓ
55. Ⓐ Ⓑ Ⓒ Ⓓ
56. Ⓐ Ⓑ Ⓒ Ⓓ
57. Ⓐ Ⓑ Ⓒ Ⓓ
58. Ⓐ Ⓑ Ⓒ Ⓓ
59. Ⓐ Ⓑ Ⓒ Ⓓ
60. Ⓐ Ⓑ Ⓒ Ⓓ

61. Ⓐ Ⓑ Ⓒ Ⓓ
62. Ⓐ Ⓑ Ⓒ Ⓓ
63. Ⓐ Ⓑ Ⓒ Ⓓ
64. Ⓐ Ⓑ Ⓒ Ⓓ
65. Ⓐ Ⓑ Ⓒ Ⓓ
66. Ⓐ Ⓑ Ⓒ Ⓓ
67. Ⓐ Ⓑ Ⓒ Ⓓ
68. Ⓐ Ⓑ Ⓒ Ⓓ
69. Ⓐ Ⓑ Ⓒ Ⓓ
70. Ⓐ Ⓑ Ⓒ Ⓓ
71. Ⓐ Ⓑ Ⓒ Ⓓ
72. Ⓐ Ⓑ Ⓒ Ⓓ
73. Ⓐ Ⓑ Ⓒ Ⓓ
74. Ⓐ Ⓑ Ⓒ Ⓓ
75. Ⓐ Ⓑ Ⓒ Ⓓ
76. Ⓐ Ⓑ Ⓒ Ⓓ
77. Ⓐ Ⓑ Ⓒ Ⓓ
78. Ⓐ Ⓑ Ⓒ Ⓓ
79. Ⓐ Ⓑ Ⓒ Ⓓ
80. Ⓐ Ⓑ Ⓒ Ⓓ

TEAR HERE

SAMPLE EXAMINATION V

THE TIME ALLOWED FOR THE ENTIRE EXAMINATION IS 3¹/₂ HOURS.

DIRECTIONS: Each question has four suggested answers lettered (A), (B), (C), and (D). Decide which one is the best answer and, on your answer sheet, darken the space for that letter.

1. The employee most likely to find the nests and runways of roaches and vermin in a public building is a

   (A) maintenance worker
   (B) night cleaner
   (C) senior building custodian
   (D) stationary fireman

2. A building custodian in charge of a building who is normally on duty during the daytime hours in a building which is cleaned at night, should

   (A) never make night inspections since he is not responsible for the cleanliness of the building
   (B) make night inspections at least once a year
   (C) never make night inspections because the cleaners will think he is spying on them
   (D) make night inspections at least twice a month

3. A custodian's written instruction to her staff on the subject of security in public buildings should include instructions to

   (A) exclude the public at all times
   (B) admit the public at all times
   (C) admit the public only if they are neat and well dressed
   (D) admit the public during specified hours

4. When the American flag is to be flown at half staff, it should always be

   (A) hoisted slowly to half staff
   (B) hoisted slowly to the peak of staff and then lowered slowly to half staff
   (C) hoisted briskly to the peak of staff and then lowered slowly to half staff
   (D) hoisted briskly to the peak of staff and then lowered briskly to half staff

5. An office has floor dimensions of 16 feet 6 inches wide by 22 feet 0 inches long. The floor area of this office, in square feet, is most nearly

   (A) 143
   (B) 263
   (C) 363
   (D) 463

6. The key figure in any custodial safety program is the

   (A) building custodian
   (B) cleaner
   (C) mayor
   (D) commissioner

7. A building custodian must inspect or have a maintenance person inspect every window cleaner's safety bolt at least

   (A) each time the windows are washed
   (B) once a month
   (C) once a year
   (D) once every second year

8. An incipient fire is one which

   (A) has just started and can be readily extinguished using an ordinary hand extinguisher
   (B) occurs only in motor vehicles
   (C) is burning out of control in a storeroom
   (D) is a banked coal fire

9. Maintaining room temperature at 75°F in the winter time will increase fuel consumption above the amount needed to maintain 70°F by approximately

   (A) 5%
   (B) 8%
   (C) 12%
   (D) 20%

10. Of the following, the one which represents the best practical combustion condition in an oil fired low pressure steam plant is

   (A) 8% CO_2–500°F stack temperature
   (B) 13% CO_2–400°F stack temperature
   (C) 10% CO_2–700°F stack temperature
   (D) 6% CO_2–400°F stack temperature

11. The floor area, in square feet, on which a properly treated dustless sweeping cloth can be used before the cloth must be washed, is

   (A) 500–1000
   (B) 2000–3000
   (C) 4000–6000
   (D) 8000–10000

12. A cleaning woman working a six-hour shift should be able to cover (clean) _____ Gilbert work units.

   (A) 100–200
   (B) 400–500
   (C) 1100–1200
   (D) 6000–7000

13. When mopping, the pails containing the cleaning solutions should be

   (A) slid along the floor to avoid injury due to lifting
   (B) kept off the floor preferably on a rolling platform
   (C) shifted from place to place using the mop
   (D) equipped with a spigot for applying the mopping solution

14. Of the following, the item that is considered a concrete floor sealer is

   (A) water wax
   (B) sodium hypochlorite
   (C) sodium silicate
   (D) linseed oil

15. A material commonly used in detergents is

   (A) rock salt
   (B) Glauber's salt
   (C) trisodium phosphate
   (D) monosodium glutamate

16. A disinfectant material is one that will

   (A) kill germs
   (B) dissolve soil and stop odors
   (C) give a clean odor and cover a disagreeable odor
   (D) prevent soil buildup

17. When scrubbing a wooden floor it is advisable to

   (A) flood the surface with the cleaning solution in order to float the soil out of all crevices
   (B) hose off the loosened soil before starting the scrubbing operation
   (C) pick up the used solution as soon as possible
   (D) mix a mild acid with the cleaning solution in order to clean the surface quickly

18. Before starting a wall washing operation it is best to

   (A) check the temperature of the water
   (B) soak the sponge to be used
   (C) check the pH of the mixed cleaning solution
   (D) dust the wall to be washed

19. Of the following, the most nearly correct statement regarding the economical operation of the heating system in a public building is that

   (A) the heat should always be shut down at 4 P.M. and turned on at 8 A.M.
   (B) the heat should be shut down only over the weekend
   (C) it is best to keep the heat on at all times so that the number of complaints are kept to a minimum
   (D) the times at which the heat is shut down and turned on should be varied depending on the prevailing outdoor temperature

20. A floor made of marble or granite chips imbedded in cement is usually called

   (A) terrazzo   (C) palmetto
   (B) linoleum   (D) parquet

21. In a 4-wire, 3-phase electrical supply system, the voltage between one phase and ground used for the lighting load is, most nearly

   (A) 440   (B) 230   (C) 208   (D) 115

22. Of the following, the one that takes the place of a fuse in an electrical circuit is a

   (A) tranformer   (C) condenser
   (B) circuit breaker   (D) knife switch

23. Gas bills are usually computed on the basis of

   (A) cubic feet   (C) pounds
   (B) gallons   (D) kilowatts

24. An operating oil-fired steam boiler explosion may sometimes be caused by

   (A) carrying too high a water level in the boiler
   (B) inadequate purging of combustion chamber between fires
   (C) overfiring the boiler
   (D) carrying too high an oil temperature

25. Of the following commercial sizes of anthracite, the largest in size is

(A) stove

(C) pea

(B) chestnut

(D) rice

26. A supervisor should know the equipment used in his work well enough to

(A) make any repairs which might be needed
(B) know what parts to remove in case of breakdown
(C) anticipate any reasonable possiblity of a breakdown
(D) know all the lubricants specified by the manufacturer

27. The *primary* responsibility of a building custodian is to

(A) make friends of all subordiantes
(B) search for new methods of doing the work
(C) win the respect of her superior
(D) get the work done properly within a reasonable time

28. When a supervisor believes that the work of a subordinate is below standard, he should

(A) assign the employee to work that is considered undesirable
(B) do nothing immediately in the hope that the employee will bring his work up to standard without any help from the supervisor
(C) reduce the privileges of the employee at once
(D) discuss it as soon as possible with the employee

29. The first objective of all fire prevention is

(A) confining fire to a limited area
(B) safeguarding life against fire
(C) reducing insurance rates
(D) preventing property damage

30. An office worker frequently complains to the building-custodian that her office is poorly illuminated. The best action for the building custodian to follow is to

(A) ignore the complaints as those of an habitual crank
(B) inform the worker that illumination is a fixed item built into the building originally and evidently is the result of faulty planning by the architect
(C) request a licensed electrician to install additional ceiling lights
(D) investigate for faulty illumination features in the room, such as dirty lamp globes and incorrect lamp wattages

31. Assume that six windows of a public building facing one street have been consistently broken by children playing ball after hours and over weekends. The best solution to this problem is to

(A) post a "No ball playing" sign on the wall
(B) erect protective screening outside the six windows
(C) post a guard on weekend patrol duty
(D) request special weekend police protection for the property

32. In the satisfactory handling of a complaint which is fancied rather than real, the complaint should be considered

    (A) as important as a real grievance
    (B) unimportant since it has no basis in fact
    (C) an attempt by the complainant to stir up trouble
    (D) indicative of overpaternalism

33. The best method or tool to use for cleaning dust from an unplastered cinderblock wall is

    (A) a tampico brush with stock cleaning solution
    (B) a vacuum cleaner
    (C) water under pressure from hose and nozzle
    (D) a feather duster

34. Of the following, the largest individual item of expense in operating a public building is generally the cost of

    (A) cleaning
    (B) heating fuel
    (C) electricity
    (D) elevator service

35. The chief purpose for changing the handle of a floor brush from one side of the brush block to the other side is to

    (A) allow the janitor to change hands
    (B) make both sides of the brush equally dirty
    (C) give both sides of the brush equal wear
    (D) change the angle of sweeping

36. Of the following, the weight of mop most likely used in the nightly mopping of corridors, halls, or lobbies is

    (A) 8 ounce
    (B) 16 ounce
    (C) 24 ounce
    (D) 50 ounce

37. After a sweeping assignment is completed, floor brushes should be stored

    (A) in a pan of water
    (B) by hanging the brushes on pegs or nails
    (C) by piling the brushes on each other carefully
    (D) in a normal sweeping position, bristles resting on the floor

38. Nylon treated scrubbing discs

    (A) require more water than scrubbing brushes
    (B) require more detergent solution than scrubbing brushes
    (C) must be used with cold water only
    (D) are generally more effective than steel wool pads

39. Of the following, the best material to use to clean exterior bronze is

    (A) pumice
    (B) paste wax
    (C) wire wheel on portable buffer
    (D) lemon oil polish

40. The use of trisodium phosphate in cleaning polished marble should be avoided because

   (A) it may cause spalling
   (B) it discolors the surface of the marble
   (C) it builds up a slick surface on the marble
   (D) it pits the glazed surface and bleaches the marble

41. Sealers for open-grained wood floors should *not* contain linseed oil because

   (A) the linseed oil would damage the wood fibers
   (B) the linseed oil would deteriorate mop strands
   (C) water wax would penetrate the linseed oil sealer and rot the wood
   (D) linseed oil on wood takes too long to dry satisfactorily before a floor finish could be applied

42. When washing painted wall areas by hand, a person should be expected to wash each hour an area in square feet equal to

   (A) 75–125   (C) 400–600
   (B) 150–300   (D) 750–1000

43. of the following, the one that is most desirable to use in dusting furniture is

   (A) a feather duster   (C) a counter brush
   (B) a paper towel   (D) a soft cotton cloth

44. The one of the following floor types on which oily sweeping compound may be used is

   (A) vinyl tile   (C) linoleum
   (B) concrete   (D) terrazzo

45. A steam heating sytem where the steam and condensate flow in the same pipe is called a

   (A) one pipe gravity return system   (C) vacuum return system
   (B) sub-atmospheric system   (D) zone control system

46. A test of a boiler by applying pressure equal to or greater than the maximum working pressure is called a

   (A) hydrostatic test   (C) hygroscopic test
   (B) barometric test   (D) gyroscopic test

47. A stackswitch as used with an oil burner

   (A) shuts down the burner in case of non-ignition
   (B) shuts down the burner in case of high stack temperatures
   (C) controls the flow of secondary air
   (D) operates the barometric damper

48. The vertical pipes leading from the steam mains to the radiators are called

   (A) drip lines   (C) radiant coils
   (B) risers   (D) expansion joints

49. Fuel oil storage tanks are equipped with vents. The purpose of these vents is to

   (A) make tank soundings
   (B) check oil flash points
   (C) fill the fuel tanks
   (D) allow air to escape during filling

50. A compound gauge in a boiler room

   (A) measures steam and water pressure
   (B) shows the quantity of boiler treatment compound on hand
   (C) measures pressures above and below atmospheric pressure
   (D) indicates the degree of compounding in a steam engine

51. Of the following, the chief purpose of insulating steam lines is to

   (A) prevent loss of heat
   (B) protect people from being burned by them
   (C) prevent leaks
   (D) protect the pipes against corrosion

52. The most important function of thermostatic traps on radiators is to

   (A) regulate the heat given off by the radiator
   (B) remove water and air from the radiator
   (C) assist the steam pressure in filling the radiator
   (D) maintain a vacuum within the radiator

53. The designation "1/8–27 N.P.T." usually indicates

   (A) machine screw thread   (C) spur gear size
   (B) pipe thread   (D) sprocket chain size

54. The size of a chisel is determined by its

   (A) length   (C) pitch
   (B) width   (D) height

55. The cause of paint blisters is usually

   (A) moisture under the paint coat
   (B) too thick a coat of paint
   (C) too much oil in paint
   (D) the plaster pores not sealed properly

56. A wood framed picture is to be attached to a plaster and hollow tile wall. Of the following, the proper installation would include the use of

   (A) wire cut nails   (C) expansion shields and screws
   (B) miracle glue   (D) self-tapping screws

57. The proper tool or method to use for driving a finishing nail to the depth necessary for puttying when installing wood trim is

   (A) a countersink
   (B) another nail of the same diameter
   (C) a nail set
   (D) a center punch

58. Faucet leakage in a large building is best controlled by periodic

(A) faucet replacement
(B) addition of a sealing compound to the water supply
(C) packing replacement
(D) faucet inspection and repair

59. Escutcheons are usually located

(A) on kitchen cabinet drawers
(B) on windows
(C) around pipes, to cover pipe sleeve openings
(D) around armored electric cable going into a gem box

60. It is advisable to remove broken bulbs from light sockets with

(A) a wooden or hard rubber wedge   (C) a hammer and chisel
(B) pliers   (D) a fuse puller

61. A room 20 feet × 25 feet in area with a ceiling height of 9 feet 6 inches is to be painted. One gallon of paint will cover 400 square feet. The minimum number of gallons necessary to give the four walls and the ceiling one coat of paint is

(A) 2   (B) 3   (C) 4   (D) 5

62. Of the following, the ones on which gaskets are most likely to be used are

(A) threaded pipe plugs
(B) cast iron pipe nipples
(C) flanged pipe fittings
(D) threaded cast iron reducing tees

63. If a 110 volt lamp were used on a 220 volt circuit, the

(A) fuse would burn out   (C) line would overheat
(B) lamp would burn out   (D) lamp would flicker

64. The third prong on the plug of portable electric power tools of recent manufacture is for

(A) using the tool on a 3-phase power outlet
(B) eliminating interference in radio or television sets
(C) grounding the tool as a safety precaution
(D) using the tool on direct current circuits

65. Of the following, the greatest emphasis in selecting employees for supervisory positions should ordinarily be placed on

(A) intelligence and educational background
(B) knowledge of the work and capacity for leadership
(C) sincere interest in the activities and objectives of the agency
(D) skill in performing the type of work to be supervised

66. A supervisor who is overworked is usually one who

(A) complains about working more than she actually works
(B) has failed to delegate sufficient responsibility to others
(C) is capable of carrying heavy responsibility
(D) is unable to enlist the cooperation of her employees

67. Of the following, the most effective way to reduce waste in cleaning equipment and tools is by

(A) requiring a worn brush or broom to be returned before issuing a new one
(B) requiring the cleaners to use all cleaning tools for specific periods of time
(C) keeping careful records of how frequently cleaning equipment and tools are issued to cleaners
(D) making sure that cleaners use the tools properly

68. If a cleaner is doing excellent work, then the proper action of his supervisor is to

(A) give him preferential assignments as a reward
(B) tell the other cleaners what excellent work he is doing
(C) praise his work at the earliest opportunity
(D) do nothing since the man may become overconfident

69. A cleaner does very good work, but she has trouble getting to work on time. To get the worker to come on time you should

(A) bring her up on charges to stop the lateness once and for all
(B) have her report directly to you every time she is late
(C) talk over the problem with her to find its cause and possible solution
(D) threaten to transfer her if she cannot get to work on time

70. Of the following, the most effective way to teach a subordinate how to store an item is to

(A) do it yourself while explaining
(B) explain the procedure verbally
(C) have him do it while you criticize
(D) let him look at photographs of the operation

71. Of the following, the most important reason for the supervisor to plan work schedules for workers under her supervision is that

(A) emergency situations can easily be handled if they should arise
(B) it insures that essential operations will be adequately covered
(C) the workers will be more satisfied if a routine is established
(D) the relationship between the supervisor and her subordinate will be clarified

72. In order to evaluate adequately the work of an individual, it is most essential for the analysis to be based on

(A) standard forms
(B) the collective opinion of several experts
(C) the individual's interest in his work
(D) standards of performance

73. A foam-type fire extinguisher extinguishes fires by

(A) cooling only
(B) drenching only
(C) smothering only
(D) cooling and smothering

74. When changing brushes on a scrubbing machine, of the following, the first step to take is to

(A) lock the switch in the off position
(B) be sure the power cable electric plug supplying the machine is disconnected from the wall outlet
(C) place the machine on top of the positioned brushes
(D) dip the brushes in water

75. In cleaning away branches that have been broken off as a result of a severe storm, one of your workers comes in contact with a live electric line and falls unconscious. After having removed her from contact, the first thing to be done is to

(A) send for an inhalator to revive her
(B) administer mouth-to-mouth resuscitation
(C) search for the switch to prevent any other such cases
(D) loosen her clothing and begin rubbing her forehead to restore circulation

76. Of the following types of fires, a soda-acid fire extinguisher is *not* recommended for

(A) electric motor controls
(B) waste paper
(C) waste rags
(D) wood desks

77. Window cleaners should carefully examine their safety belts

(A) once a week
(B) before they put them on each time
(C) once a month
(D) once before they enter a building

78. One of your cleaners was injured as a result of slipping on an oily floor. This type of accident is most likely due to

(A) defective equipment
(B) the physical condition of the cleaner
(C) failure to use proper safety appliances
(D) poor housekeeping

79. One important use of accident reports is to provide information that may be used to reduce the possibility of similar accidents. The most valuable entry on the report for this purpose is the

(A) name of the victim
(B) injury sustained by the victim
(C) cause of the accident
(D) location of the accident

80. Fires in buildings are of such complexity that

(A) no plans or methods of attack can be formulated in advance
(B) no planned procedures can be relied on
(C) an appointed committee is necessary to direct fighting at the fire
(D) the problem must be considered in advance and methods of attack formulated

Answer Key

1. B	11. C	21. D	31. B	41. D	51. A	61. C	71. B
2. D	12. C	22. B	32. A	42. B	52. B	62. C	72. D
3. D	13. B	23. A	33. B	43. D	53. B	63. B	73. D
4. C	14. C	24. B	34. A	44. B	54. B	64. C	74. B
5. C	15. C	25. A	35. C	45. A	55. A	65. B	75. B
6. A	16. A	26. C	36. C	46. A	56. C	66. B	76. A
7. C	17. C	27. D	37. B	47. A	57. C	67. D	77. B
8. A	18. D	28. D	38. D	48. B	58. D	68. C	78. D
9. D	19. D	29. B	39. D	49. D	59. C	69. C	79. C
10. B	20. A	30. D	40. A	50. C	60. A	70. A	80. D

Explanatory Answers
Sample Examination V

1. **(B)** Roaches tend to come out of their nests in the dark, at night when the night cleaners are likely to see them.

2. **(D)** The custodian has ultimate responsiblity for the building's upkeep and maintenance.

3. **(D)** A public building, one that houses public agencies, is only considered open to the public during the hours when business is being transacted.

4. **(C)** Hoisting the flag briskly to the peak and lowering it slowly to half staff is the proper flag protocol.

5. **(C)** $6'' = \frac{1}{2}'$. $16\frac{1}{2}' \times 22' = 363$ sq. ft.

6. **(A)** The building custodian is a vital part of any safety program because he must show the workers safe working procedures and encourage them to use them.

7. **(C)** A year is a reasonable time between inspections of a window cleaner's safety belt if the inspections are made properly.

8. **(A)** Incipient means it is at the beginning, or in the early stages.

9. **(D)** A great deal of additional heat energy (and therefore fuel consumption) is needed to raise the room temperature in a building. This is why slightly lower temperatures yield significant fuel conservation.

10. **(B)** The best air-to-fuel ratio in an oil-fired low pressure steam plant comes when the stack temperature is 400°F and there is 6% CO_2.

11. **(C)** A generous amount of treatment spray on a clean dust cloth will go a long way before the cloth needs to be washed. After more than 4000–6000 square feet of cleaning the dust will no longer be picked up, just moved around.

12. **(C)** A Gilbert work unit is a measurement of electricity converted into physical force. A cleaner should cover just under 200 Gilbert work units per hour.

13. **(B)** Keep pails containing cleaning solution on a rolling platform. This will save time and energy.

14. **(C)** A salt/silicon element such as sodium silicate will protect a concrete floor.

15. **(C)** Trisodium phosphate is commonly used in detergent.

16. **(A)** Disinfectant kills germs while cleaning.

17. **(C)** Cleaning solution should not be allowed to sink into a wood floor. It can stain the floor.

18. **(D)** Dusting the wall first will allow the cleaner to begin removing the stains on the wall's surface.

19. **(D)** The operation of the heating system should be varied depending on the outside temperature. This is the most economical method and will help reduce complaints of overheating and underheating. Weather forecasts can play a large part in this procedure.

20. **(A)** Terrazzo is attractive, but it can present maintenance problems.

21. **(D)** One leg to ground equals 115 volts.

22. **(B)** A circuit breaker does the same job as as a fuse and does not have to be replaced. A simple activation resets the circuit.

23. **(A)** Utility companies measure the amount of gas used in cubic feet.

24. **(B)** The residue left in an oil-fired steam boiler becomes flammable. Purging the boiler is essential to prevent buildup of fuel or gases in the fire chamber.

25. **(A)** Pea is the smallest commercial size of anthracite; stove is the largest.

26. **(C)** It is unreasonable to expect the custodial engineer to know everything about repairing the equipment; that is the job of the maintenance mechanic. The supervisor should be aware of what the equipment can and cannot do, and should keep its performance within its abilities.

27. **(D)** The supervisor is primarily responsible for getting the work done in the most efficient and expeditious manner.

28. **(D)** If a worker is performing poorly, the supervisor must first identify the reason. The solution may be as simple as giving additional training.

29. **(B)** Life should always be considered before property.

30. **(D)** A custodian should respond to complaints of poor lighting by checking for faulty illumination fixtures.

31. **(B)** Put protective screening over windows which are often broken by children playing ball. A sign would probably be ignored, and additional guards are expensive and probably unwarranted.

32. **(A)** Any complaint is real enough in the mind of the complainer and should not be taken lightly.

33. **(B)** A vacuum cleaner will clean a cinderblock wall efficiently.

34. **(A)** Labor is always the biggest expense involved in daily operation of a building—more expensive than any commodity.

35. **(C)** A floor brush will last much longer if both sides get equal use and wear.

36. **(C)** A 24 oz. mop is heavy, but not too heavy. 8 oz. or 16 oz. would be too light for commercial buildings.

37. **(B)** Hang a brush up on a peg to help it keep its shape. This takes the weight of the brush off the bristles when the brush is not in use.

38. **(D)** Nylon is not as abrasive as steel wool, which may damage the surface it is scrubbing.

39. **(D)** Besides cleaning the bronze, a lemon polish will protect it from the elements. Pumice and wire wheels may damage the surface, and paste wax will create a filmy buildup.

40. **(A)** The sodium element in trisodium phosphate can eat away or erode marble, concrete, etc. Do not use it to clean marble; the chemical reaction could be devastating.

41. **(D)** Linseed oil on wood takes too long to dry, so it should not be used as a wood sealer on a wood floor.

42. **(B)** An experienced worker should be able to wash 150–300 sq. ft. of a painted wall in an hour under normal conditions.

43. **(D)** A soft cotton cloth is absorbent and will not blow dust around as a feather duster will nor scratch the furniture as a counter brush might.

44. **(B)** An oily sweeping compound may damage vinyl tile, linoleum, and terrazzo. It can be used safely on a concrete floor.

45. **(A)** In a one pipe gravity return system, the steam in the single pipe is used for heating, after which it turns to condensate and returns to the boiler to start the cycle over again.

46. **(A)** A hydrostatic test is a water pressure test done on a boiler to check for leaks or damage due to low water levels or after any extensive repairs.

47. **(A)** A stackswitch senses draft and gases of combustion. It indicates to the control panel that ignition did not occur. The boiler then shuts off to prevent a fuel buildup in the fire chamber.

48. **(B)** Steam rises through the "risers" of a steam heating system to heat the building.

49. **(D)** Oil is heavier than air. When filling a tank the oil replaces the air which rises to the top and escapes through the vent.

50. **(C)** Compound means combination. A compound gauge in a boiler room measures pressures both above and below atmospheric pressure.

51. **(A)** Steam lines are insulated so that the heat generated is not wasted.

52. **(B)** A thermostatic trap allows the water or condensate to be removed, but not the steam which is needed for heating.

53. **(B)** On a pipe designation of "⅛″–27 N.P.T.," ⅛″ is the diameter and 27 is the number of threads per inch.

54. **(B)** A chisel's size is measured by its width.

55. **(A)** The moisture trapped under a coat of paint will fight its way through to the surface of the paint and cause blisters.

56. **(C)** An expansion shield expands when the screw is tightened into the shield, thus gripping the wall.

57. **(C)** A nail set countersinks a nail below the surface of the wood trim to allow for puttying so the nail will not be seen.

58. **(D)** Periodic inspections are the only way to find and repair worn washers before they leak.

59. **(C)** Located where the pipe enters the wall, escutcheons present a more attractive finishing.

60. **(A)** Wood and rubber do not conduct electricity.

61. **(C)** 2 walls: 20′ × 9½′ × 2 = 380 sq. ft.
    2 walls: 25′ × 9½′ × 2 = 475 sq. ft.
    ceiling: 25′ × 20′ = 500 sq. ft.

    Total: 1355

    1355 sq. ft. divided by 400 = slightly more than 3; 4 gallons of paint are required.

62. **(C)** A flange is used to attach one pipe to another with nuts and bolts. The gasket is put between the two flanges. When the nuts and bolts are tightened, the gasket will be compressed, sealing any leak.

63. **(B)** The force of voltage rated above a lamp's rating will be too much for the lamp to endure.

64. **(C)** The third prong on a plug helps to prevent electrical shock by grounding it.

65. **(B)** Both knowledge and leadership ability must be present in an effective leader. Many knowledgeable workers are poor supervisors because they cannot lead. A good leader is able to function through subordinates by getting them to produce work. However, a supervisor must also understand the work in order to direct and train subordinates.

66. **(B)** An effective supervisor must delegate some responsibility. He or she cannot be overwhelmed by the tasks that need to be done. Delegation should take place as far down as effective decisions can be made.

67. **(D)** An improperly used cleaning tool will deteriorate more quickly because it is not being used as it was intended to be.

68. **(C)** Praise in public, rebuke in private. Preferential treatment will have negative effects on the other workers.

69. **(C)** Once you identify the cause of a problem it can be corrected.

70. **(A)** The best method of on-the-job training is to demonstrate the procedure and correct the trainee's mistakes.

71. **(B)** A work schedule is a control the supervisor uses to ensure that work is completed on schedule.

72. **(D)** If an employee meets the pre-set standards of performance he or she should be considered a satisfactory worker.

73. **(D)** A foam fire extinguisher cools and smothers the fire at the same time.

74. **(B)** Always unplug power tools before replacing their parts. If the motor should start while the parts are being changed, it would be very dangerous.

75. **(B)** The most important consideration after an electrical shock is to get the victim breathing as quickly as possible. Delay can cause serious complications.

76. **(A)** The water that is used in a soda-acid fire extinguisher will not put out an electrical fire, and it may cause electrocution. Foam will extinguish an electrical fire.

77. **(B)** Window cleaners' lives depend on checking their safety belts.

78. **(D)** Oil on the floor should be taken care of immediately. An oily floor is dangerously slippery.

79. **(C)** Include the cause of an accident in an accident report so that it can be corrected.

80. **(D)** Proper planning to cope with fires is vitally important. Problems can be isolated, and procedures to deal with them can be developed.

Answer Sheet
Sample Examination VI

1. Ⓐ Ⓑ Ⓒ Ⓓ
2. Ⓐ Ⓑ Ⓒ Ⓓ
3. Ⓐ Ⓑ Ⓒ Ⓓ
4. Ⓐ Ⓑ Ⓒ Ⓓ
5. Ⓐ Ⓑ Ⓒ Ⓓ
6. Ⓐ Ⓑ Ⓒ Ⓓ
7. Ⓐ Ⓑ Ⓒ Ⓓ
8. Ⓐ Ⓑ Ⓒ Ⓓ
9. Ⓐ Ⓑ Ⓒ Ⓓ
10. Ⓐ Ⓑ Ⓒ Ⓓ
11. Ⓐ Ⓑ Ⓒ Ⓓ
12. Ⓐ Ⓑ Ⓒ Ⓓ
13. Ⓐ Ⓑ Ⓒ Ⓓ
14. Ⓐ Ⓑ Ⓒ Ⓓ
15. Ⓐ Ⓑ Ⓒ Ⓓ
16. Ⓐ Ⓑ Ⓒ Ⓓ
17. Ⓐ Ⓑ Ⓒ Ⓓ
18. Ⓐ Ⓑ Ⓒ Ⓓ
19. Ⓐ Ⓑ Ⓒ Ⓓ
20. Ⓐ Ⓑ Ⓒ Ⓓ

21. Ⓐ Ⓑ Ⓒ Ⓓ
22. Ⓐ Ⓑ Ⓒ Ⓓ
23. Ⓐ Ⓑ Ⓒ Ⓓ
24. Ⓐ Ⓑ Ⓒ Ⓓ
25. Ⓐ Ⓑ Ⓒ Ⓓ
26. Ⓐ Ⓑ Ⓒ Ⓓ
27. Ⓐ Ⓑ Ⓒ Ⓓ
28. Ⓐ Ⓑ Ⓒ Ⓓ
29. Ⓐ Ⓑ Ⓒ Ⓓ
30. Ⓐ Ⓑ Ⓒ Ⓓ
31. Ⓐ Ⓑ Ⓒ Ⓓ
32. Ⓐ Ⓑ Ⓒ Ⓓ
33. Ⓐ Ⓑ Ⓒ Ⓓ
34. Ⓐ Ⓑ Ⓒ Ⓓ
35. Ⓐ Ⓑ Ⓒ Ⓓ
36. Ⓐ Ⓑ Ⓒ Ⓓ
37. Ⓐ Ⓑ Ⓒ Ⓓ
38. Ⓐ Ⓑ Ⓒ Ⓓ
39. Ⓐ Ⓑ Ⓒ Ⓓ
40. Ⓐ Ⓑ Ⓒ Ⓓ

41. Ⓐ Ⓑ Ⓒ Ⓓ
42. Ⓐ Ⓑ Ⓒ Ⓓ
43. Ⓐ Ⓑ Ⓒ Ⓓ
44. Ⓐ Ⓑ Ⓒ Ⓓ
45. Ⓐ Ⓑ Ⓒ Ⓓ
46. Ⓐ Ⓑ Ⓒ Ⓓ
47. Ⓐ Ⓑ Ⓒ Ⓓ
48. Ⓐ Ⓑ Ⓒ Ⓓ
49. Ⓐ Ⓑ Ⓒ Ⓓ
50. Ⓐ Ⓑ Ⓒ Ⓓ
51. Ⓐ Ⓑ Ⓒ Ⓓ
52. Ⓐ Ⓑ Ⓒ Ⓓ
53. Ⓐ Ⓑ Ⓒ Ⓓ
54. Ⓐ Ⓑ Ⓒ Ⓓ
55. Ⓐ Ⓑ Ⓒ Ⓓ
56. Ⓐ Ⓑ Ⓒ Ⓓ
57. Ⓐ Ⓑ Ⓒ Ⓓ
58. Ⓐ Ⓑ Ⓒ Ⓓ
59. Ⓐ Ⓑ Ⓒ Ⓓ
60. Ⓐ Ⓑ Ⓒ Ⓓ

61. Ⓐ Ⓑ Ⓒ Ⓓ
62. Ⓐ Ⓑ Ⓒ Ⓓ
63. Ⓐ Ⓑ Ⓒ Ⓓ
64. Ⓐ Ⓑ Ⓒ Ⓓ
65. Ⓐ Ⓑ Ⓒ Ⓓ
66. Ⓐ Ⓑ Ⓒ Ⓓ
67. Ⓐ Ⓑ Ⓒ Ⓓ
68. Ⓐ Ⓑ Ⓒ Ⓓ
69. Ⓐ Ⓑ Ⓒ Ⓓ
70. Ⓐ Ⓑ Ⓒ Ⓓ
71. Ⓐ Ⓑ Ⓒ Ⓓ
72. Ⓐ Ⓑ Ⓒ Ⓓ
73. Ⓐ Ⓑ Ⓒ Ⓓ
74. Ⓐ Ⓑ Ⓒ Ⓓ
75. Ⓐ Ⓑ Ⓒ Ⓓ
76. Ⓐ Ⓑ Ⓒ Ⓓ
77. Ⓐ Ⓑ Ⓒ Ⓓ
78. Ⓐ Ⓑ Ⓒ Ⓓ
79. Ⓐ Ⓑ Ⓒ Ⓓ

SAMPLE EXAMINATION VI

THE TIME ALLOWED FOR THE ENTIRE EXAMINATION IS 3½ HOURS.

DIRECTIONS: Each question has four suggested answers lettered (A), (B), (C), and (D). Decide which one is the best answer and, on your answer sheet, darken the space for that letter.

1. There are a considerable number of forms and reports to be submitted on schedule by a senior building custodian. The advisable method of accomplishing this duty is to

   (A) fill out the reports at odd times during the days when you have free time
   (B) schedule a definite period of the work week for completing these forms and reports
   (C) assign your supervisor or cleaner to handle all these forms for you and to have them available on time
   (D) classify or group the forms and reports and fill out only one of each group and refer the other forms or reports to the ones completed

2. In enforcing compliance with safety regulations, you should take the attitude that they must be complied with because

   (A) every accident can be prevented
   (B) safety regulations are based on reason and experience with the best methods of accident prevention
   (C) compliance with safety regulations will make other safety efforts unnecessary
   (D) they are the law and law enforcement is an end in itself

3. When instructing employees in regard to their duties in case of fire, a supervisor should

   (A) tell employees to take no action until the fire department equipment has arrived
   (B) tell all employees to go to the scene of the fire
   (C) assign each employee specific duties
   (D) tell employees to extinguish the fire before calling the supervisor or the fire department

4. The principal value of a good report is that it

   (A) is always available for reference
   (B) impresses department heads with the need for immediate action
   (C) reflects upon the writer of the report
   (D) expedites official business

5. The quality of work performed by personnel engaged in building cleaning is best evaluated by

   (A) studying building cleaning expenditures
   (B) studying time records of personnel
   (C) analyzing complaints by building occupants
   (D) inspecting the building periodically

6. Of the following, a senior building custodian need *not* be kept informed of

(A) departmental management policies
(B) terms of union contracts covering his subordinates
(C) developments of current interest in custodial operations
(D) current rate of interest on municipal bonds

7. The best way to make work assignments to persons required to clean a multistory building is to

(A) allow the persons to pick their room or area assignments out of a hat
(B) make specific room or area assignments to each person separately
(C) rotate room and area assignments daily according to a chart posted on the bulletin board
(D) each week let a different member of the group make the room or area assignment

8. One important use of accident reports is to provide information that may be used to reduce the possibility of similar accidents. The most valuable entry on the report for this purpose is the

(A) name of the victim
(B) injury sustained by the victim
(C) cause of the accident
(D) location of the accident

9. Suppose that an emergency has arisen which requires you to cancel some of the jobs scheduled for that day. Of the following jobs, the one that can be eliminated for that day with least effect on the proper operation and maintenance of the building is

(A) mopping and cleaning toilet rooms
(B) checking public stairs and corridors for hazards
(C) improving the location of supplies in the storeroom
(D) replacing broken window panes in offices

10. Of the following, a senior building custodian's attitude toward grievances should be to

(A) pay little attention to little grievances
(B) be very alert to grievances and make adjustments in existing conditions to appease all of them
(C) know the most frequent causes of grievances and strive to prevent them from arising
(D) maintain rigid discipline of a nature that "smooths out" all grievances

11. A heavy snowfall must be removed from the sidewalks around the building. You, as senior building custodian, have assigned two workers to shovel snow from the walks. After an interval you check and find they are bickering as to how much each is shoveling and no snow is being removed. In this situation you should

(A) stand with them to supervise the snow removal and to be sure the work is divided evenly
(B) assign two other workers to snow removal and send the original two back to their usual chores
(C) put the worker with seniority in full charge of the other worker
(D) separate the workers by sending them to opposite ends of the walk to shovel alone, with a warning that you will be checking on their progress at short intervals

12. Of the following, safety on the job is best assured by

(A) keeping alert
(B) following every rule
(C) working very slowly
(D) never working alone

13. A foam type fire extinguisher extinguishes fires by

(A) cooling only
(B) drenching only
(C) smothering only
(D) cooling and smothering

14. The extinguishing agent in a soda-acid fire extinguisher is

(A) carbon dioxide
(B) water
(C) carbon-tetrachloride
(D) calcium chloride solution

15. The proper extinguisher to use on an electrical fire in an operating electric motor is

(A) foam
(B) carbon dioxide
(C) soda and acid
(D) water

16. When an extension ladder is in place and ready to be used, the rope used to extend the ladder should be

(A) left hanging free out of the way of the climber's feet
(B) used to raise and lower tools to the man on the ladder
(C) used as a means of steadying the climber
(D) tied securely around a lower rung

17. The principal characteristic of panic locks or bolts on doors of places of public assembly is that they

(A) allow the doors to open outwardly with sufficient pressure on the bars of the lock
(B) allow the doors to open inwardly with sufficient pressure on the bars of the lock
(C) prevent the door from opening under impact load
(D) may be opened with any tumbler lock key

18. The main purpose of periodic inspections and tests of electrical equipment is to

(A) encourage the workers to take better care of the equipment
(B) make the workers familiar with the equipment
(C) discover minor faults before they develop into major faults
(D) keep the workers busy during otherwise slack periods

19. Standard, extra strong, and double extra strong welded steel pipe of a given size all have the same

(A) outside diameter
(B) inside diameter
(C) average diameter
(D) flow capacity for any given flow velocity

20. In reference to domestic gas piping,

(A) couplings with running threads are used to join pipes
(B) risers must have a drip leg and cap at bottom
(C) gasketed unions may be used in joining pipe
(D) composition disc globe valves are used to throttle the gas

21. Chewing gum should be removed from rubber, asphalt, or linoleum flooring with

(A) a putty knife
(B) steel wool
(C) gritty compounds
(D) a solvent

22. Of the following, the best procedure to follow when the linoleum floor of a meeting room containing movable furniture is to be mopped is to

(A) move the furniture by sliding it along the floor to prevent injury to the cleaners
(B) not move the furniture
(C) move the furniture by lifting it and carrying it to a clear spot to prevent damage to the linoleum
(D) use very little water in order to prevent the legs of the furniture from getting wet

23. Asphalt tile flooring that has been subjected to oily compounds

(A) may last indefinitely
(B) must be removed and replaced with new asphalt tile immediately
(C) may be restored to hardness and lustre by several moppings with hot water and several applications of water wax
(D) must be restored to original condition by several moppings with kerosene

24. The use of alcohol in water for washing windows is *not* recommended because it

(A) is a hazard to cleaners in that they may be affected by the fumes
(B) will damage the paint around the edges of the glass
(C) pits the surface of the glass
(D) destroys the bristles of the brush applying the solution to the pane

25. Of the following, the best material to use for removing grass stains on marble or wood is

(A) oxalic acid
(B) chloride of lime
(C) sodium silicate
(D) sodium hypochlorite

26. Shades or Venetian blinds are preferably cleaned with a

(A) feather duster
(B) counter brush
(C) damp sponge
(D) vacuum cleaner

27. Asphalt tile floors are preferably polished with

(A) water emulsion wax
(B) wax in solution in benzol
(C) a high fatty acid soap
(D) sodium metaphosphate

28. Washing soda is used to

(A) eliminate the need for rinse mopping or wiping
(B) make the cleaning compound abrasive
(C) decrease the wetting power of water
(D) increase the wetting power of water

29. Varnish or lacquer may be used as a sealer on floors finished with

(A) asphalt tiles
(B) linoleum
(C) rubber tiles
(D) cork tiles

30. A long-handled deck scrub brush is most effective when scrubbing

(A) large open areas   (C) small flat areas
(B) stair treads   (D) long corridors

31. The best method for preventing the infestation of a building by rats is to

(A) use cats
(B) use rat traps
(C) eliminate rat harborages in the building
(D) use poisoned bait

32. The one of the following foodstuffs which if allowed to remain on ordinary asphalt tile will most likely be most injurious to it is

(A) milk   (B) maple syrup   (C) ketchup   (D) salad oil

33. Employees engaged in cleaning operations who are issued rubber gloves to protect their hands against caustic solutions should be warned that

(A) if such solution spills over the glove top into the space between the glove and the hand, it may damage the skin of the hand
(B) rubber gloves have a very short life in contact with caustic solutions
(C) harmful gases can penetrate the rubber and harm even dry hands
(D) contact of the hands with glove type rubber for over an hour is harmful

34. Pyrethrins are used as

(A) insecticides   (B) germicides   (C) waxes   (D) detergents

35. Water hammer is

(A) a special hammer used to remove scale from a radiator
(B) caused by water in steam lines
(C) caused by excessive boiler pressure
(D) caused by low water level in the boiler

36. Of the following, the one usually used in the construction of a steam pressure gauge is

(A) perfect circle tube   (C) bourdon tube
(B) venturi tube   (D) elastic linkage

37. Usually, when a large room is gradually filled with people the room

(A) temperature and humidity both decrease
(B) temperature increases and the humidity decreases
(C) temperature and humidity increase
(D) temperature decreases and humidity increases

38. A foot valve at the intake end of the suction line of a pump serves mainly to

(A) maintain pump prime
(B) filter out large particles in the fluid
(C) increase the maximum suction lift of the pump
(D) increase pump flow rate

39. A pressure gauge attached to a standpipe system shows a pressure of 36 pounds per square inch. The head of water in feet above the gauge is most nearly

(A) 24   (B) 36   (C) 60   (D) 83

40. Of the following, the term "vapor barrier" would most likely be associated with

(A) electric service installation   (C) fuel oil tank installation
(B) insulation materials   (D) domestic gas piping

41. Pitot tubes are used to

(A) test feed water for impurities
(B) measure air or gas flow in a duct
(C) prevent overheating of elements of a steam gauge
(D) control the ignition system of an oil burner

42. In warm air heating and in ventilating systems, laboratories and kitchens should not be equipped with return ducts in order to

(A) keep air velocities in other returns as high as possible
(B) reduce fire hazards
(C) reduce the possibility of circulating odors through the system
(D) keep the temperature high in these rooms

43. One square foot of equivalent direct steam radiation (EDR) is equivalent to a heat emission of

(A) 150 BTU per hour   (C) 150 BTU per minute
(B) 240 BTU per minute   (D) 240 BTU per hour

44. Of the following, the one which is *least* likely to cause continuous vibration of an operating motor is

(A) a faulty starting circuit
(B) excessive belt tension
(C) the misalignment of motor and driven equipment
(D) loose bearings

45. The function of a steam trap is to

(A) remove sediment and dirt from steam
(B) remove air and non-condensable gases from steam
(C) relieve excessive steam pressure to the atmosphere
(D) remove condensate from a pipe or an apparatus

46. The temperature at which air is just saturated with the moisture present in it is called its

(A) relative humidity   (C) humid temperature
(B) absolute humidity   (D) dew point

47. If scale forms on the seat of a float-operated boiler feed water regulator, the most likely result is

(A) internal corrosion of the boiler shell
(B) insufficient supply of water to the boiler
(C) flooding of the boiler
(D) shutting down of the oil burner by the low water cutout

48. The compound gauge in the oil suction line shows a high vacuum. This is usually an indication of

(A) a dirty oil strainer
(B) low oil level in the fuel oil storage tank
(C) a leak in the fuel oil preheater
(D) an obstruction in the fuel oil preheater

49. Of the following, the information which is *least* important on a boiler room log sheet is the

(A) stack temperature readings   (C) number of boilers in operation
(B) CO_2 readings   (D) boiler room humidity

50. Pitting and corrosion of the water side of the boiler heating surfaces is due mainly to the boiler water containing dissolved

(A) oxygen   (B) hydrogen   (C) soda-ash   (D) sodium sulphite

51. The combustion efficiency of a boiler can be determined with a CO_2 indicator and the

(A) flue gas temperature   (C) outside air temperature
(B) boiler room humidity   (D) under fire draft

52. The try cocks of steam boilers are used to

(A) find the height of water in the boiler
(B) test steam pressure in the boiler
(C) empty the boiler of water
(D) act as safety valves

53. The reason for sweating inside a refrigerator cabinet is

(A) high per cent running time of compressor unit
(B) high cabinet air temperature
(C) defective expansion valve
(D) a poor door seal

54. The slope or slant of a soil line is 1/4 inch per foot. If this drainage line is 50 feet long, the difference in elevation from one end to the other is, in feet, most nearly

(A) 0.55   (B) 1.04   (C) 2.08   (D) 12.5

55. Oil is used with sharpening stones when sharpening wood chisels in order to

(A) reduce the effort needed to move the blade over the stone
(B) maintain the oil temper of the steel used for the chisel
(C) flush off the small metal chips and clear the cutting edges of the abrasive grit
(D) reduce the temperature due to friction

56. A maintenance mechanic checking a refrigerator for a freon leak would use a

(A) soap and water solution
(B) halide torch
(C) glycerine solution
(D) linseed oil and whiting solution

57. A basement floor area of 5000 square feet is under 9 inches of water. If this water is to be pumped out of the basement in one hour, the required capacity of the portable pump in gallons per minute is most nearly

    (A) 63   (B) 470   (C) 1020   (D) 2810

58. A major advantage of keeping a perpetual inventory of supplies is that it

    (A) gives a current record of the supplies available at all times
    (B) reduces the work required to distribute supplies
    (C) avoids the need for periodic physical inventories
    (D) shows who is using excessive supplies

59. Employees generally do not object to strict rules and regulations if they

    (A) are enforced without bias or favor
    (B) result in more material gain
    (C) deal with relatively unimportant phases of the work
    (D) affect the supervisors more than their subordinates

60. In order to have building employees willing to follow standardized cleaning and maintenance procedures, the supervisor must be prepared to

    (A) work alongside the employees
    (B) demonstrate the reasonableness of the procedures
    (C) offer incentive pay for their use
    (D) be adamant in opposing changes in the standardized procedures

61. Of the following, the most important step, when accepting incoming shipments of standard items normally carried in stock, is to check the items for

    (A) electrical performance   (C) quantity delivered
    (B) chemical composition   (D) mechanical performance

62. The orderly arrangement of supplies in storage usually

    (A) takes too much time to be worthwhile
    (B) is important only in large warehouses
    (C) is essential for stock selection and inventory purposes
    (D) cannot be accomplished when package sizes vary

63. A steam heating boiler is classified as a low pressure boiler when it generates steam at a gauge pressure of

    (A) not more than 30 pounds per   (C) not more than 20 pounds per
        square inch   square inch
    (B) not more than 25 pounds per   (D) 15 pounds per square inch or less
        square inch

64. A hot water heating boiler is classified as a low pressure boiler when it produces hot water at a gauge pressure

    (A) not more than 200 pounds per   (C) not more than 160 pounds per
        square inch   square inch
    (B) not more than 175 pounds per   (D) equal to an absolute pressure of 200
        square inch   pounds per square inch

65. Of the following processes, the one which is *not* involved in the transfer of heat in a boiler from the hot gases to the water is

(A) radiation   (B) conduction   (C) convection   (D) evaporation

66. The Ringelmann chart is a device that is used for checking

(A) smoke density from a chimney
(B) boiler water condition
(C) percent CO_2 of the flue gas
(D) the carbon content of coal

67. Low voltage control circuits for oil burners usually operate at a voltage of

(A) six (6) volts
(B) twelve (12) volts
(C) twenty-five (25) volts
(D) fifty (50) volts

68. The connection known as a "Hartford Loop" is usually found on

(A) radiators
(B) high pressure hot water heaters
(C) low pressure unit heaters
(D) low pressure steam boilers

69. Of the following types of fuel, the one which has the highest heat content per pound (Btu/lb) is

(A) #2 fuel oil
(B) semibituminous coal
(C) semianthracite coal
(D) wood

70. Of the following types of fuel oils, the one that has the greatest heat value per gallon is

(A) diesel oil   (B) #2 oil   (C) #4 oil   (D) #6 oil

71. The atomization of oil in the average domestic gun type burner is accomplished by the

(A) air pressure
(B) pressure and centrifugal action of the oil
(C) low steam pressure
(D) draft effect of the stack

72. The type of fuel oil pump most commonly used with gun type oil burners is the

(A) centrifugal type
(B) external or internal gear type
(C) volute type
(D) propeller type

73. Chimney draft is usually measured in

(A) inches of mercury
(B) inches of water
(C) feet of water
(D) pounds per square inch

74. "Draft" that is produced over the fire or in a chimney without the use of any mechanical aids is generally known as

(A) balanced draft   (B) induced draft   (C) positive draft   (D) natural draft

75. Assume that a residential heating control system consists of a room thermostat, a limit control, a combustion control, a safety control and a control relay. These controls would most likely be used with

(A) automatic gas fired burners
(B) automatic oil fired burners
(C) coal fired stokers
(D) electric heating systems

76. A gauge that can be used for measuring either a vacuum or positive pressure in pounds per square inch is generally called a

(A) compound gauge   (C) boiler gauge
(B) pressure gauge   (D) vacuum gauge

77. The purpose of a goose-neck connection to a Bourdon type steam gauge is to

(A) prevent water getting into the gauge tube
(B) prevent steam getting into the gauge tube
(C) correct for trapped air in the line
(D) allow impurities to settle in the tube

78. The device that is generally used to reduce high pressure steam to low pressure steam is called a

(A) pressure relief valve   (C) condenser
(B) pressure regulating valve   (D) bypass control valve

79. The maximum size of boiler safety valve that can be used on a low pressure boiler is

(A) 2 inches   (B) 3½ inches   (C) 4½ inches   (D) 5½ inches

Answer Key

1. B	9. C	17. A	25. D	33. A	41. B	49. D	57. B	65. D	73. B
2. B	10. C	18. C	26. D	34. A	42. C	50. A	58. A	66. A	74. D
3. C	11. D	19. A	27. A	35. B	43. D	51. A	59. A	67. C	75. B
4. D	12. A	20. B	28. D	36. C	44. A	52. A	60. B	68. D	76. A
5. D	13. D	21. A	29. D	37. C	45. D	53. D	61. C	69. A	77. B
6. D	14. B	22. C	30. C	38. A	46. D	54. B	62. C	70. D	78. B
7. B	15. B	23. C	31. C	39. D	47. C	55. C	63. D	71. B	79. B
8. C	16. D	24. B	32. D	40. B	48. A	56. B	64. D	72. B	

Explanatory Answers
Sample Examination VI

1. **(B)** Submitting required forms is important for control of an organization. The forms are also the basis of many administrative decisions that cannot be delayed or neglected. Ignoring them can be costly. A system makes the procedure easier.

2. **(B)** An accident is costly to both the worker involved and the organization. Safety regulations are based on proven preventive measures and they should not be omitted.

3. **(C)** If each employee is assigned specific duties in case of fire, then the different aspects of fire fighting will be performed and important steps will not be overlooked during the actual emergency.

4. **(D)** Reports are not an end in themselves but a means to achieving desired results in a timely fashion. They form the basis for administrative decisions.

5. **(D)** The interval between inspections of subordinates' work should be determined by how often they must be done to achieve the desired productivity.

6. **(D)** Management policies, union contracts, and new custodial operations are all important to the custodian's work performance. The current rate of interest on bonds is not.

7. **(B)** By making specific work assignments, a custodian ensures that every area will be covered.

8. **(C)** By pinpointing the cause of an accident, its cause can be rectified and similar accidents can be prevented in the future.

9. **(C)** Rearranging the store room can be put off to a later day; broken window panes, dirty toilet rooms, and hazards on public stairways cannot be ignored without reducing the efficiency of the building personnel.

10. **(C)** It is almost impossible to eliminate all grievances, but with some effort they can be kept to a minimum.

11. **(D)** If a dispute arises between two workers who are shoveling a walk, separate them and give each a separate area to shovel.

12. **(A)** Studies have shown that individuals who are not alert and who are not giving their full attention to their duties are more prone to accidents.

13. **(D)** A foam fire extinguisher cools and smothers a fire.

14. **(B)** The carbon dioxide, carbon tetrachloride, and calcium chloride solution in a soda-acid extinguisher react and force the water out to extinguish the fire.

15. **(B)** Only a carbon dioxide extinguisher will not spread and promote an electrical fire.

16. **(D)** If the extension rope is not secured, it will be a safety hazard for those climbing the ladder.

17. **(A)** A panic bolt is designed so that people may exit quickly in an emergency but the door is still locked from the outside to keep out unwanted visitors.

18. **(C)** Doing periodic tests and inspections is known as preventive maintenance.

19. **(A)** The outside diameter (OD) of a given size pipe must be the same. The extra steel which increases the strength of the pipe is added to the inside.

20. **(B)** In domestic gas piping the risers have a moisture trap at the bottom.

21. **(A)** Chewing gum should be removed from a floor with a putty knife.

22. **(C)** Sliding furniture mars a floor, but cleaning around the furniture will not clean the floor adequately. Lift the furniture to a clean place.

23. **(C)** Any oil must be entirely removed from a floor before applying wax.

24. **(B)** Alcohol often acts as a paint remover.

25. **(D)** Remove grass stains on marble or wood with sodium hypochlorite.

26. **(D)** A vacuum cleaner will get all the loose dust off a Venetian blind. A duster or a brush will only transfer the dust from one slat to another.

27. **(A)** Polish asphalt floors with a water emulsion wax.

28. **(D)** Washing soda is a hydrated sodium carbonate used as a general cleaner. It is effective because it increases the wetting power of water.

29. **(D)** Varnish will harm asphalt, rubber, and linoleum. It is a good cork sealer.

30. **(C)** In a large area using a long handled deck scrub brush will be too time-consuming and will require a lot of energy.

31. **(C)** Eliminating rat harborages can be difficult, but it must be done.

32. **(D)** Oil in any form, even salad oil, is harmful to asphalt tile.

33. **(A)** Gloves are worn so that caustic solutions do not touch the cleaners' skin.

34. **(A)** Pyrethins are either of two viscous liquid esters that are extracted from pyrethaun flowers and used as insecticides.

35. **(B)** Water hammer occurs when water is carried over into the steam lines.

36. **(C)** A bourdon tube is an oval tube that looks like a question mark; one end of the tube is connected to the steam side of the boiler while the other end is closed and connected to a needle. As pressure builds up, the bourdon tube tries to straighten out and moves the needle over a scale to indicate the pressure.

37. **(C)** Human bodies give off heat and moisture.

38. **(A)** Foot valves are installed at the intake end of the suction pump so that when the system is not pumping the pump will stay primed and ready to lift.

39. **(D)** 83 feet of water is equal to 36 lbs. Gravity creates the pressure.

40. **(B)** A vapor barrier keeps moisture from seeping through a wall.

41. **(B)** The valve in a pitot tube is sensitive to pressure and thus measures air and gas flow.

42. **(C)** Kitchens and laboratories often have foul odors, so their ventilating systems should not be equipped with return ducts.

43. **(D)** 240 BTUs per hour will be emitted from one square foot of equivalent direct steam radiation.

44. **(A)** Excessive tension, misalignment of the motor, or loose bearings will cause continuous vibration of an operating motor. A faulty starting circuit will not.

45. **(D)** A steam trap removes condensate, not steam.

46. **(D)** The dew point is the temperature at which air becomes saturated with moisture and produces dew.

47. **(C)** If scale forms on the seat of a float-operated boiler feed water regulator, the seat cannot be fully closed and water will be allowed to enter the boiler.

48. **(A)** A dirty strainer will restrict the flow of oil, creating a higher vacuum.

49. **(D)** Stack temperature, CO_2, and the number of boilers in operation are all important to the proper operation of the boiler.

50. **(A)** The free oxygen in the water is liberated when the water is heated and the air containing the oxygen is driven from the water. This oxygen causes corrosion (rusting) and pitting of the boiler metal. Proper chemical treatment is important.

51. **(A)** Combustion efficiency or complete combustion is the burning of all the fuel with the proper amount of excess air. If heat is not transferred properly, the temperature of the discharged gases will rise.

52. **(A)** The top try cock allows only steam to exit, the bottom try cock allows only water, and the middle try cock allows a combination of steam and water. Try cocks are on the water column found at the normal operating level.

53. **(D)** A faulty door seal will cause a refrigerator to sweat.

54. **(B)** ¼″ slope per foot
1″ per 4′
50′ divided by 4 = 12′½″
Approximately 1.04′

55. **(C)** Oil cleans wood chisels when they are being sharpened.

56. **(B)** A halide torch detects freon leaks.

57. **(B)** There are approximately 28,200 gallons of water in the basement. To be pumped out in one hour, you need to pump about 470 gallons per minute (470 × 60 = 28,200).

58. **(A)** When an item is removed from the shelf it is subtracted from the inventory; when it is placed on the shelf it is added to the inventory. This procedure keeps an accurate record of available supplies.

59. **(A)** No favoritism can be shown by a supervisor; it hurts morale, cooperation, etc.

60. **(B)** A standardized procedure will be accepted by workers if they are convinced that it is the best way to accomplish what has to be done.

61. **(C)** Always check incoming shipments; you must make sure you are getting what you ordered (and what you will pay for).

62. **(C)** Without an orderly stockroom, items are difficult to locate quickly. Items are also likely to run out of stock because it is not obvious when an item is running low and needs to be reordered.

63. **(D)** A low pressure steam heating boiler generates steam at 15 psi or less.

64. **(D)** A low pressure hot water heating boiler produces hot water at a gauge pressure of 200 psi.

65. **(D)** Evaporation is the change from liquid to gas form.

66. **(A)** A Ringelmann chart has a scale of different colors to show the amount of smoke. Smoke is passed through a filter and then is compared to the chart.

67. **(C)** More than 25 volts is not needed for the low voltage control circuits of an oil burner. Higher voltage can cause damage to the relays or controls.

68. **(D)** A Hartford loop is the connection of one low-pressure steam boiler to another boiler with piping to the water sides and steam sides. They share the same amount of water and pressure.

69. **(A)** #2 fuel oil contains 140,000 BTU's per pound. Coal and wood have much less.

70. **(D)** #6 fuel oil is the most commonly used in large buildings, and also has the greatest heat value per pound. #6 oil has 150,000 BTU/lb.

71. **(B)** Atomization is the breaking up of oil into small particles to allow it to burn. This is done with pressure from a pump and centifugal force from a rapidly rotating cup.

72. **(B)** A gear type pump is external if the oil is pumped back to the oil tank, internal if the oil is only returned to the suction side of the pump.

73. **(B)** Chimney draft is calibrated in tenths of inches of water. It is the difference in pressure between the atmosphere and the boiler fire box (the breeching, or stack).

74. **(D)** Natural draft is caused by the difference in weight between a column of warm air and an equal column of cold air.

75. **(B)** Thermostat, limit control, combustion control, safety control, and a control relay are all parts of an automatic oil-fired burner.

76. **(A)** A compound gauge has a midpoint. One side (the negative side) measures vacuum, and the positive side measures pressure.

77. **(B)** A bourdon tube is very delicate and steam entering the tube will warp it so that it gives a false reading. To prevent steam from entering, a goose neck connection or siphon is installed.

78. **(B)** A pressure regulating valve maintains a constant pressure by opening and closing a bypass port as pressure is increased or decreased.

79. **(B)** The huddling chamber is 3½ inches, which is wider than the valve seat, thus giving the steam a larger area to push against so that the total force will increase from 106 lbs. to 144 lbs. and push the valve open.

Answer Sheet
Sample Examination VII

1. Ⓐ Ⓑ Ⓒ Ⓓ
2. Ⓐ Ⓑ Ⓒ Ⓓ
3. Ⓐ Ⓑ Ⓒ Ⓓ
4. Ⓐ Ⓑ Ⓒ Ⓓ
5. Ⓐ Ⓑ Ⓒ Ⓓ
6. Ⓐ Ⓑ Ⓒ Ⓓ
7. Ⓐ Ⓑ Ⓒ Ⓓ
8. Ⓐ Ⓑ Ⓒ Ⓓ
9. Ⓐ Ⓑ Ⓒ Ⓓ
10. Ⓐ Ⓑ Ⓒ Ⓓ
11. Ⓐ Ⓑ Ⓒ Ⓓ
12. Ⓐ Ⓑ Ⓒ Ⓓ
13. Ⓐ Ⓑ Ⓒ Ⓓ
14. Ⓐ Ⓑ Ⓒ Ⓓ
15. Ⓐ Ⓑ Ⓒ Ⓓ
16. Ⓐ Ⓑ Ⓒ Ⓓ
17. Ⓐ Ⓑ Ⓒ Ⓓ
18. Ⓐ Ⓑ Ⓒ Ⓓ
19. Ⓐ Ⓑ Ⓒ Ⓓ

20. Ⓐ Ⓑ Ⓒ Ⓓ
21. Ⓐ Ⓑ Ⓒ Ⓓ
22. Ⓐ Ⓑ Ⓒ Ⓓ
23. Ⓐ Ⓑ Ⓒ Ⓓ
24. Ⓐ Ⓑ Ⓒ Ⓓ
25. Ⓐ Ⓑ Ⓒ Ⓓ
26. Ⓐ Ⓑ Ⓒ Ⓓ
27. Ⓐ Ⓑ Ⓒ Ⓓ
28. Ⓐ Ⓑ Ⓒ Ⓓ
29. Ⓐ Ⓑ Ⓒ Ⓓ
30. Ⓐ Ⓑ Ⓒ Ⓓ
31. Ⓐ Ⓑ Ⓒ Ⓓ
32. Ⓐ Ⓑ Ⓒ Ⓓ
33. Ⓐ Ⓑ Ⓒ Ⓓ
34. Ⓐ Ⓑ Ⓒ Ⓓ
35. Ⓐ Ⓑ Ⓒ Ⓓ
36. Ⓐ Ⓑ Ⓒ Ⓓ
37. Ⓐ Ⓑ Ⓒ Ⓓ
38. Ⓐ Ⓑ Ⓒ Ⓓ

39. Ⓐ Ⓑ Ⓒ Ⓓ
40. Ⓐ Ⓑ Ⓒ Ⓓ
41. Ⓐ Ⓑ Ⓒ Ⓓ
42. Ⓐ Ⓑ Ⓒ Ⓓ
43. Ⓐ Ⓑ Ⓒ Ⓓ
44. Ⓐ Ⓑ Ⓒ Ⓓ
45. Ⓐ Ⓑ Ⓒ Ⓓ
46. Ⓐ Ⓑ Ⓒ Ⓓ
47. Ⓐ Ⓑ Ⓒ Ⓓ
48. Ⓐ Ⓑ Ⓒ Ⓓ
49. Ⓐ Ⓑ Ⓒ Ⓓ
50. Ⓐ Ⓑ Ⓒ Ⓓ
51. Ⓐ Ⓑ Ⓒ Ⓓ
52. Ⓐ Ⓑ Ⓒ Ⓓ
53. Ⓐ Ⓑ Ⓒ Ⓓ
54. Ⓐ Ⓑ Ⓒ Ⓓ
55. Ⓐ Ⓑ Ⓒ Ⓓ
56. Ⓐ Ⓑ Ⓒ Ⓓ
57. Ⓐ Ⓑ Ⓒ Ⓓ

58. Ⓐ Ⓑ Ⓒ Ⓓ
59. Ⓐ Ⓑ Ⓒ Ⓓ
60. Ⓐ Ⓑ Ⓒ Ⓓ
61. Ⓐ Ⓑ Ⓒ Ⓓ
62. Ⓐ Ⓑ Ⓒ Ⓓ
63. Ⓐ Ⓑ Ⓒ Ⓓ
64. Ⓐ Ⓑ Ⓒ Ⓓ
65. Ⓐ Ⓑ Ⓒ Ⓓ
66. Ⓐ Ⓑ Ⓒ Ⓓ
67. Ⓐ Ⓑ Ⓒ Ⓓ
68. Ⓐ Ⓑ Ⓒ Ⓓ
69. Ⓐ Ⓑ Ⓒ Ⓓ
70. Ⓐ Ⓑ Ⓒ Ⓓ
71. Ⓐ Ⓑ Ⓒ Ⓓ
72. Ⓐ Ⓑ Ⓒ Ⓓ
73. Ⓐ Ⓑ Ⓒ Ⓓ
74. Ⓐ Ⓑ Ⓒ Ⓓ
75. Ⓐ Ⓑ Ⓒ Ⓓ
76. Ⓐ Ⓑ Ⓒ Ⓓ

77. Ⓐ Ⓑ Ⓒ Ⓓ
78. Ⓐ Ⓑ Ⓒ Ⓓ
79. Ⓐ Ⓑ Ⓒ Ⓓ
80. Ⓐ Ⓑ Ⓒ Ⓓ
81. Ⓐ Ⓑ Ⓒ Ⓓ
82. Ⓐ Ⓑ Ⓒ Ⓓ
83. Ⓐ Ⓑ Ⓒ Ⓓ
84. Ⓐ Ⓑ Ⓒ Ⓓ
85. Ⓐ Ⓑ Ⓒ Ⓓ
86. Ⓐ Ⓑ Ⓒ Ⓓ
87. Ⓐ Ⓑ Ⓒ Ⓓ
88. Ⓐ Ⓑ Ⓒ Ⓓ
89. Ⓐ Ⓑ Ⓒ Ⓓ
90. Ⓐ Ⓑ Ⓒ Ⓓ
91. Ⓐ Ⓑ Ⓒ Ⓓ
92. Ⓐ Ⓑ Ⓒ Ⓓ
93. Ⓐ Ⓑ Ⓒ Ⓓ
94. Ⓐ Ⓑ Ⓒ Ⓓ
95. Ⓐ Ⓑ Ⓒ Ⓓ

SAMPLE EXAMINATION VII

THE TIME ALLOWED FOR THE ENTIRE EXAMINATION IS 4 HOURS.

DIRECTIONS: Each question has four suggested answers lettered (A), (B), (C), and (D). Decide which one is the best answer and, on your answer sheet, darken the space for that letter.

1. Before starting any lawn mowing, the distance between the blade and a flat surface should be measured with a ruler. This distance should be such that the cut of the grass above the ground is

(A) 1 inch
(B) 1½ inches
(C) 2 inches
(D) 3 inches

2. Strainers in a number 6 fuel oil system should be checked

(A) once a day
(B) once a week
(C) once a month
(D) once a year

3. The spinning cup on a rotary cup oil burner should be cleaned once

(A) a day
(B) a week
(C) every two weeks
(D) a month

4. Terrazzo floors should be cleaned daily with a

(A) damp mop using clear water
(B) damp mop using a strong alkaline solution
(C) damp mop using a mild acid solution
(D) dust mop treated with vegetable oil

5. New installations of vinyl-asbestos floors should

(A) never be machine scrubbed
(B) be dry buffed weekly
(C) be swept daily, using an oily compound
(D) never be swept with treated dust mops

6. Standpipe fire hose shall be inspected

(A) monthly
(B) quarterly
(C) semi-annually
(D) annually

7. All portable fire extinguishers shall be inspected

(A) once a year
(B) once a month
(C) once a week
(D) once every 3 months

8. Soda-acid and foam type fire extinguishers shall be discharged and recharged at least once

(A) each year
(B) every two years
(C) every six months
(D) each month

9. Elevator "safeties" under the car shall be tested once each

(A) day
(B) week
(C) month
(D) quarter

10. Key type fire alarms in public school buildings shall be tested

(A) daily
(B) weekly
(C) monthly
(D) quarterly

11. Combustion efficiency can be determined from an appropriate chart used in conjunction with

(A) steam temperature and steam pressure
(B) flue gas temperature and percentage of CO_2
(C) flue gas temperature and fuel heating value
(D) oil temperature and steam pressure

12. In the combustion of common fuels, the major boiler heat loss is due to

(A) incomplete combustion
(B) moisture in the fuel
(C) heat radiation
(D) heat lost in the flue gases

13. The most important reason for blowing down a boiler water column and gauge glass is to

(A) prevent the gauge glass level from rising too high
(B) relieve stresses in the gauge glass
(C) insure a true water level reading
(D) insure a true pressure gauge reading

14. The secondary voltage of a transformer used for ignition in a fuel oil burner has a range of most nearly

(A) 120 volts to 240 volts   (C) 660 volts to 1,200 volts
(B) 440 volts to 660 volts   (D) 5,000 volts to 15,000 volts

15. Assume that during the month of April there were 3 days with an average outdoor temperature of 30°F, 7 days with 40°F, 10 days with 50°F, 3 days with 60°F, and 7 days with 65°F. The number of degree-days for the month was

(A) 330   (C) 595
(B) 445   (D) 1,150

16. The pH of boiler feedwater is usually maintained within the range of

    (A) 4 to 5   (C) 10 to 12
    (B) 6 to 7   (D) 13 to 14

17. The admission of steam to the coils of a domestic hot water supply tank is regulated by a (an)

    (A) pressure regulating valve   (C) check valve
    (B) immersion type temperature gauge   (D) thermostatic control valve

18. The device which senses primary air failure in a rotary cup oil burner is usually called a (an)

    (A) vaporstat   (C) venturi
    (B) anemometer   (D) pressure gauge

19. The device which starts and stops the flow of oil into an automatic rotary cup oil burner is usually called a (an)

    (A) magnetic oil valve   (C) oil check valve
    (B) oil metering valve   (D) relief valve

20. A vacuum breaker, used on a steam heated domestic hot water tank, is usually connected to the

    (A) circulating pump   (C) aquastat
    (B) tank wall   (D) steam coil flange

21. A vacuum pump in a low pressure steam heating system which is equipped with a float switch, a vacuum switch, a magnetic starter, and a selector switch, can be operated on

    (A) float, vacuum, or automatic   (C) vacuum, automatic, or continuous
    (B) float, vacuum, or continuous   (D) float, automatic, or continuous

22. If the temperature of the condensate returning to the vacuum pump in a low pressure steam vacuum heating system is above 180 degrees Fahrenheit, the trouble may be caused by

    (A) faulty radiator traps
    (B) room thermostats being set too high
    (C) uninsulated return lines
    (D) too many radiators being shut off

23. A feedwater regulator operates to

    (A) shut down the burner when the water is low
    (B) maintain the water in the boiler at a predetermined level
    (C) drain the water from the boiler
    (D) regulate the temperature of the feedwater

24. An automatically fired steam boiler is equipped with an automatic low water cut-off. The low water cut-off is usually actuated by

    (A) steam pressure   (C) float action
    (B) fuel pressure   (D) water temperature

25. Low pressure steam or an electric heater is usually required for heating

(A) #1 fuel oil   (C) #4 fuel oil
(B) #2 fuel oil   (D) #6 fuel oil

26. A compound gauge is calibrated to read

(A) pressure only   (C) vacuum and pressure
(B) vacuum only   (D) temperature and humidity

27. In a mechanical pressure-atomizing type oil burner, the oil is atomized by using an atomizing tip and

(A) steam pressure   (C) compressed air
(B) pump pressure   (D) a spinning cup

28. A good over-the-fire draft in a natural draft furnace should be approximately

(A) 5.0 inches of water positive pressure
(B) 0.05 inches of water positive pressure
(C) 0.05 inches of water vacuum
(D) 5.0 inches of water vacuum

29. When it is necessary to add chemicals to a heating boiler it should be done

(A) immediately after boiler blowdown
(B) after the boiler has been cleaned internally of sludge, scale, and other foreign matter
(C) at periods when condensate flow to the boiler is small
(D) at a time when there is a heavy flow of condensate to the boiler

30. The modutrol motor on a rotary cup oil burner burning #6 fuel oil automatically operates the

(A) primary air damper, secondary air damper, and oil metering valve
(B) primary air damper, secondary air damper, and magnetic oil valve
(C) primary air damper, oil metering valve, and magnetic oil valve
(D) primary air damper and magnetic oil valve

31. The manual-reset pressuretrol is classified as a

(A) safety and operating control
(B) limit and operating control
(C) limit and safety control
(D) limit, operating, and safety control

32. Sodium sulphite is added to boiler feedwater to

(A) avoid caustic embrittlement
(B) increase the pH value
(C) reduce the tendency of foaming in the steam drum
(D) remove dissolved oxygen

33. Neat cement is a mixture of

(A) cement, putty, and water   (C) cement, lime, and water
(B) cement and water   (D) cement, salt, and water

34. In a concrete mix of 1:2:4, the 2 refers to the amount of

    (A) sand
    (B) cement
    (C) stone
    (D) water

35. The volume in cubic feet of a cylindrical tank 6 feet in diameter × 35 feet long is most nearly

    (A) 210
    (B) 990
    (C) 1,260
    (D) 3,960

36. Plated metal surfaces which are protected by a thin coat of clear lacquer should be cleaned with a (an)

    (A) abrasive compound
    (B) liquid polish
    (C) mild soap solution
    (D) lemon oil solution

37. Wet mop filler replacements are ordered by

    (A) length
    (B) weight
    (C) number of strands
    (D) trade number

38. The best way to determine the value of a cleaning material is by

    (A) performance testing
    (B) manufacturer's literature
    (C) written specifications
    (D) interviews with manufacturer's salesman

39. The instructions on a container of cleaning compound state: "Mix one pound of compound in 5 gallons of water." Using these instructions, the amount of compound which should be added to 15 quarts of water is most nearly

    (A) 3 ounces
    (B) 8 ounces
    (C) 12 ounces
    (D) 48 ounces

40. The most common cause of paint blisters is

    (A) too much oil in the paint
    (B) moisture under the paint coat
    (C) a heavy coat of paint
    (D) improper drying of the paint

41. The floor that should *not* be machine scrubbed is the floor of a (an)

    (A) lobby
    (B) lunchroom
    (C) gymnasium
    (D) auditorium aisle

42. Pick-up sweeping in a school building is the occasional removal of the more conspicuous loose dirt from corridors and lobbies. This type of sweeping should be done

    (A) after scrubbing or waxing of floors
    (B) with the aid of a sweeping compound
    (C) at night after school hours
    (D) during regular school hours

43. According to recommended practice, when a steam boiler is taken out of service for a long period of time, the boiler drums should first be

(A) drained completely while the water is hot (above 212°F)
(B) drained completely after the water has been cooled down to 180°F
(C) filled completely without draining
(D) filled to the level of the top try cock

44. If it is not possible to plant new shrubs immediately upon delivery in the spring, they should be stored in a (an)

(A) sheltered outdoor area   (C) boiler room
(B) unsheltered outdoor area   (D) warm place indoors

45. Peat moss is generally used for its

(A) food value   (C) alkalinity
(B) nitrogen   (D) moisture retaining quality

46. The prevention and control of vermin and rodents in a school building is primarily a matter of

(A) maintaining good housekeeping on a continuous basis
(B) periodic use of an exterminator's service
(C) calling in the exterminator when necessary
(D) cleaning the building thoroughly during school vacation

47. The main classification of lumber used for construction purposes is known as

(A) industrial lumber   (C) finish lumber
(B) commercial lumber   (D) yard lumber

48. Oil-soaked waste and rags should be

(A) deposited in a self-closing metal can
(B) piled in the open
(C) stored in the supply closet
(D) rolled up and be available for the next job

49. Inspection for safety should be included as part of the custodian engineer's

(A) daily inspection   (C) monthly inspection
(B) weekly inspection   (D) quarterly inspection

50. Of the following classifications, the one which pertains to fires in electrical equipment is

(A) Class A   (C) Class C
(B) Class B   (D) Class D

51. The type of portable fire extinguisher which is particularly suited for extinguishing flammable liquid fires is the

(A) soda-acid type   (C) pump tank type
(B) foam type   (D) loaded stream type

52. Of the following liquids, the one which has the lowest flash point is

(A) kerosene

(B) gasoline

(C) benzene

(D) carbon tetrachloride

53. Of the following, you should *not*, when giving first aid to an injured person

(A) administer medication internally

(B) send for a physician

(C) control bleeding

(D) treat for shock

54. In reference to fire fighting, fires are of such complexity that

(A) no plans or methods of attack can be formulated in advance

(B) the problem must be considered in advance and methods of attack formulated

(C) an appointed committee is necessary to direct fighting at the fire

(D) no planned procedures can be relied on

55. The heat of a soldering copper should be tested

(A) with solder

(B) by holding it near kraft paper

(C) by holding it near your hand

(D) with water

56. Safety on the job is best assured by

(A) keeping alert

(B) following every rule

(C) working very slowly

(D) never working alone

57. One important use of accident reports is to provide information that may be used to reduce the possibility of similar accidents. The most valuable entry on the report for this purpose is the

(A) time lost due to accident

(B) date of the occurrence

(C) injury sustained by the victim

(D) cause of the accident

58. If the directions given by your superior are *not* clear, the best thing for you to do is to

(A) ask to have the directions repeated and clarified

(B) proceed to do the work taking a chance on doing the right thing

(C) do nothing until some later time when you can find out exactly what is wanted

(D) ask one of the other workers in your crew what to do under the circumstances

59. Of the following procedures concerning grievances of subordinate personnel, the custodian engineer should maintain an attitude of

(A) paying little attention to little grievances

(B) being very alert to grievances and make adjustments in existing conditions to appease all personnel

(C) knowing the most frequent causes of grievances and strive to prevent them from arising

(D) maintaining rigid discipline of a nature that "smooths out" all grievances

60. Of the following, the best course of action to take to settle a dispute or conflict between two employees is to

(A) insist that the two employees settle the case between themselves
(B) call in each one separately and after hearing their cases presented, decide the issue
(C) bring both in for a conference at the same time and make the decision in their presence
(D) have both present their points of view and arguments in a written memorandum and on this basis make your decision

61. If, as a custodian engineer, you discover an error in your report submitted to the main office, you should

(A) do nothing, since it is possible that one error will have little effect on the total report
(B) wait until the error is discovered in the main office and then offer to work overtime to correct it
(C) go directly to the supervisor in the main office after working hours and ask him unofficially to correct the error
(D) notify the main office immediately so that the error can be corrected, if necessary

62. There are a considerable number of forms and reports to be submitted on schedule by the custodian engineer. The advisable method of accomplishing this duty is to

(A) fill out the reports at odd times during the days when you have free time
(B) schedule a definite period of the work week for completing these forms and reports
(C) assign your supervisor or cleaner to handle all these forms for you and to have them available on time
(D) classify or group the forms and reports and fill out only one of each group and refer the other forms or reports to the ones completed

63. A school custodian engineer can best evaluate the quality of work performed by custodial personnel by

(A) periodic inspection of the building's cleanliness
(B) studying the time records of personnel
(C) reviewing the building cleaning expenditures
(D) analyzing complaints of building occupants

64. Assume that you are the custodian engineer and one of your employees wants to talk with you about a grievance. Of the following actions, the *least* desirable action for you to take is to

(A) listen sympathetically
(B) conduct the discussion openly in the presence of the workforce
(C) try to get his point of view
(D) endeavor to obtain all the facts

65. Of the following factors, the one which is *least* important in evaluating an employee and his work is her

(A) dependability
(B) quantity of work done
(C) quality of work done
(D) education and training

66. Supervision of a group of people engaged in building cleaning operations should *not* include supervision of

(A) time spent in cleaning operations
(B) utilization of official rest and lunch periods
(C) cleaning methods
(D) materials used for various cleaning jobs

67. Of the following methods, the best one to utilize in assigning custodial personnel to clean a multi-floor school building is to

(A) allow the cleaners to pick their room or area assignments out of a hat
(B) have the supervisor make specific room or area assignments to each cleaner separately
(C) rotate room and area assignments daily according to a chart posted on the bulletin board
(D) let a different member of the group make the room or area assignments each week

68. Of the following items, the one which is the *least* important in the preparation of a report is that the report

(A) is brief, but to the point
(B) uses the prescribed form if there is one
(C) contains extra copies
(D) is accurate

69. In order to have building employees willing to follow standardized cleaning and maintenance procedures, the supervisor must be prepared to

(A) work alongside the employees
(B) demonstrate the reasonableness of the procedures
(C) offer incentive pay for their utilization
(D) allow the employees the free use of the time saved by their adoption

70. Suppose that you are the custodian engineer and one of your employees has gross earnings of $210.70 for the week, all of which is subject to Social Security deductions at the rate of 7.15%. The amount which should be deducted from the employee's gross earnings for the week is most nearly

(A) $ 6.65
(B) $14.44

(C) $13.79
(D) $15.07

71. Suppose that you are a custodian engineer and an employee works for you at the rate of $5.80 per hour with time and one-half paid for time worked after 40 hours in one week. The gross pay for working 53 hours in one week is most nearly

(A) $307.40
(B) $321.40

(C) $325.10
(D) $345.10

72. The minimum number of gate valves usually required in a bypass around a steam trap is

(A) 1
(B) 2

(C) 3
(D) 4

73. A 2-inch standard steel pipe, as compared with a 2-inch extra heavy steel pipe, has the same

(A) wall thickness   (C) outside diameter
(B) inside diameter   (D) weight per linear foot

74. A short piece of pipe with a standard male pipe thread on one end and a locknut thread on the other end is usually called a

(A) close nipple   (C) coupling
(B) tank nipple   (D) union

75. Dies are used by plumbers to

(A) ream out the inside of pipes   (C) bevel the ends of pipes
(B) thread pipes   (D) make up solder joints

76. Of the following types of pipe, the one which is most brittle is

(A) brass   (C) cast iron
(B) copper   (D) wrought iron

77. The primary function of a trap in a drainage system is to

(A) prevent gases from flowing into the building
(B) produce an efficient flushing action
(C) prevent articles accidentally dropped into the drainage system from entering the sewer
(D) prevent the water backing up

78. If a plumbing fixture is allowed to stand unused for a long time, its trap is apt to lose its seal by

(A) evaporation   (C) siphonage
(B) capillary action   (D) condensation

79. The pipe fitting used to connect a 1¼ inch pipe directly to a 1 inch pipe in a straight line is called a

(A) union   (C) elbow
(B) nipple   (D) reducer

80. The best procedure to follow when replacing a blown fuse is to

(A) immediately replace it with the same size fuse
(B) immediately replace it with a larger size fuse
(C) immediately replace it with a smaller size fuse
(D) correct the cause of the fuse failure and replace it with the correct size

81. The amperage rating of the fuse to be used in an electrical circuit is determined by the

(A) size of the connected load
(B) size of the wire in the circuit
(C) voltage of the circuit
(D) ambient temperature

82. In a 208 volt, 3 phase, 4 wire circuit the voltage, in volts, from any line to the grounded neutral is approximately

(A) 208
(B) 150
(C) 120
(D) zero

83. The device commonly used to change an a.c. voltage to a d.c. voltage is called a

(A) transformer
(B) rectifier
(C) relay
(D) capacitor or condenser

84. Where conduit enters a knock-out in an outlet box, it should be provided with a

(A) bushing on the inside and locknut on the outside
(B) locknut on the inside and bushing on the outside
(C) union on the outside and a nipple on the inside
(D) nipple on the outside and a union on the inside

85. The electric circuit to a ten kilowatt electric hot water heater which is automatically controlled by an aquastat will also require a

(A) transistor
(B) choke coil
(C) magnetic contactor
(D) limit switch

86. An electric power consumption meter usually indicates the power used in

(A) watts
(B) volt-hours
(C) amperes
(D) kilowatt-hours

87. Of the following sizes of copper wire, the one which can safely carry the greatest amount of amperes is

(A) 14 gauge stranded
(B) 12 gauge stranded
(C) 12 gauge solid
(D) 10 gauge solid

88. A flexible coupling is primarily used to

(A) allow for imperfect alignment of two joining shafts
(B) allow for slight differences in shaft diameters
(C) insure perfect alignment of the joining shafts
(D) reduce fast starting of the machinery

89. Of the following statements concerning lubricating oil, the correct one is

(A) SAE 10 is heavier and more viscous than SAE 30
(B) diluting lubricating oil with gasoline increases its viscosity
(C) oil reduces friction between moving parts
(D) in hot weather, thin oil is preferable to heavy oil

90. The main purpose of periodic inspections and tests made on mechanical equipment is to

(A) make the operating workers familiar with the equipment
(B) keep the maintenance mechanics busy during otherwise slack periods
(C) discover minor faults before they develop into serious breakdowns
(D) encourage the workers to take better care of the equipment

91. Of the following bearing types, the one which is *not* classified as a roller bearing is

(A) radial
(B) angular
(C) thrust
(D) babbit

92. In a wire rope, when a number of wires are laid left-handed into a strand and the strand laid right-handed around a hemp rope center, the wire rope is commonly known as a

(A) right-lay, Lang-lay rope
(B) left-lay, Lang-lay rope
(C) left-lay, regular-lay rope
(D) right-lay, regular-lay rope

93. The chemical which is *not* used for disinfecting swimming pools is

(A) ammonia
(B) calcium hypochlorite
(C) chlorine
(D) liquefied chlorine

94. An air compressor which is driven by an electric motor is usually started and stopped automatically by a (an)

(A) unloader
(B) pressure regulator valve
(C) float switch
(D) pressure switch

95. If the water level in a steam heating boiler is unsteady, the most probable cause is

(A) overfiring of the boiler
(B) the use of a poor grade of fuel
(C) insufficient radiation in the heating system
(D) use of an oversize boiler

Answer Key

1. C	13. C	25. D	37. B	49. A	61. D	73. C	85. C
2. A	14. D	26. C	38. A	50. C	62. B	74. B	86. D
3. A	15. B	27. B	39. C	51. B	63. A	75. B	87. D
4. A	16. C	28. C	40. B	52. B	64. B	76. C	88. A
5. B	17. D	29. D	41. C	53. A	65. D	77. A	89. C
6. B	18. A	30. A	42. D	54. B	66. B	78. A	90. C
7. B	19. A	31. C	43. B	55. A	67. B	79. D	91. D
8. A	20. D	32. D	44. A	56. A	68. C	80. D	92. D
9. C	21. D	33. B	45. D	57. D	69. B	81. B	93. A
10. A	22. A	34. A	46. A	58. A	70. D	82. C	94. D
11. B	23. B	35. B	47. D	59. C	71. D	83. B	95. A
12. D	24. C	36. C	48. A	60. C	72. C	84. A	

Explanatory Answers
Sample Examination VII

1. **(C)** If the lawn mower blade is any lower than 2 inches it can cause damage to the lawn.

2. **(A)** #6 oil is very thick or viscous, and the mesh screening on strainer baskets is very fine. If the fuel line is not cleaned every 24 hours it can clog.

3. **(A)** Clean the spinning cups daily to prevent build-up at the burner.

4. **(A)** Only a damp mop and clear water are necessary to clean a terrazzo floor.

5. **(B)** To keep the luster of a new vinyl-asbestos floor, dry-buff it weekly.

6. **(B)** Quarterly inspection of fire hose is mandated by most fire codes. In the event of a fire you want to be sure that all the hose is sound.

7. **(B)** Inspect portable fire extinguishers once a month to make sure they have not been tampered with, even though most fire codes only require inspections once a year.

8. **(A)** Soda-acid and foam extinguishers tend to lose their charge after a year of inactivity.

9. **(C)** Elevator safeties should be inspected at least monthly, usually by an elevator maintenance company.

10. **(A)** Inspect key type fire alarms at the beginning of each day.

11. **(B)** Combustion efficiency can be determined by the percentage of burnt fuel and the flue gas temperature in the stack.

12. **(D)** Improper air-to-fuel ratio causes improper or inefficient combustion and heat loss through the flue gases.

13. **(C)** A proper level of water is essential to the efficient operation of a boiler.

14. **(D)** The secondary voltage of a transformer used for ignition is related to the temperature needed to ignite the fuel. This is 5,000 to 15,000 volts.

15. **(B)**

Days	Degrees	Deviation from 65°		Degree-Days
3	30	35	3 × 35	105
7	40	25	7 × 25	175
10	50	15	10 × 15	150
3	60	5	3 × 5	15
7	65	0	–	0
			Total:	445

16. **(C)** pH is a measure of alkalinity and acidity. The pH of boiler feedwater should be between 10 and 12.

17. **(D)** A thermostatic control valve regulates domestic hot water temperature.

18. **(A)** A vaporstat is a very low pressure switch which senses pressure in inches of water column and thus senses primary air failure.

19. **(A)** The magnetic oil valve will shut off the flow of oil for safety purposes.

20. **(D)** The flange is the closest to the steam coil that you can get. The rest of the piping is submerged.

21. **(D)** For seasonal temperature control strategies a vacuum pump in a steam heating system can be operated on float, automatic, or continuous.

22. **(A)** If the temperature of condensate returning to the vacuum pump is over 180°F, this is a sign that live steam is returning to the tank instead of condensate.

23. **(B)** A feed water regulator is located at the normal operating water level. Sometimes referred to as a pump control, it maintains a constant water level in the boiler by means of a float, starting the pump when the water level drops and stopping it when it returns to the normal level.

24. **(C)** The low water cut-off is a little below the normal operating water level. As the water level drops to an unsafe level, the float in the low water cut-off drops and breaks (opens) the electric circuit, shutting off the burner.

25. **(D)** #6 fuel oil must be heated to reduce its viscosity.

26. **(C)** Compound means having more than one function. A compound gauge measures both vacuum and pressure. Temperature is measured with a thermometer, and humidity with a barometer.

27. **(B)** The pump in a mechanical pressure atomizing burner moves the oil at a high pressure so that it hits the atomizing tip and the oil is atomized.

28. **(C)** .05 inches of water vacuum in a natural draft furnace will allow ample air for combustion and will allow enough draft for the gases to leave the furnace.

29. **(D)** Chemicals are usually added to the condensate by the vacuum pump. Water or condensate flows through the chemical feeder and forces the chemicals into the boiler.

30. **(A)** The modutrol motor on a rotary cup oil burner burning #6 fuel oil automatically operates the primary air damper, secondary air damper, and magnetic oil valve for a proper air-to-fuel ratio of 10 parts air to 1 part fuel.

31. **(C)** A pressuretrol is a switch that starts or stops a boiler on pressure. It also controls its operating range. It is a limit and safety control.

32. **(D)** Sodium sulfite added to boiler feed water helps avoid a scale or rust build-up in the boiler waterside. Rust is created by dissolved oxygen.

33. **(B)** Neat cement is not mixed or diluted with any substances other than water.

34. **(A)** A concrete mix ratio of 1:2:4 stands for 1 part cement, 2 parts sand, and 4 parts water.

35. **(B)** The volume of a cylinder is computed with the formula $(pi)r^2h$.
$3.14 (pi) \times (3')^2 \times 35' = 989.1$ cubic feet, or approximately 990 cu. ft.

36. **(C)** Nothing caustic should be used on a surface protected by clear lacquer—just a mild cleaning agent.

37. **(B)** The greater the weight, the larger the mop.

38. **(A)** To test a new cleaning material, use it properly and inspect the results.

39. **(C)** 5 gallons of water is equal to 20 quarts.
1 lb. is equal to 16 oz.
$15/20 = 3/4$
3/4 of 16 oz. = 12 oz.

40. **(B)** Moisture trapped under a coat of paint will eventually blister the paint.

41. **(C)** The polished finish of a gymnasium floor will be marred by machine scrubbing.

42. **(D)** "Pick-up" sweeping is done to maintain appearances only. A thorough sweeping should be done after school is out.

43. **(B)** Cool the water from a steam boiler drum before emptying it to prevent damage to the sewer lines.

44. **(A)** If you store new shrubs in a sheltered outdoor area they will remain acclimatized to the environment in which they will ultimately be planted.

45. **(D)** Peat moss is a porous medium that will retain water.

46. **(A)** Vermin control is a continuous process. Neglect for any period of time will bring infestation.

47. **(D)** Yard lumber is used for construction. It usually has some surface imperfections.

48. **(A)** Oil-soaked rags are a fire hazard and should be kept away from any possible flame.

49. **(A)** Accidents are costly to an organization and to the affected worker. They can be largely prevented by keeping the workplace as free from hazards as possible.

50. **(C)** *Class A* fires are fires in wood, paper, coal, rubbish, buildings, and most common materials. *Class B* fires are fires in liquids such as oil, gasoline, paint, fats, and similar materials that create a gas when heated. *Class C* fires are fires in live electrical equipment such as motor switches, fuse boxes, and appliances.

51. **(B)** A foam extinguisher cools and smothers the flames at the same time.

52. **(B)** Gasoline has a relatively low flash point.

53. **(A)** A person giving first aid should never administer medication internally. External medication may be acceptable if used with discretion. The first aid person should send for a doctor, try to control bleeding, and treat for shock.

54. **(B)** Extensive planning for possible fires, including fire drills, will help keep personal and property damage to a minimum if a fire should occur.

55. **(A)** Testing with solder is the only way to determine whether a soldering copper's heat is adequate.

56. **(A)** Studies have shown that workers who are not alert or who are inattentive and lack proper concentration are the most accident-prone.

57. **(D)** If the cause of an accident can be identified it can be corrected or eliminated so that similar accidents do not happen in the future.

58. **(A)** There is no harm in asking questions. One does not display ignorance by asking; instead, one shows attentiveness and interest in the work.

59. **(C)** It is impossible to eliminate grievances entirely, but it is possible to keep them to a minimum by eliminating the most common causes of employee complaints.

60. **(C)** Holding a conference to solve a dispute between two employees can be beneficial, but it must be done with considerable skill and tact to prevent the conference itself from exacerbating the dispute.

61. **(D)** An incorrect report can have severe unwanted consequences, since actions may or may not be taken as a result of it. Correct errors at once. Reports must be accurate.

62. **(B)** Reports are essential to agency control. They must be submitted on time without exception. A late or missing report can mean that inappropriate action is taken or that necessary action is not taken.

63. **(A)** Observation and inspection are the best way to determine the quality of custodial work.

64. **(B)** Always hear a grievance in private. Airing it in public may be embarrassing to both parties.

65. **(D)** The most important factor in evaluating an employee is how much work is being done and how well it is performed. Education and training are important in the placement of a worker initially, but after that the most important evaluating factor is how well the work is performed.

66. **(B)** Lunch and rest periods are the workers' time to do whatever they please, within reason.

67. **(B)** The supervisor should make specific cleaning assignments. This course of action ensures that all the necessary work is performed.

68. **(C)** Only the required number of copies of a report should be submitted. Extra copies waste time, effort, and paper.

69. **(B)** If the workers do not accept the standardized procedures and the reasons for them, they will not follow them.

70. **(D)** $210.70 × .0715 = $15.065 or $15.07

71. **(D)** $5.80 × 40 = $232
$5.80 × 1½ = $8.70
$8.70 × 13 = $113.10
$232 + $113.10 = $345.10

72. **(C)** To bypass a steam trap, one valve is located at the intake, and one at the outtake. These two will be closed. A third will be opened as the bypass after the trap is thus isolated.

73. **(C)** The extra steel that is the difference between a standard steel pipe and an extra heavy steel pipe is on the inside of the pipe. The ID (inside diameter) of the two pipes will be different.

74. **(B)** A tank nipple is designed so that it will not fall into the tank.

75. **(B)** There are many different sizes of pipe dies to thread pipes of different sizes. Most pipes, especially longer lengths, come unthreaded.

76. **(C)** Cast iron is a hard, brittle, non-malleable iron and carbon alloy containing 2.0 to 4.5 percent carbon.

77. **(A)** A trap in a drainage system is usually shaped like a U or a P. There is always water in the bottom of the U or the P to prevent sewer gas from flowing back out of the fixture drain.

78. **(A)** The water in a trap which prevents the back flow of sewer gases will evaporate after a long period of disuse.

79. **(D)** A reducer, by connecting a 1¼″ pipe to a 1″ pipe, is effectively "reducing" the 1¼″ pipe to a 1″ pipe.

80. **(D)** If the cause of a fuse failure is not corrected before the replacement fuse is installed, the new fuse will also blow.

81. **(B)** The heavier the wire, the higher the amperage of the fuse to be used.

82. **(C)** In a 208 volt circuit the voltage from any line to the grounded neutral is 120 volts, because that is the voltage the circuit is designed for.

83. **(B)** A rectifier changes a.c. voltage to d.c. voltage.

84. **(A)** To remove any possible friction, a conduit entering a knock-out box should be provided with a bushing on the outside and a locknut on the inside.

85. **(C)** A magnetic contactor is an on/off switch controlled via aquastat temperature.

86. **(D)** Electrical use is measured in kilowatt-hours.

87. **(D)** The heaviest copper wire can carry the most amperes safely. The lower the gauge, the higher the load it can carry.

88. **(A)** A flexible coupling is usually made of rubber. Since it is rubber, if it is placed between two joining shafts the only wear will be on the coupling, which is relatively inexpensive to replace compared to the shafts.

89. **(C)** Oil reduces friction between moving parts.

90. **(C)** Periodic inspections are used as preventive maintenance.

91. **(D)** A babbit does not swing, it rolls.

92. **(D)** A right-lay, regular-lay rope has wires laid left-handed into the strand which is then laid right-handed around a hemp rope center.

93. **(A)** Calcium hypochlorite and chlorine are commonly used to disinfect swimming pools. Ammonia is not.

94. **(D)** An air compressor is designed to hold a certain amount of air pressure. When that pressure is reached the pressure switch will shut off the motor.

95. **(A)** Unsteady water level in a steam boiler can be caused by water contaminated with grease, dirt, or other impurities, or by overfiring.

OIL BURNER OPERATION

The primary function of an oil burner is to break up the oil into fine particles and mix it with air so that proper combustion will result under suitable conditions of temperature. Combustion, or burning, is any kind of chemical combination in which heat is liberated. In domestic heating, combustion is caused by the combining of the elements of the fuel with oxygen of the air. When this combustion is completely carried out, the maximum heating value of the fuel is realized.

Oil Burner Classification

Oil burners operate upon one or another of two broad principles—namely, the vaporization or the atomization of the oil prior to burning. Burners may be classed, then, as either vaporizing, comprising the so called gravity-feed type, or atomizing, including those in which the oil is broken by mechanical or spray devices.

GRAVITY-FEED VAPORIZING TYPE

This is the simplest type of burner, very often consisting merely of one or two rough castings which are set inside the furnace, and its initial cost is low. Some device such as a "hot plate" is essential for volatilizing the oil so that a vapor will be produced. The air to support combustion is generally brought into the furnace by the natural draft produced by the chimney. Some rather ingenious methods are used to induce an intimate mingling of this air with the vaporized fuel, but in general, good combustion is not obtained by this method unless a highly volatile fuel is used.

ATOMIZING TYPE

The atomizing type of oil burners may be subdivided into those which break up the oil by purely mechanical means and those which atomize the oil by spray devices. In one mechanical type atomizing burner, oil is put under pressure and forced through a small opening to break it up into minute particles, and it enters the furnace as a vapor spray. Air is supplied by a blower or pump and so regulated as to bring about the proper combustion of the fuel.

In another type of mechanical atomizing burner the oil is broken up by being thrown from the periphery of a revolving disk or cup. The disk or cup speed is relatively high and is sometimes obtained by positive gear drive or by friction drive from an electric motor.

The spray type of atomizing burner consists of air and oil nozzles arranged so that air supplied by a motor driven compressor blows directly over the oil nozzle and creates a partial vacuum. The oil is drawn up from the supply reservoir by the vacuum thus formed and is atomized or broken into minute particles by the air pressure, in preparation for ignition. The rate of feed is governed by the air pressure and the size of the nozzle openings. This principle is not unlike that of the ordinary carburetor employed in the gasoline engine.

Combustion

Oil fuel used by domestic oil burners contains principally hydrogen and carbon, with much smaller quantities of oxygen, nitrogen, and sulphur. Of these elements, the carbon, hydrogen, and sulphur are the ones that burn or combine with oxygen. The oil fuels that are employed for domestic heating are for the most part uniform in composition and contain roughly 84 per cent carbon and 13 per cent hydrogen; the oxygen, nitrogen, and sulphur taken together compose the other 3 per cent. A pound of fuel of this composition will require about 14½ pounds of air for perfect and complete combustion.

Accumulation of carbon in oil-burning furnaces may be due either to insufficient atomization of oil by the burners or to an insufficient (or inefficiently distributed) air supply. The accumulation of carbon may be prevented by careful overhauling of the burner to make sure that the tip is clean and not burned, that passages are clear and, that, if a mechanical burner, it is revolving at full speed. Also, oil should be heated to at least 150°F., but not over 200° at a pressure of at least 25 pounds per square inch.

Insufficient air will be shown by black smoke at the stack, and the remedy is to admit more air. Even with express air, carbon may form if the air is not supplied at the right point. Some air should be admitted around the burner, the rest through the checkerwork in the furnace floor. Air spaces clear across the furnace will produce cool corners at the front end. Openings starting in front of the burner and extending to the end of the furnace will result in carbon at the rear wall.

Ignition

Burners may be subclassified according to the manner in which the fuel is ignited. With the manually-controlled gravity burner, the hot plate is preheated by a wick which is saturated with oil and ignited by a torch. The plate must be heated to a temperature sufficient to vaporize the oil falling upon it. The heat of combustion is supposed to do this once the flame is started. The temperature of the building is maintained at a desired point by increasing or decreasing the intensity of the flame by means of a valve in the oil line; or the burner may be operated at a fixed intensity and then completely shut off as the condition may demand. Whenever the burner is off for a few minutes, the hot plate must be preheated again before the oil can again be vaporized and ignited.

In some automatically controlled vaporizing burners, a gas flame is used both for heating the hot plate and as a pilot light for igniting the fuel. The gas flame burns continuously and keeps the hot plate at such a temperature as to cause the oil to vaporize when it is admitted to the apex of the plate and trickles down over the corrugations. At the same time, the pilot flame licks through holes drilled in the hot plate and ignites the mixture of vaporized oil and air. The automatic device in this case merely shuts off or opens a valve in the oil line to the burner.

With the atomizing type of burner, it is necessary to introduce a flame or electric arc within a region which is filled with an intimate mixture of oil and air in such proportions as to make it comparatively easy to ignite. Ignition methods used may be roughly classified as gas, electric, electric-gas, or electric-oil. With a gas pilot, ordinary illuminating gas is used to provide a continuous source of heat and is so placed as most effectively to bring the mixture of oil and air to such a temperature as to cause combustion. The pilot flame is sometimes expanded at the time the burner "comes on." By this means the danger of extinguishing the pilot light is somewhat lessened, and ignition is presumably hastened.

In case of electric ignition, a spark is introduced into the region of the charge. Electric-spark machines are either continuous or intermittent. In the continuous-spark type the spark continues during the entire time the burner is in operation.

In the intermittent type the spark is active only during the time necessary to ignite the charge, and then ceases. Various advantages are claimed for each type by the designers.

In the electric-gas type, a gas pilot is turned on, the gas being ignited by a spark. The pilot light then ignites the charge. Still another device is the electric-oil ignition in which an independent atomized mixture is ignited by an electric arc and is utilized as a source of heat energy to ignite the charge of the burner proper.

Automatic Devices for Control of Oil Burner

The oil heats extremely rapidly and if not controlled in some manner will build up temperatures and pressures in the heating system which may prove dangerous. If the drafts of a coal furnace are inadvertently left open the worst that can happen is that the coal in the furnace will burn up. It is true that temporary overheating or increase in pressures might occur, but in all probability no serious effects would be produced. With the oil burner, however, overheating would go on as long as the oil supply lasted.

In automatic oil-burner installations there are boiler controls. The boiler controls are termed hydrostats in hot-water systems and pressurestats in steam systems. (Steam in this case is used in the general sense to include vapor, vacuum, and low-pressure steam plants.) These control conditions at the boiler. By use of the hydrostat the temperature of the water in the boiler is kept within certain limits, and in the case of the pressurestat the steam pressure is kept within certain limits regardless of the temperature conditions in the rooms.

These boiler controls make for safety by limiting the boiler pressures and temperatures prevailing.

Emergency or Safety Controls

In addition to the controls which regulate heat, it is essential that precaution be taken to cut off the burner in the event that ignition fails to take place. In such burners as permit, a drip bucket or sump is provided to catch the unburned fuel which flows to it when ignition fails. This device trips when a certain quantity has been delivered to it and either cuts off the oil supply or breaks the power circuit, in either case rendering the burner inoperative. The machine must then be reset by hand before operation can be resumed. One of the chief objections to this control is the clogging of the line which delivers the unburned oil to the drip bucket or sump, owing to the accumulation of soot, scale, etc. Liberal passages offset this tendency to a great extent.

Another emergency control is designed on the assumption that so long as the pilot light burns the charge will be ignited; and, accordingly, a thermostatic member which is exposed to the heat of the pilot light breaks the power circuit when the pilot light is extinguished.

When the general design of the burner is such as to make the catching of unburned oil and its subsequent delivery to a sump or drip bucket impracticable, the "stack control" is utilized. A thermostatic member is placed in the stack and if, after a predetermined period, it does not become heated, indicating that the burner has failed to function, the thermostatic member breaks the power circuit and stops the motor and supply of oil.

Adjustment of Burner

After a burner has been installed in a boiler, it must be properly adjusted for efficient service. Assuming that the burner has been properly set and such details as impingement of burning gases directly against water-cooled surfaces have been guarded against, the next step is to establish the fuel and air rates.

With the gravity type of burner, using natural-draft air supply and manual fuel control, the adjustments are simple but as a rule not very satisfactory. Adjustment is made by hand as the heating demand changes. When the room temperature is high enough, the burner is cut down or entirely stopped, depending on weather conditions. When the room temperature is too low the opposite procedure is followed. These adjustments are made by altering the fuel valve setting. The air admitted to the burner is controlled by the stack damper, also manually operated. Thus with this type of burner no fixed setting of the fuel valve or air damper can be made; these settings are continually being altered as the heating demand is changed. Often with this type of burner, the air supplied is much in excess of that actually required and inefficient operation is the result.

The burner is adjusted by regulating the quantities of oil and air admitted. The rate of oil consumption depends, of course, on the heating load, that is, size and character of the building, temperature to be maintained, etc. The adjustment of the air admission depends upon the quantity of fuel to be burned.

The regulation of the air supply can best be made with the aid of an apparatus for analyzing the products of combustion, although the appearance of the flame is also an indication of the mixture of air and fuel.

Very often, in the adjuster's zeal to cut down the loss of heat (up the stack), he or she will almost entirely close the stack damper, resulting in a leaking of burned gases into the rooms of the building. This should be guarded against. Very frequently odor from an oil burner can be traced to this leakage of gases into the rooms of the building when the damper has been closed. One simple method of determining whether or not this leakage is occurring is to place a candle flame or flame of a match near the fire door which has been slightly opened. The flame should be drawn into the furnace; if it is not, there may be pressure in the furnace caused by a blocked chimney passage.

Efficiency

With fuels ordinarily used in oil burners, the maximum amount of carbon dioxide passing up the stack is about 15%. More air than that theoretically required is generally supplied, and the carbon dioxide content may fall as low as 10 or 12%. This may be done to avoid soot deposits and without greatly impairing the combustion. An oil burner which, with a reasonable excess of air, is not capable of burning oil fuels without smoke, cannot be satisfactory.

"Overall efficiency" is a term applied to a complete installation, including the heater itself, which indicates the percentage of the heating value of the oil that is utilized for warming the building. The overall efficiency is the ratio between the heat energy of the fuel which is used in heating the water or air (not air passing up the stack), as the case may be, to the total amount of heat contained in the fuel. For example, suppose that for each gallon of an oil containing 140,000 heat units, 70,000 heat units, are actually made available for heating; then the overall efficiency would be 70,000 divided by 140,000 or 50%. No other "efficiency" is significant. It is true that a high so-called burner efficiency is imperative, but this does not insure high overall efficiency.

Combustion

COMBUSTION OF FUEL OIL

Combustion of fuel oil as applied to boilers and furnaces may be defined as the process wherein the combustible elements in the fuel oil combine in chemical union with the oxygen of the air to produce other substances (gases of combustion) accompanied by the formation of a flame and the liberation of heat. Before combustion can take place, the combustible elements in the fuel oil must be heated to their ignition temperatures, and they must have access to a supply of oxygen (contained in air).

In order for complete and efficient combustion to take place, the fuel oil must be broken up into small particles (atomized) of uniform size and projected at a constant rate together with the correct amount of air properly directed into the combustion zone.

Fuel oil consists of a great many different hydrocarbon compounds, i.e., substances containing various combinations of hydrogen and carbon. The average fuel oil will be found to consist of these elements:

Carbon	84% by weight
Hydrogen	12.7% by weight
Oxygen	1.2% by weight
Sulphur	.2% by weight
Nitrogen	1.9% by weight

Carbon, hydrogen, and sulphur are the combustible elements in fuel oil. The oxygen in the fuel oil is a desirable element because it is used in the combustion process. Sulphur, even though it is combustible and is practically impossible to eliminate completely from fuel oil (or from other fuels such as gas or coal) is not considered a desirable element as its combustion produces gases that form sulphurous and sulphuric acids when mixed with the water or water vapor that is usually found in air and is always produced when hydrogen is burned. The nitrogen is not a desirable element as it plays no part in combustion other than to carry away valuable heat.

AIR

Air consists almost completely of a mixture of two gases, oxygen and nitrogen. These gases are not in chemical combination with each other; they are both in a free state although they are mixed together. The percentage of oxygen and nitrogen in air is as follows:

	By volume	*By weight*
Oxygen	20.91%	32.15%
Nitrogen	79.09%	76.85%

STACK GAS ANALYSIS

The ususal method of analyzing stack gases is by means of an "Orsat" instrument. This instrument basically consists of a "burette" or graduated cylinder into which a measured quantity of the gas is drawn from the stack. The entire quantity of the gases taken into the instrument is then passed into contact with different chemical solutions which completely absorb the CO_2 gas, the O_2 gas, and the CO gas alternately as the stack gas is passed from one solution to the other. Most generally the average analysis is confined to the CO_2 gas, and, in this case, the stack gases are passed into the bottle containing the caustic potash solution. This solution completely absorbs the CO_2 gas. The rest is brought back into the measuring burette to determine the amount of CO_2 gas removed.

EXCESS AIR

More air than is required for practical operation of the burner is, of course, wasteful as it carries away heat up the chimney that might otherwise be absorbed by the boiler or furnace.

The amount of CO_2 in the stack gases that represents good practice in burning oil will vary according to the size of the fire, the boiler or furnace, the quality of the oil, draft conditions, etc. Generally speaking, it is easier to maintain a higher CO_2 with a large fire than it is with a small fire. For example: it is comparatively easy to obtain a CO_2 reading of 13% to 14% on large industrial jobs whereas on some of the small fires from 1.00 gallons to 1.35 gallons, 9% of CO_2 or better would be considered good practice. On fires from 1.5 gallons to 6 gallons, 10% to $11\frac{1}{2}$% CO_2 would be good practice.

General Information

BTU OR BRITISH THERMAL UNIT

The British Thermal Unit, commonly designated BTU, is the unit of heat used in this and practically all other English speaking countries. It may be defined as that amount of heat which is necessary to raise the temperature of one pound of water one degree Fahrenheit. The following are examples:

How much heat is required to raise the temperature of 50 pounds of water from 40°F. to 200°F.? Ans. $50 \times (200 - 40) = 8000$ BTU.

1 gallon No. 3 fuel oil contains approximately 142,000 BTU.

1 gallon water weighs approximately 8.33 lbs. and requires 8.33 BTU to raise its temperature one degree F.

1 pound of air requires .24 BTU to raise its temperature one degree F.

RADIATORS

In the common steam or hot water heating system the cast iron radiator is most generally used. The rate at which the radiator gives off its heat to the room depends on the temperature of the steam or hot water inside the radiator together with the temperature of the room or air surrounding the radiator as well as the speed with which the air circulates around the radiator.

In figuring the amount of radiation required to heat a given space, heating engineers have adopted a standard representing the amount of heat one square foot of cast iron radiator surface will give off into a room in a given time under standard conditions. This standard is 240 BTU per square foot of radiator surface per hour for steam radiators and 150 BTU per square foot of radiator surface per hour for hot water radiators. These heat emission rates are based on the room temperature in each case being at 70°F., the temperature of the steam (for steam radiators) being at 215°F. or 1 pound gauge pressure, and the temperature of the water in the radiators (for hot water radiators) being at 170°F.

TYPES OF HEATING SYSTEMS

You should familiarize yourself with the various types of heating systems which you are likely to encounter.

Generally speaking, heating systems are classified as follows:

1. The one-pipe steam system is one in which only one pipe connects to each radiator. Both the steam supplied to the radiator and the condensate returning from the radiator to the boiler pass through the same pipe.

2. The two-pipe steam, vapor, or vacuum system is one in which two pipes connect to each radiator, one for supplying steam either under pressure or vacuum, as the case may be, to the radiator and the other pipe for returning the condensate from the radiator to the boiler.

3. The two-pipe gravity hot water system has two pipes connected to each radiator and a supply and return main connected to the boiler, either closed type wherein a pressure regulating water valve, relief valve, and pressure tank are used, or open type wherein an expansion tank placed at a point above the highest radiator is used. In this system the water circulates from the boiler to the radiators and back to the boiler by "gravity," the natural circulation that takes place when water is heated such as it would be in the boiler.

4. The two-pipe forced circulation hot water system has two pipes connected to each radiator and a supply and return main connected to the boiler, usually closed pipe wherein the heated water in the boiler is circulated to the radiators and back to the boiler by means of a circulating water pump.

5. The one-pipe forced circulation hot water system has two pipes connected to each radiator from a circulating main forming a loop from the outlet of boiler to the return of same. The inlet sides of the radiators are connected to the main with special one-pipe circulating fittings. In operation, a circulating water pump forces the hot water to circulate around the main and the special one-pipe circulating fittings cause a certain amount of the hot water to pass through each radiator. One-pipe forced circulation hot water systems are used both at the standard hot water temperature of 170°F and as high as 220°F. The former case is called the standard temperature one-pipe system and the latter case is called the high temperature one-pipe system.

6. The gravity warm air system is one in which air is heated in a furnace and passed through ducts to the rooms. The circulation of the air takes place by "gravity," i.e., the heated air rises by its own momentum into the ducts, and the cold air actually

falls into the cold air returns to the furnace. Sometimes this system is used with only one large opening into one room for the warm air to pass through. In a case of this kind, the system is called a "pipeless furnace system."

7. A forced circulation warm air system may be either a converted gravity system or one of the modern wintertime air conditioning systems wherein air is heated in a furnace and forced through ducts to the rooms and then returned to the furnace by means of a fan or blower.

PIPING LOSSES

The various pipes and fittings communicating between the boiler and the different radiators in a steam or hot water system naturally will dissipate a certain amount of heat into the basement and space between the outside walls where they usually are located. This heat is commonly called "piping losses" and the boiler must have sufficient capacity to provide for this "pipe loss," over and above the actual amount of heat required to satisfy the radiators under the variable conditions of room temperatures, etc., to which they may be subjected.

It would be very difficult to attempt to figure out the actual surface of the various pipes and fittings in a heating system and then try to calculate the actual amount of heat that would be dissipated from them. In lieu of this it has been generally recognized by experienced heating engineers that the piping losses on the average heating system under extreme conditions will average 20% of the standard radiation load when the pipes and fittings are well insulated and 30% of the standard radiation load when the pipes and fittings are not insulated. For example:

Assume we have a job with an actual radiator load of 400 square feet. If the pipes are insulated we would figure the piping losses to be $\frac{400 \times 20}{100}$ = 80 square feet of radiation. If the pipes are not insulated the piping loss would be $\frac{400 \times 30}{100}$ = 120 square feet of radiation.

DRAFT, CHIMNEYS, ETC.

A considerable amount of carbon dioxide is formed when combustion takes place. Carbon dioxide and excess quantities of nitrogen will smother and extinguish a fire if permitted to remain in contact with it. For this reason it is necessary to have a chimney of proper dimensions and construction connected to the boiler in which oil or other fuel is being burned to carry away the combustion gases from the zone of combustion as fast as they are being formed. The larger the oil fire, the more gases of combustion we produce and consequently the larger the chimney capacity must be. Other factors such as the amount of excess air supplied to the burner and the stack temperature also affect the volume of combustion gases that must be disposed of.

DRAFT INTENSITY

The term "draft intensity" refers to the force or pull of the draft, as measured by means of a draft gauge. It should not be confused with the actual capacity a chimney might have for removing a certain volume of combustion gases in a given time. If we have two chimneys, both 30 feet high, one having a cross-sectional area of 10 square inches, and the other having a cross-sectional area of 80 square inches, the temperature inside and outside of both chimneys being the same, we would obtain the same draft intensity from both chimneys; however, the one having a cross-sectional area of only 10 square inches would have so little volumetric capacity that it would not be practical to use on any boiler either coal or oil fired. The other chimney would have a much greater volumetric capacity and would be very satisfactory on many of the oil burner installations used in house heating.

CHIMNEY CAPACITY

The capacity a chimney has for removing combustion gases depends on its draft intensity, cross-sectional area, and the friction or resistance it may present to the flow of gases, through it. The draft intensity varies according to the height of the chimney, the temperature of the gases inside the chimney, and the temperatures of the outside air as well as the barometric condition of the air.

DRAFT LOSS IN BOILERS AND FURNACES

If a draft gauge tube is inserted in the smoke pipe of a boiler and a reading taken while the burner is running, we would find that the draft intensity at this point would be greater than it would be if a similar reading were taken in the fire box of the boiler. This difference in draft instensity between the two points of the boiler represents the "draft loss" or draft intensity drop through the boiler. By measuring the draft loss on different makes and types of boilers and furnaces under different firing rates, we will find that the draft loss varies considerably; in some cases it may be as low as .01 inch of water column, in other cases it may be as great as .20 inches of water column. This difference in draft loss in one boiler compared to another is due to the differences in the length of the flue travel, the area of the flue passages, and the friction or resistance the flue passes offer to the flow of the hot combustion gases; consequently a chimney that might be of proper height and area for one boiler might not be satisfactory for another boiler even though both boilers had the same rating and were being fired at the same combustion rate.

For example, given two boilers each of which is being fired at two gallons of oil per hour: In both cases we will require a minimum of .01 inch draft in the firebox to keep the combustion gases moving out. In the first boiler we have a draft loss of .07 inches of water. The chimney in each case will have to handle the same volume of combustion gases per hour. However, the chimney in the second boiler, in order to overcome its own friction and the draft loss through the boiler will have to provide more draft intensity, will have to be higher than the chimney on the first boiler, and preferably have more cross-sectional area.

BOILER OPERATION

Care of Steel Boilers When in Service

GETTING READY TO START

Open System – An open-type hot water heating system is provided with an expansion tank located at the highest point of system. An overflow pipe is connected to the tank to prevent excess pressure. An altitude gauge indicates height of water in expansion tank.

1. When filling boiler, notice movement of altitude gauge hand and ascertain that black and red hands are together just before water overflows from expansion tank.

2. Admit sufficient water to make sure that overflow pipe is clear.

3. *Do not run overflow outside.*

Closed System – A closed-type hot water heating system is provided with a reducing valve and a relief valve to prevent excess pressure and also with an altitude gauge or a pressure gauge to indicate amount of water in system.

1. Black and red hands of altitude gauge should be together when water stops flowing into system.

2. Relief valve should be tested by pulling hand lever, if there is one, to determine that it works properly and that disc is not corroded to seat.

Steam Heating System – A steam heating system is provided with a safety valve to prevent excess pressure; a steam pressure gauge to indicate pressure within boiler; and a gauge glass and gauge cocks to show level of water in boiler.

1. Observe rise of water level in gauge glass and open gauge glass drain cock and gauge cocks as boiler fills with water.

2. Test the accuracy of gauge glass by using try or pet cocks on water column.

3. If water does not flow out freely, obstructed cock should be cleaned immediately.

4. It is of great importance that water level indicators operate properly, for low water may ruin boiler or cause a boiler explosion.

5. Valves at top and bottom of water gauge glass should always be open.

6. Safety valve should be tested by pulling hand lever to be certain that it works properly and that disc of valve is not corroded to seat. (Always pull when there is at least 70% pressure so as not to damage the valve.)

7. Make sure that steam gauge cock is always open. (Have two gauges because the code requires that the boiler be shut down when the gauge is broken.)

STARTING THE BOILER

1. Make certain that valves in piping to heating system are open before starting fire.

2. Dampers must be opened and firebox thoroughly vented.

3. Breeching must fit tightly into chimney and should not extend into stack beyond thickness of wall.

4. Follow instructions of manufacturer of burner. (These should be posted in boiler room.) Do not turn on fuel supply at any time until firebox has been thoroughly ventilated or until sure a lighted torch or ignition system will ignite fuel immediately at low fire.

5. Increase temperature gradually—watch water level carefully. If it appears necessary to admit more water, do so, but determine reason why more water is needed (loss of water from system indicates there is a leak). Do not confine investigation to boiler but examine entire system.

6. If at any time boiler is shut down, dampers should be kept open after fuel is shut off to free firebox of inflammable vapors which otherwise may accumulate. (Vent the fire box.)

7. Oil and gas fuel are automatically controlled, but do not leave boiler room after starting fire until it has been determined that burner and automatic regulators are in working order. Do not depend entirely upon automatic controls but make a practice of visiting boiler room periodically to see that everything is working properly.

ROUTINE OPERATION

1. Do not carry more steam pressure than is absolutely required to heat building.

2. Do not try to operate multiple boiler heating system with one boiler when weather is cold and two boilers are required.

3. If only one boiler is needed during part of day, do not close valves of idle boiler but allow it to remain warm and connected to system so that it can be fired up at any time—operation of system is simplified in that way.

4. If steam and return valves have been closed for any reason during the time one boiler or battery was out of service, those valves should not be opened again until pressure of entire system is equalized, preferably by reducing pressure to zero on boiler that is in service.

5. If it is impossible to reduce pressure, idle boiler should be fired up and pressure raised to an amount exactly equal to that of boiler in service before valves are opened.

6. Return valves should be opened first and steam valve immediately thereafter. (Open slowly.)

7. Operation of boiler with respect to both pressure and water level should be observed carefully for some time after boilers are connected together.

8. Water level in gauge glass of steam boiler should not vary greatly.

9. If water disappears from the gauge glass as temperature is increased each morning and again appears at its usual level when fire is low, a thorough investigation should be made.

10. Hot water must not be drawn from heating boiler for any purpose whatsoever; to do so may result in damage to boiler.

11. Water returning from system is ample for boiler if system is tight. Need of additional water to greater extent than one inch in gauge glass of steam system or 1 foot, according to altitude gauge of water system, per month is indication that water is being lost from system.

12. Excess amounts of make-up water results in formation of scale within boiler.

13. Water, when needed, should be added slowly and at time when load is lightest.

14. Determine from experience the pressure or temperature of system that affords best results with changing weather conditions and maintain proper pressure or temperature as nearly constant as possible with uniform fire covering entire grate.

LOW WATER

1. If at any time water is not visible in gauge glass or its height does not register on altitude gauge, put out the fire at once. Allow boiler to cool until crown of firebox is comfortable to touch before adding water. Inspect if you have any doubts.

2. If no burns are found after increasing amount of water in boiler to normal level, determine cause of low water condition and correct difficulty before starting fire.

SAFETY APPLIANCES

1. Gauge cocks, gauge glass, and safety valve of steam system should be operated by hand each day.

2. Water relief valve of closed hot water system must be piped to discharge in safe place so that it may be operated by hand at least once each month. No valve can be connected after the valve discharge or between the boiler relief valve. The discharge line diameter must not be reduced and must not be in an area where the temperature will freeze the discharge water. It must discharge in a safe place.

3. Overflow from expansion tank of open hot water system must discharge in safe place, and sufficient water should be added to system each week to ascertain that overflow pipe is clear and that altitude gauge registers correctly.

4. Safety valve of steam heating boiler should operate freely before steam gauge registers more than 15 pounds. If it does not, pressure should be reduced to zero, and boiler should be cooled as promptly as possible so that safety valve or pressure gauge may be adjusted or repaired. No valve should be connected between the boiler and the safety valve or between the safety valve and discharge pipe. The discharge pipe

must be reduced. It must discharge to a safe place. It must be mounted without damage to its body by a tool.

BLOWING OFF

1. Under normal conditions a heating boiler does not need blowing off, emptying, or cleaning during the heating season if chemical is added.

2. If it becomes necessary to empty boiler for any reason, be sure that fire is out and that firebox is comfortable to the touch.

Care of Steel Boilers When Not in Service

CLEANING

1. Clean boiler thoroughly inside and outside.

2. Scrape tubes down to metal.

3. Brush down front and rear heads, inside of firebox and crown sheet.

4. Remove all soot, scale, rust, or other deposits with steel brush.

5. Clean out smokehood and breeching.

6. Clean outside of boiler where uncovered.

WASHING

1. Drain boiler.

2. Remove handhole and handhole covers and washout plugs.

3. Wash boiler out thoroughly with hose, using sufficient water pressure to remove all sediment and scale.

4. Place hose in openings to flush out water legs on all four sides.

5. Leave off all manhole and handhole covers and washout plugs so air may circulate through boiler.

6. Keep feed valve closed so no water can enter boiler.

DRYING

1. Dry boiler by placing small lighted single burner kerosene stove or single burner gas plate inside of firebox.

2. Let it burn until boiler is dry.

3. Do not dry boiler by building fire upon grate; there is danger of damaging boiler even though very light materials are used.

Oiling and Painting

1. Swab all tube surfaces with a rag soaked in mineral oil.

2. Apply coat of boiler paint or mineral oil to exposed outside surface of boiler.

Caution

1. If boiler remains empty when not in service, extreme caution must be taken to see that fire is not started.

2. Place a seal or a caution sign on fire door.

3. If hazard is too great replace manhole, handhole covers, and washout plugs.

4. Fill boiler with water until heat is required.

5. Then drain all water, refill, and place in service.

6. If boiler has been without water during idle period, replace manhole and handhole covers and washout plugs; then fill with water to correct level.

7. A steel boiler which remains filled with water and coated with soot when not in service deteriorates rapidly.

8. Keep boiler room dry to avoid rusting in summer.

9. Leave flue doors and fire doors wide open during the entire period while boiler is not in use; this will keep the flues dry.

Inspection

1. At the end of heating season clean and inspect boiler and accessories. Clean gauge glass or replace. Make sure the gauge connections are not plugged with dirt.

2. Place in good working condition for next heating season.

3. Repair parts are more readily obtained during summer season, and installation charges are frequently less than in fall.

4. Do not neglect boiler—clean as directed above.

5. More damage can occur in one month when boiler is idle than in entire heating season if care is not taken to properly prepare boiler for idle period.

Automatically Fired Boilers

STARTING NEW BOILER

Before starting the burner make certain that there is water in the boiler. Water level should be carried approximately at the middle of water gauge glass for a steam boiler. The required amount of water in a hot water heating system may be determined from indication of the hand on altitude of the boiler. Water will appear at the air valves of every radiator when the system is full of water.

A feedwater line with valve will be connected into the return main near the boiler for the purpose of adding water. This valve must be kept closed. The boiler blowoff valve and any drain valves to the heating system must also be closed.

When provided, the valves in supply and return mains to the heating system must be kept wide open when the heating plant is operated. If these are closed for summertime hot water service, both valves must be closed tight.

WATER GAUGE

The valves at top and bottom of the water gauge glass provided with steam boilers must be kept open so that the true boiler water level will be shown in the gauge glass.

The try cocks or gauge cocks at the side of the water glass are for the purpose of checking the indication of the water gauge. Open these occasionally when there is pressure on the boiler.

With the drain cock at bottom of gauge glass open and with steam pressure on the boiler, the valves should be occasionally closed and opened alternately to blow them clean of any sediment. Do this two or three times each heating season. Keep the stuffing box on the valves tightened to prevent air leakage.

Put a spoonful of muriatic acid (hydrochloric) in a cup of water. With pressure on the boiler, close both water gauge valves and open drain cock at bottom of glass, allowing water to flow out. Open top valve allowing steam to flow through glass and out of drain cock; allow the steam to flow until glass is thoroughly heated. Then close the top valve and place cup of solution so that the drain cock is submerged causing the solution to be drawn into the water glass. By keeping the drain cock in the solution and alternately opening and closing the top gauge valve the glass will be thoroughly cleaned.

Be sure when the cleaning is completed that both top and bottom gauge valves are again opened. Safety valve should be tested once a month by pulling the lever when the boiler has 75% pressure or at the time when the pressure throw shuts off.

Automatically fired boilers should be provided with water level controls and these must be tested at least once a week as follows: With the thermostat set up so the burner will operate and with the water level normal, open the blowoff valve to let out water. The low water cut-off control should stop the burner when the water level is within $\frac{1}{4}$ inch from the bottom of the glass.

Some low water devices have a valve that is spring loaded to shut off the water drained from the device, or else they have a gate valve or a ball valve with the opening the diameter of the drain. Keeping running water on it until it is free of rust and mud.

Close the blow-off valve and open the feedwater valve. When the water level is raised back to $\frac{3}{4}$ inches in the glass, the cut-off control should again allow the burner to operate. Where an automatic water feeder is used it should stop feeding water to the boiler when the level is 1 inch above the bottom of gauge glass. The drain valve should be opened at regular intervals, and always directly after cleaning the boiler, to clear the chamber of any sediment.

Steam heating boilers are equipped with a pressure limit control switch and hot water boilers with a temperature control switch to govern the operating range of pressure or temperature. The pressure or temperature at the boiler should be no higher than is required to heat the building in coldest weather.

DRAFT ADJUSTER

The draft adjuster is designed to maintain a uniform draft on the boiler. Regulate the damper plate to swing freely. For strong chimney drafts the damper should be set to swing nearly wide open and for low drafts it should be kept practically closed. Leakage of furnace gases into the boiler room is usually an indication of low draft.

CHIMNEY

The smokepipe connecting the boiler with chimney must have tight fitting joints. All cracks should be sealed with boiler putty or cement. Separately fired water heaters, incinerators, or fireplaces must not be connected to the same chimney flue with the heating boiler.

BOILER OPERATION AND MAINTENANCE QUIZZER

1. Of the following, the one which is *not* the name of a heat control system for large buildings or a group of buildings is

   (A) Warren-Webster (C) Dunham
   (B) Johnson (D) Allis-Chalmers

2. The number of BTU's per gallon in No. 6 oil at 60°F is usually

   (A) the same as for No. 2 oil
   (B) double that of No. 2 oil
   (C) about 25% greater than for No. 2 oil
   (D) about 10% greater than for No. 2 oil

3. Analysis of the flue gases shows that as the percentage of excess air

   (A) increases, the percentage of CO_2 increases
   (B) increases, the percentage of oxygen decreases
   (C) increases, the percentage of CO_2 decreases
   (D) decreases, the percentage of oxygen decreases

4. A correct statement concerning a subatmospheric steam heating system is

   (A) in mild weather, the steam is under a higher vacuum than in cold weather
   (B) in cold weather, the steam is placed under a higher vacuum to increase the circulation rate
   (C) the steam pressure is below atmospheric pressure only during severe weather
   (D) a controllable vacuum is maintained only on the return side of the system

5. The device which is used in a vacuum or subatmospheric heating system to allow the passage of condensate, but not of steam, from a radiator is best described as a (an)

   (A) air valve
   (B) P trap
   (C) thermostatic trap
   (D) modulating valve

6. A vacuum steam heating system has the following characteristic:

   (A) a vacuum is carried on the steam side at all times
   (B) the boiler operates at a pressure lower than atmospheric
   (C) a vacuum is carried on the return side almost constantly
   (D) only one pipe to each radiator

7. The function of a zone control system of heating is to

   (A) prevent overheating of the various buildings of a housing project
   (B) eliminate heating complaints by tenants
   (C) assign each boiler to heat one or two buildings of a housing project
   (D) limit hazards of explosion or fire to a small area

8. The main purpose of a loop or pigtail in the line leading to a steam pressure gauge is to

   (A) keep the gauge temperature at a moderate level
   (B) reduce steam pressure in the gauge
   (C) prevent steam changing to water in the gauge
   (D) collect scale or sediment which might block steam flow to the gauge

9. Steam traps in heating systems are devices which serve to

   (A) bypass steam flow where radiators are filled with steam
   (B) shut down rate of steam flow where radiators are filled with steam
   (C) separate air and condensate from steam in steam heating systems
   (D) prevent the development of high steam pressures by releasing excess steam

10. The temperature of oil from the storage tank should not exceed 130°F on the suction side of the transfer pump. The most important reason for this operating rule is

(A) the pump will not operate effectively if its temperature is above 130°F

(B) vapor lock in the pump may occur if the oil temperature is too high

(C) the oil may ignite before reaching the burner

(D) a vacuum condition may result, causing excessive strain on the pump

11. The barometric damper in the breeching operates so that it

(A) opens wider when draft exceeds the desired maximum

(B) closes when draft exceeds the desired maximum

(C) causes boiler room air to enter the stack only when natural draft under the fire is insufficient

(D) remains in fixed position unless manually changed

12. Information which is *not* necessary on a boiler room log sheet is

(A) number of boilers in operation

(B) amount of oil on hand

(C) stack temperature reading

(D) temperature in boiler room

13. A mixing valve in a domestic hot water system blends cold water with

(A) hot boiler water

(B) hot water from a coil submerged in the boiler water

(C) steam

(D) condensate

14. A scale pocket is most often found on

(A) the bottom of a steam riser

(B) a hot air exhaust grille

(C) a hot water radiator

(D) the side of a steam radiator

15. The purpose of an air valve in a heating system is to

(A) prevent pressure from building up in a room due to the heated air

(B) relieve the air from steam radiators

(C) allow excessive steam pressure in the boiler to escape to the atmosphere

(D) control the temperature in the room

16. In HRT boilers, the lowest safe water level is

(A) at least 6 inches above the top row of tubes

(B) at least one inch above the top row of tubes

(C) at the level of the top row of tubes

(D) one-third the height of the rows of tubes

17. Boilers used in the heating plants of the Housing Authority housing projects are classified as low pressure boilers. This means that they are designed to operate at a steam pressure no higher than

(A) 10 pounds per square inch

(B) 15 pounds per square inch

(C) 25 pounds per square inch

(D) 100 pounds per square inch

Questions 18 to 21 inclusive are based on the following sketch of a boiler.

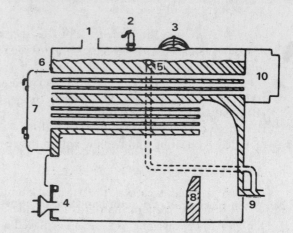

18. The boiler shown in this sketch is a

(A) one pass fire tube boiler

(B) two pass fire tube boiler

(C) one pass water tube boiler

(D) two pass water tube boiler

19. The part of the boiler numbered 3 is a (an)

(A) exit for steam

(B) safety valve

(C) exit for flue gases

(D) manhole

20. The fusible plug is most likely to be located at part numbered

(A) 10   (C) 2
(B) 5   (D) 6

21. When the boiler is emptied of water, the water leaves the boiler at part numbered

(A) 5   (C) 1
(B) 9   (D) 4

22. The feedwater line to a boiler always has a check valve before the boiler. The purpose of this valve is to

(A) control the rate of flow of water into the boiler
(B) close when feedwater temperature is too high
(C) close when feedwater temperature is too low
(D) prevent backflow from the boiler into the feedwater line

23. A primary cause of spalling of the refractory lining in the furnace of a steam boiler is

(A) a change in fuel size and quality
(B) continuous surface blowdown
(C) slag accumulations on furnace walls
(D) uneven heating and cooling within the refractory brick

24. When placing a cover on a handhole of a low pressure boiler

(A) no gasket should be used
(B) the minimum thickness of gasket to be used is 1/4″
(C) the thinnest gasket practical should be used
(D) shellac, grease, or oil should be used

25. The ratio of the amount of fuel oil used for supplying heat to the amount used for providing hot water in a large project is, on the average, most nearly

(A) 1 to 1   (C) 2 to 1
(B) 1.5 to 1   (D) 3 to 1

26. In the steam heating system used in large projects, the differential pump

(A) controls the amount of steam pumped into the supply lines in accordance with varying heat requirements
(B) creates the higher pressure needed in the return piping to cause a positive circulation of steam
(C) exhausts the air and vapor from the return piping
(D) provides the vacuum pressure which prevents the radiator traps from releasing the condensate

27. The device which is used to prevent fuel oil from entering the combustion chamber of the oil burner before the oil has reached the proper temperature is the

(A) aquastat
(B) magnetic oil valve
(C) thermostatic coupling
(D) vaporstat

28. The purpose of the pressuretrol in the oil burner heating system is to

(A) keep the boiler steam pressure from exceeding a predetermined amount
(B) keep the fuel oil pressure from exceeding a predetermined amount
(C) prevent operation of the oil burner until the fuel oil pressure has reached the proper amount
(D) prevent operation of the oil burner when there is an inadequate supply of air

29. Generally, for each gallon of oil burned per hour the effective volume of the combustion chamber or firebox should be not less than

(A) 4½ cubic feet   (C) 1½ cubic feet
(B) 2 cubic feet   (D) 6 cubic feet

30. Generally, the air nozzle of a horizontal rotary cup oil burner terminates about ⅛ in. back of the cup edge. The most important reason for this arrangement is to

(A) reduce possible friction between the cup and the walls of the nozzle
(B) prevent misalignment of the cup
(C) avoid having the oil spray strike the air nozzle
(D) permit the igniting flame to come into closer contact with the atomized oil

31. The oil supplied to horizontal rotary cup burners is usually maintained at a pressure of approximately

    (A) 80 pounds to enable proper mixing of oil and air in the rotating cup
    (B) 100 pounds to insure proper atomization of the oil
    (C) 40 pounds to supply the rotating cup with a continuous oil supply
    (D) 150 pounds to keep the oil from cooling rapidly before reaching the burner

32. In the operation of a boiler heated by a horizontal-rotary cup oil burner, it is correct to say that the

    (A) greater part of the air required for the combustion of oil is secondary air
    (B) greater part of the air required for combustion of the oil is introduced by the blower of the burner
    (C) most important function of secondary air is to atomize the oil sprayed by the rotating cup
    (D) primary air is not usually controlled by a damper motor

33. The purpose of the warp switch in a relay of an oil burner is to

    (A) shut down the burner in case of ignition failure
    (B) energize the stackswitch when the oil has been ignited
    (C) control the amount of current flowing to the burner motor and ignition transformer
    (D) cut the motor in as soon as a call for heat is received from a thermostat

34. Duplicate strainers are often placed in the suction line between the oil tank and the oil pump. The main advantage of using duplicate strainers instead of a single strainer is

    (A) oil pressure to the burner is less likely to be reduced
    (B) it permits cleaning of one strainer without interrupting pump operation
    (C) less oil will be wasted
    (D) the strainers become self-cleaning, eliminating this maintenance job

35. In the electric-gas ignition system of a fully-automatic horizontal rotary cup oil burner, the oil is ignited by

    (A) both the electric spark and gas flame
    (B) the gas flame alone
    (C) the electric spark, with gas flame applied only in case of electric spark failure
    (D) continuous electric sparking

36. The pressure of oil in the oil supply piping to a rotary cup oil burner is about 40 pounds. This pressure is maintained mainly in order to

    (A) bring the oil into the atomizing cup
    (B) mix the oil together with the primary air
    (C) operate the magnetic oil valve
    (D) avoid having the oil spray strike the edge of the oil nozzle

37. Of the following, the most common cause of black smoke in oil-burning installations is

    (A) too much oil fed into a cold furnace in starting with consequent failure or partial failure of combustion
    (B) fuel oil adulterated with carbon substances
    (C) insufficient draft through the boiler due to faulty brick setting of boiler
    (D) excessive secondary air through dampers not properly controlled

38. In an oil fired plant, the emergency or remote control switch is usually located

    (A) at the entrance to the boiler room
    (B) next to the oil burner
    (C) at the panel board in the boiler room
    (D) at the electrical distribution panel in the basement

39. A safety device which is commonly used in oil burner operation to detect flame failure and shut down the burner is a (an)

    (A) thermostat   (C) aquastat
    (B) stackswitch   (D) pressuretrol

40. Of the following devices, the one that responds to low room temperature resulting in the starting up of an oil burner is

    (A) stackswitch   (C) thermostat
    (B) airstat   (D) pyrostat

41. Of the following, the most important step which a fireman should take in his daily routine when starting up morning operation of his boiler room is

    (A) give each boiler to be operated a short surface blow after the burners are in full operation
    (B) make sure that low suction is used on oil supply lines
    (C) make sure that breeching dampers are in closed position before starting up
    (D) take a CO_2 reading and record same in log book

42. When a radiator valve leaks around the stem, the trouble is most commonly due to a

    (A) defective supply line to the valve
    (B) defective line from the valve to the radiator
    (C) worn packing inside the packing nut
    (D) cracked or worn valve stem

43. Tube failures are occurring in a fire tube boiler with unusual frequency. Of the following, the *least* likely cause is

    (A) scale formation
    (B) high water level
    (C) soot accumulation
    (D) expansion and contraction strains

44. If in a vacuum heating system the water level in the tank of the vacuum pump rises and overflows the vent while the pump is in operation, it is most probable that the

    (A) float in the receiving tank is water logged
    (B) vacuum system has air leaks, affecting the build-up of vacuum
    (C) discharge valve lever is broken or defective
    (D) boiler is priming and throwing over an excessive amount of water

45. If scale forms on the seat of a float-operated boiler feed valve, the most likely result is

    (A) insufficient supply of water to the boiler
    (B) flooding of the boiler
    (C) shutting down of the oil burner by the low-water cutout
    (D) internal corrosion of the boiler shell

46. When it is found necessary to shut off one steam circuit in order to repair a leak, the *first* step of the following operations is to

    (A) open drain valve
    (B) close return valve
    (C) close the steam valve
    (D) close drain valve

47. Of the following statements concerning heating systems with vacuum traps and vacuum pumps, the one that is most correct is

    (A) a radiator steam valve which is partially open will cause "pounding"
    (B) a defective trap with the valve held open will cause "no heat" complaints
    (C) eccentric pipe fittings are usually used to form pockets to maintain a "wet condition" in a return line
    (D) radiator traps require inspection only when heat complaints are received

48. To check combustion efficiency of a hearing system, the best of the following combinations of instruments to use is

    (A) stack thermometer, Orsat apparatus, and draft gauge
    (B) petrometer, stack thermometer, and Orsat apparatus
    (C) vaporstat, Orsat apparatus, and potromotor
    (D) vaporstat, stack thermometer, and draft gauge

49 You observe that the water line in the water column of a boiler is unsteady. Of the following, the most likely cause of this condition is

    (A) too low a rate of fuel combustion
    (B) water level in boiler is much higher than that specified for normal operation
    (C) the boiler is operating below rated output
    (D) grease and dirt in the boiler

50. Of the following, the most common cause of poor steam circulation is

    (A) improper pitch of pipes connecting steam and return risers to radiators
    (B) poor quality or improper grade of fuel oil
    (C) improperly insulated steam lines
    (D) limit controls of heating system improperly adjusted or defective

51. Of the following, the one that is *not* usually a cause of low CO_2 in an oil burning boiler is

(A) leakage through the boiler setting
(B) insufficient quality of oil being burned
(C) improper fire due to a fouled nozzle or cup
(D) excessive rate of output

52. Of the following values of draft in the furnace, the one which is best for a fully automatic rotary cup oil burner using No. 6 oil is

(A) −4.0 inches of water
(B) −0.4 inches of mercury
(C) −0.04 inches of water
(D) +0.04 inches of mercury

53. The part of a fully automatic oil burning heating system which usually requires cleaning *most* frequently is

(A) stack switch helix
(B) oil strainer
(C) magnetic oil valve
(D) relay contacts

54. If the gauge glass breaks and the water level in the boiler is to be checked, the first thing to do is to

(A) test for water with the bottom try cock
(B) test for water with the middle try cock
(C) test for water with the top try cock
(D) insert a measuring stick through the manhole

55. General operating procedure is to test the low water cutout each watch. The proper test is to

(A) blow down the boiler
(B) open the drain valve of the water column
(C) shut off the feedwater line
(D) open all try cocks

56. The best way of testing the stackswitch to see if it operates in the event of flame failure is to

(A) cut off the oil supply of the operating burner
(B) cut off current to the burner motor and transformer
(C) adjust the pressure range of the pressure-stats
(D) cut off the air supply to the burner

57. When a radiator return trap is checked and taken apart, the diaphragm and valve seat are found to be dirty. The most common method of cleaning these parts is to wash them with

(A) weak lye solution
(B) machine oil
(C) very hot water
(D) kerosene

58. A boiler smokes through the fire doors. The one of the following that is *not* a cause of this condition is

(A) excess air through the fire box
(B) air leaks into boiler or breeching
(C) defective draft in chimney
(D) primary and secondary air dampers shut

59. When a building superintendent tells you that the transformer of one of the oil burners is defective, he is referring to the device which

(A) atomizes the liquid oil prior to ignition
(B) changes low pressure steam to high pressure steam
(C) increases the voltage for oil ignition
(D) regulates oil temperature prior to atomization

60. Of the following, the one which is most essential to efficient operation of a large oil burner is that the

(A) exact proportion of air be admitted which will theoretically permit complete combustion of the fuel oil
(B) flash point of the fuel oil used must not exceed 160°F
(C) fuel oil be finely atomized
(D) fuel oil be pre-heated to reduce its viscosity

61. A site building has a coal-fired steam boiler as the heating plant. In checking the boiler while it is in use, proper examination of the water gauge fails to reveal the presence of any water. Of the following, it would be best that

(A) a small amount of water be let into the boiler immediately, increasing the amount of water gradually until the proper level is reached
(B) the fire be put out immediately by covering with sand
(C) the fire be put out immediately by spraying with warm water
(D) the required amount of water be put into the boiler immediately

62. If a small leak occurs in the boiler of a heating plant

   (A) no repairs should be authorized unless the leak becomes large
   (B) the boiler may continue to be used, deferring repairs until the boiler is next removed from service
   (C) the boiler should be taken out of service immediately but other emergency action is not necessary
   (D) the fire must be killed immediately on an emergency basis

63. It is generally agreed that soot accumulations in boiler tubes are undesirable because of the poor heat conduction properties of soot. A frequently used rule-of-thumb comparison of the insulating properties of soot and asbestos indicates that 1/8 inch of soot is approximately equal to

   (A) 1/16 inch of asbestos
   (B) 1/8 inch of asbestos
   (C) 1/4 inch of asbestos
   (D) 1/2 inch of asbestos

64. Preheating of No. 6 oil is necessary because

   (A) it is impossible to ignite the oil unless it is preheated
   (B) the viscosity of the oil must be lowered for proper atomization
   (C) No. 6 oil will not pass through the fuel pump freely unless heated to at least 140°F
   (D) No. 6 oil is solid at room temperatures

65. Suppose that the vent pipe of an oil storage tank is completely clogged, preventing passage of air into the tank. Assuming that the tank is full and is located below the level of the pump, this stoppage will usually result in

   (A) failure of the oil pump to draw oil from the tank
   (B) reduction in the amount of vacuum required to draw oil from the tank
   (C) excessive preheating of oil in the tank
   (D) excessive sludge in the oil drawn from the tank

66. Suppose that the rotary pumps supplying oil to oil burners fail to deliver oil at the burner. Of the following, the first item to check is the

   (A) oil temperature at the burner
   (B) possibility of air leaks in the suction line of the pump
   (C) oil level in the storage tanks
   (D) viscocity of the oil delivered to the pump

67. The air nozzle and the atomizing cup of an oil burner show carbon deposits. Of the following, the most desirable way to remove these deposits is to

   (A) use a scraper, followed by light rubbing with 00 sandpaper
   (B) wash the cup and nozzle with a mild trisodium phosphate solution
   (C) use kerosene to dissolve the deposits and wipe with a soft cloth
   (D) apply a hot flame to the carbonized surfaces to burn the carbon deposits

68. The most likely result of failure to clean carbon from the rotary cup of an oil burner is

   (A) carbon formation on the back wall of the combustion chamber
   (B) oil drip from the burner to the floor of the combustion chamber
   (C) increased firing rate
   (D) pitting of the inner surface of the cup

69. A fireman who is on the last watch in a large low-pressure, fully automatic oil burning heating plant should as his *first* step in closing down the plant

   (A) shut off the oil supply to the burners
   (B) shut off the feedwater supply to the boilers
   (C) open the remote control switch
   (D) blow down the boilers

70. In an oil-fired plant, a high vacuum on an oil suction line would indicate

   (A) a broken line between gauge and oil pump
   (B) a dirty strainer
   (C) an open valve in the suction line
   (D) a clogged line at the rotary cup

71. Suppose that an oil burner starts, but shuts down shortly thereafter because no fuel is being delivered to it. After checking the fuel supply in the tank, the *next* step should be to check

(A) if valves in the suction and delivery lines are open
(B) oil strainers
(C) oil pump
(D) piping from the pump to the burner

72. The average temperature of a certain month of 30 days is 52°F. The number of degree-days for that month is therefore

(A) 390   (C) 540
(B) 1560   (D) 39

Answer Key

1. D	13. B	25. C	37. A	49. D	61. B
2. D	14. A	26. C	38. A	50. A	62. B
3. C	15. B	27. A	39. B	51. D	63. D
4. A	16. B	28. A	40. C	52. C	64. B
5. C	17. B	29. A	41. B	53. B	65. A
6. C	18. B	30. C	42. C	54. A	66. C
7. A	19. D	31. C	43. B	55. A	67. C
8. A	20. A	32. A	44. A	56. A	68. D
9. C	21. B	33. A	45. B	57. D	69. A
10. B	22. D	34. B	46. C	58. A	70. B
11. A	23. D	35. B	47. B	59. C	71. A
12. D	24. C	36. A	48. A	60. C	72. A

PLUMBING QUIZZER

DIRECTIONS: For each question read all choices carefully. Then select that answer you consider correct or most nearly correct. Write the letter preceding your best choice next to the question.

1. The most accurate of the following statements concerning the venting of soil and waste systems is that

   (A) vent lines must not enter a soil line above the first floor
   (B) vent lines equalize the pressure on both sides of the water seal of a trap
   (C) venting is not required when fresh air inlets are provided
   (D) venting prevents the development of unsanitary and harmful conditions by introducing fresh air

2. The type of pump that is most commonly used in pumping water to a roof tank of recently constructed high rise apartment houses is

   (A) rotary   (C) deep well
   (B) reciprocating (D) centrifugal

3. When a centrifugal pump is directly connected to an electric motor, a flexible coupling is preferable to a rigid flange coupling mainly because

   (A) transfer of power is more efficiently maintained
   (B) a stronger joint is usually provided with a flexible coupling
   (C) slight misalignment of motor and pump is less likely to affect operation
   (D) there is less chance of the motor overheating

4. The *least* likely cause of rapid wear of packing in a pump is

   (A) pressure too high for the packing used
   (B) misalignment of pump and its driver
   (C) slight leakage through the stuffing box
   (D) stuffing box gland too tight

5. Automatic operation of a sump pump is controlled by the

   (A) pneumatic switch
   (B) float
   (C) foot valve
   (D) centrifugal driving unit

6. A characteristic of a rotary pump is

   (A) a rapidly rotating impeller moves the liquid through the discharge piping
   (B) two gears, meshed together and revolving in opposite directions move the liquid to the discharge pipe
   (C) valves are required on the discharge side of the pump
   (D) it is usually operated at high speeds up to 3600 rpm

7. Condensation on cold water pipes is frequently prevented by

   (A) insulating the pipe
   (B) keeping the temperature of cold water at least 10° above the freezing point
   (C) keeping the cold water lines near the hot water lines
   (D) oiling or greasing the outside of the pipe

8. Sweating usually occurs on pipes that

   (A) contain cold water
   (B) contain hot water
   (C) are chrome plated
   (D) require insulation

9. The method that is *not* used to overcome water hammer in a water line is the installation of

   (A) air chambers
   (B) shock absorbers
   (C) relief valves
   (D) quick closing valves

10. When the hot and cold handles of a combination faucet are in the normal "off" position,

water leaks from the swivel mounting of the spout. The proper way of correcting this leak is to

(A) repack the stem glands of the hot and cold water valves
(B) replace the valve seat washers on both hot and cold stems as well as the washer in the swivel mounting
(C) tighten the gland nuts of the hot and cold valve stems
(D) tighten the gland nut on the swivel mounting

11. The one of the following that is correct concerning roof water supply tanks is

(A) the overflow pipe should be larger than the supply pipe
(B) wherever possible the overflow pipe should not discharge above the roof
(C) where an overflow pipe is provided, an emergency drain is unnecessary
(D) the top of the overflow pipe should be not more than one inch below the top of the tank

12. Of the following statements concerning venting of drain lines, the one that is correct is

(A) vent lines cannot converge into the soil line at the top floor
(B) vent lines prevent emptying of the water seal of traps by equalizing pressure on both sides of the seal
(C) venting is required only where fresh air inlets are not provided
(D) a vent line should be connected to the drain line as far away as possible from the trap to avoid possible clogging of the vent line

13. Of the following statements concerning a roof tank used for water supply for both standpipe and ordinary consumption, the one that is most correct is

(A) the intake of the line for fire service is lower than the intake of the blow off line
(B) the elevation of the intake for fire service is higher than that for ordinary consumption
(C) the overflow line usually empties onto the roof or gutter
(D) both blow off and overflow lines are controlled with gate valves

14. A complaint is received that water is continually leaking from the low-down tank into the bowl of a water closet. An inspection reveals that the ball cock and float are operating properly. Of the following, the most probable cause of leakage is

(A) the overflow tube has become clogged
(B) the supply valve does not close when the tank is full
(C) the rubber ball flush valve is defective
(D) there is siphonic action between the tank and the closet bowl

15. A tenant complains that sewer odors are present in her kitchen, and appear to come from the sink drain. Of the following, the first item to check is

(A) water pressure in the water supply lines in the kitchen
(B) the vent pipe of the sink trap
(C) water seal in the trap
(D) pitch of the waste line

16. The main purpose of a house trap is to

(A) exclude sewer air from the drainage pipes of the building
(B) trap sediment in the waste line
(C) reduce the back pressure resulting from the trapping of fixtures
(D) provide easy access to drainage lines for cleaning purposes

17. The main purpose of a float in a flush tank is to regulate the

(A) water pressure
(B) water velocity
(C) rate of discharge
(D) water supply

18. The pipe which receives the discharge of water closets is the

(A) soil pipe   (C) vent pipe
(B) waste pipe   (D) leader pipe

19. To permit the fullest discharge from a blowdown valve and prevent the building up of sediment or sludge, the type of valve that should be used is a

(A) check valve   (C) globe valve
(B) gate valve   (D) butterfly valve

20. A tenant complains that the water from the cold water tap has a milky appearance which clears up shortly after standing. The action that should be taken is

(A) advise the tenant to attach a filter to the tap
(B) advise the tenant that there is nothing wrong with the water
(C) inspect the water supply line for defects and corrosion
(D) recommend cleaning the water service line

21. A major disadvantage of self-closing faucets in lines operating under moderate water pressure is that they

(A) close too rapidly
(B) frequently produce water hammer
(C) open too easily
(D) tend to become filled with sediment

22. Joints of vent pipe at the roof of a building are made watertight by means of

(A) flashings   (C) flanges
(B) ferrules   (D) drip pipes

23. To help prevent leaks at the joints of water lines, the threads are frequently covered with

(A) tar   (C) oakum
(B) cup grease   (D) white lead

24. When it is necessary to select a fitting to make a right angle turn in a pipe line, the proper ell to use is

(A) 22½″   (C) 60°
(B) 45°   (D) 90°

25. A fitting that has one side outlet at right angles to the run is a

(A) reducer   (C) elbow
(B) wye   (D) tee

26. The name of a fitting commonly used to make a turn in the direction of a pipe line is

(A) union   (C) elbow
(B) bushing   (D) coupling

27. A condensate trap is used on a

(A) steam radiator
(B) hot water radiator
(C) hot air register
(D) freon refrigerator

28. The *first* tool or method to try in clearing a drainage stoppage in a toilet bowl is

(A) a plumber's friend
(B) a hot lye solution
(C) a wire snake or auger
(D) to remove the cleanout plug on the trap

Answer Key

1. B	7. A	13. C	19. B	25. D
2. D	8. A	14. C	20. B	26. C
3. C	9. D	15. C	21. B	27. A
4. C	10. B	16. A	22. B	28. A
5. B	11. A	17. D	23. D	
6. B	12. B	18. A	24. D	

ELECTRICAL MAINTENANCE QUIZZER

1. When changing a burned out fuse it is important to use a fuse of the same size.

   (A) correct
   (B) wrong
   (C) only with fuses of high amperage
   (D) only with fuses of low amperage

2. The significance of the reading of demand meters is that such meters indicate

   (A) the cumulative total of the electricity used during a specific period
   (B) the greatest use of electricity at any given time during a specific period
   (C) whether total usage of electricity has exceeded the quantity upon which the budget is based
   (D) whether usage of electricity has exceeded safe operating loads

3. When lamps are wired in parallel, the failure of one lamp will

   (A) break the electric circuit to the other lamps
   (B) have no effect on the power supply to the other lamps
   (C) increase noticeably the light production of the other lamps
   (D) cause excessive current to flow through the other lamps

4. S.P.S.T. would be used to identify a

   (A) rheostat   (C) fuse
   (B) conduit   (D) switch

5. A tenant complains that her refrigerator does not run at all. Of the following, the first item to check is

   (A) condition of the condenser of the refrigerator
   (B) current in the outlet to which the refrigerator is connected
   (C) motor protector relay
   (D) float valve

6. A rheostat is commonly used to

   (A) change D.C. current to A.C. current
   (B) break a circuit if current is too high
   (C) change A.C. current to D.C. current
   (D) regulate speed of motors

7. When compressed air is used to clean motor windings, it is most important that the air be

   (A) heated
   (B) dry
   (C) at a pressure of 50 psi or more
   (D) at very low velocity

8. If a polyphase motor hums but does not run when the switch is thrown, it is most likely that

   (A) air surrounding motor is moist
   (B) brushes need adjustment
   (C) a fuse in the line has blown
   (D) voltage is below rated voltage

9. The proper method of changing the direction of rotation on a polyphase motor is

   (A) insert a converter in the line to the motor
   (B) interchange any two wires at the line switch
   (C) interchange all three leads at the line switch
   (D) reverse the polarity of the rotor circuit

10. A procedure which should not be followed in the maintenance of electric motors is

    (A) the commutator should be smoothed down occasionally with 00 sandpaper
    (B) vasoline can be used to lubricate commutators
    (C) if sparking is due to a rough commutator surface, it should be ground down with fine emery paper
    (D) oil for the bearings of motors should be renewed every 6 months on the average

11. Several split phase motors operating apartment refrigerators have burned out. The most probable reason is

(A) refrigerators overloaded due to too much food stored
(B) fan belt is slipping
(C) line voltage at least 10-15% above or below rated motor voltage
(D) refrigerators are confined in a poorly ventilated corner

12. Two insulated copper wires protected by a spirally wound strip of galvanized steel is known as

(A) lead cable   (C) conduit
(B) BX cable   (D) service cable

13. The Electrical Code requires that in housing projects

(A) appliance branch circuits in kitchens be wired with no. 14 wire
(B) appliance branch circuits in kitchens be wired with no. 12 wire
(C) branch lighting circuits in kitchens be wired with no. 12 wire if less than 40 feet from the basement
(D) branch lighting circuits in kitchens must be wired with no.10 wire

14. The electric service to a housing project is a 3 phase, 4 wire, AC system. The available voltages between any two wires is about

(A) 120/208   (C) 150/300
(B) 115/230   (D) 120/240

15. A light bulb socket should have the threaded shell connected to

(A) the ground wire
(B) neither the hot nor ground wires
(C) the hot or live wire
(D) both hot and ground wires

16. A 20 ampere fuse is placed in a circuit usually fused at 30 amperes. It is most likely that

(A) an excessive amount of current will pass through that circuit
(B) a short circuit will occur
(C) the fuse will burn out
(D) the wires in the circuit will burn out

17. A tenant asks for the replacement of a refrigerator because it does not refrigerate sufficiently, although the unit does run. Of the following the most likely cause for inadequate refrigeration in this situation is

(A) broken thermostatic switch
(B) broken wires in the electrical supply cord
(C) noisy compressor
(D) shortage of refrigerant

18. The average temperature of a household electric refrigerator should be maintained at about

(A) 15°   (C) 32°
(B) 25°   (D) 40°

19. A 2000 watt, 110 volt sterilizer should be connected to a branch circuit protected by a fuse with a rating of

(A) 10 amperes   (C) 20 amperes
(B) 15 amperes   (D) 60 amperes

Answer Key

1. A	5. B	9. B	13. B	17. D
2. B	6. D	10. C	14. A	18. D
3. B	7. B	11. C	15. A	19. C
4. D	8. C	12. B	16. C	

SAFETY AND JUDGMENT IN ELECTRICAL WORK QUIZZER

1. An electrician should consider all electrical equipment "alive" unless he definitely knows otherwise. The main reason for this practice is to avoid

   (A) doing unnecessary work
   (B) energizing the wrong circuit
   (C) personal injury
   (D) de-energizing a live circuit

2. When working on live 600-volt equipment where rubber gloves might be damaged, an electrician should

   (A) work without gloves
   (B) carry a spare pair of rubber gloves
   (C) reinforce the fingers of the rubber gloves with rubber tape
   (D) wear leather gloves over the rubber gloves

3. When connecting a lamp bank or portable tool to a live 600-volt DC circuit, the best procedure is to make the negative or ground connection first and then the positive connection. The reason for this procedure is that

   (A) electricity flows from positive to negative
   (B) there is less danger of accidental shock
   (C) the reverse procedure may blow the fuse
   (D) less arcing will occur when the connection is made

4. If a live conductor is contacted accidentally, the severity of the electrical shock is determined primarily by

   (A) the size of the conductor
   (B) the current in the conductor
   (C) whether the current is AC or DC
   (D) the contact resistance

5. A corroded electrical connection in a circuit generally has a tendency to develop a high spot temperature. This is because the corrosion

   (A) increases the flow of current through the connection
   (B) decreases the voltage drop across the connection
   (C) increases the voltage drop across the connection
   (D) decreases the effective resistance of the connection

6. With respect to the safety value of insulation on electrical maintenance tools it can be said properly that

   (A) they insure the safety of the user
   (B) the insulation provides very little real protection
   (C) they are of value mainly to the new helper
   (D) the insulation should not be used as the only protective measure

7. Before using rubber gloves on high tension work they should be

   (A) given to the helper and he should try them out
   (B) treated with neat's-foot oil
   (C) washed inside and out
   (D) tested to withstand the required voltage

8. Metal cabinets used for lighting circuits are grounded to

   (A) eliminate electrolysis
   (B) assure that the fuse in a defective circuit will blow
   (C) reduce shock hazard
   (D) simplify wiring

9. When working near lead acid storage batteries extreme care should be taken to guard against sparks, essentially to avoid

   (A) overheating the electrolyte
   (B) an electric shock
   (C) a short circuit
   (D) an explosion

10. To prevent accidental starting of a motor which is to be worked on

(A) remove the fuses
(B) connect a lamp across the motor leads
(C) ground the frame
(D) ground the motor leads

11. Most electric power tools, such as electric drills, come with a third conductor in the power lead which is used to connect the case of the tool to a grounded part of the electric outlet. The reason for this extra conductor is to

(A) protect the user of the tool should the winding break down to the case
(B) prevent accumulation of a static charge on the case
(C) provide for continued operation of the tool should the regular grounded line-wire open
(D) eliminate sparking between the tool and the material being worked upon

12. A good practical test that can be used in the field for detecting punctures in rubber gloves just before putting them on is to

(A) seal the gloves by rolling down the cuffs, and then compress them against a flat surface
(B) fill the gloves with water, hang them up, and watch for leaks
(C) tie the cuffs to compressed-air line outlets and slowly inflate
(D) dip the gloves in soap suds and then blow into them, watch for bubbles

13. It is always essential that a foreman in charge of a crew of men preparing to work on a low tension circuit caution them to

(A) wait until the circuit has been killed
(B) work only when the load is zero
(C) consider the circuit alive at all times
(D) never work on any circuit alone

14. It is best, as a safety measure, not to use water to extinguish fires involving electrical equipment. The main reason is that water

(A) may damage wire insulation
(B) will not extinguish an electrical fire
(C) may transmit shock to the user
(D) will turn to steam and hide the fire

15. When cleaning the insulation of electrical equipment in confined quarters it is *least* desirable to do the cleaning by

(A) wiping with a dry cloth
(B) blowing with compressed air
(C) wiping with a cloth moistened with carbon tetrachloride
(D) wiping with a cloth moistened with water

16. A steel measuring tape is undesirable for use around electrical equipment. The *least* important reason is the

(A) magnetic effect
(B) short circuit hazard
(C) shock hazard
(D) danger of entanglement in rotating machines

Answer Key

1. C	5. C	9. D	13. C
2. D	6. D	10. A	14. C
3. B	7. D	11. A	15. C
4. D	8. C	12. A	16. A

ELECTRICAL EQUIPMENT QUIZZERS

DIRECTIONS for questions 1–10: Each DEFINITION *in Column I refers to one of the* TERMS *in Column II. Select the letter which corresponds to the defined* TERM *and write that letter next to the appropriate* DEFINITION *in Column I.*

Column I—DEFINITIONS

1. Current-consuming equipment fixed or portable.
2. That portion of a wiring system extending beyond the final overcurrent device protecting the circuit.
3. Any conductors of a wiring system between the main switchboard or point of distribution and the branch circuit overcurrent device.
4. Not readily accessible to persons unless special means for access are used.
5. A point on the wiring system at which current is taken to supply fixtures, lamps, heaters, motors and current consuming equipment.
6. The rigid steel conduit that encloses service entrance conductors.
7. That portion of overhead service conductors between the last line pole and the first point of attachment to the building.
8. Conductors of a wiring system between the lines of the public utility company or other source of supply and the main switchboard or point of distribution.
9. A wire or cable or other form of metal suitable for carrying electrical energy.
10. Surrounded by a case which will prevent accidental contact with live parts.

Column II—TERMS

A. Mains   H. Appliances

B. Switchboard   J. Branch circuit

C. Fuse   K. Fitting

D. Outlet   L. Conductor

E. Service raceway   M. Enclosed

F. Feeder   N. Surrounded

G. Isolated   O. Service drop

DIRECTIONS for questions 11–15: In this test the numbered MATERIALS *in Column I have corresponding* USES, *which are lettered in Column II. Next to each* MATERIAL *in Column I write the letter of its most appropriate* USE.

Column I—MATERIALS

11. Silver   14. Phosphor bronze

12. Mica   15. Transite

13. Porcelain

Column II—USES

(A) Strain insulators
(B) Arc shields
(C) Heater wire
(D) Commutators
(E) Batteries
(F) Relay contact points
(G) Relay springs

DIRECTIONS for questions 16–22: In this test the numbered MATERIALS *in Column I are to be matched up with the* ELECTRICAL EQUIPMENT PARTS *listed and lettered in Column II. Next to each of the* MATERIALS *in Column I write the letter of the corresponding Column II* PART.

Column I—MATERIALS		Column II—ELECTRICAL EQUIPMENT PARTS
16. Steel	20. Rubber	(A) Acid storage battery plates
17. Lead	21. Copper	(B) Transformer cores
18. Mica	22. Carbon	(C) DC motor brushes
19. Porcelain		(D) Insulating tape
		(E) Cartridge fuse cases
		(F) Commutator insulation
		(G) Strain insulators
		(H) Knife-switch blades

DIRECTIONS for questions 23–27: In this test each numbered PART *in Column I is commonly associated with one of the* PIECES OF ELECTRICAL EQUIPMENT *listed and lettered in Column II. Match up the* PARTS *in Column I with the* PIECES *in Column II. Next to each of the* PARTS *in Column I write the letter of the* PIECE *with which it is most commonly associated.*

Column I—PARTS		Column II—PIECES OF ELECTRICAL EQUIPMENT
23. Current setting plug	26. Thermostat	(A) Oil circuit breaker
24. Lead connectors	27. Pothead	(B) AC power cable
25. Closing solenoid		(C) Induction overload relay
		(D) Storage battery
		(E) Electric water heater

DIRECTIONS for questions 28–37: In this quiz Column I consists of numbered EQUIPMENT PARTS, *each of which is made from one of the* MATERIALS *listed and lettered in Column II. Match up the* PARTS *in Column I with their corresponding* MATERIALS *in Column II. Write next to the numbered* PART *in Column I the letter of the* MATERIAL *from which it is commonly made.*

Column I—EQUIPMENT PARTS	Column II—MATERIALS	
28. DC circuit breaker arcing-tips	(A) Copper	(F) Wood
29. Cartridge fuse casing	(B) Silver	(G) Lead
30. Pig-tail jumpers for contacts	(C) Porcelain	(H) Brass
31. Commutator bars	(D) Carbon	(J) Phosphor bronze
32. Bearing oil-rings	(E) Transite	(K) Fiber
33. Cores for wound heater/coils		
34. Center contact in screw lamp/sockets		
35. Acid storage battery terminals		
36. Arc chutes		
37. Operating sticks for disconnecting switches		

DIRECTIONS for questions 38–49: Column I lists various JOB DESCRIPTIONS *in numerical order. Column II lists a variety of* TOOLS, *one of which is used for each of the* JOBS *in Column I. Match up the* TOOLS *in Column II with the* JOBS *in Column I. Write next to each* JOB *the letter preceding the proper* TOOL *to use for that job.*

Column I—JOB DESCRIPTIONS

38. Testing an armature for a shorted coil
39. Measurement of electrical pressure
40. Measurement of electrical energy
41. Measurement of electrical power
42. Direct measurement of electrical insulation resistance
43. Direct measurement of electrical resistance (1 ohm to 10,000 ohms)
44. Direct measurement of electrical current
45. Testing to find if supply is DC or AC
46. Testing the electrolyte of battery
47. Cutting an iron bar
48. Soldering a rat-tail splice
49. A standard for checking the size of wire

Column II—TOOLS

A. Neon light
B. Growler
C. Iron-vane voltmeter
D. Ohmmeter
E. Wattmeter
F. Hot-wire ammeter
G. Megger
H. Watthour meter
J. Manometer
K. Cable clamp pliers
L. Pair of test lamps
M. Hack saw
N. Hydrometer
O. Electrician's blow-torch
P. American wire gauge
Q. Micrometer
R. Hygrometer
S. Rip saw

Answer Key

1. H	11. F	21. H	31. A	41. E
2. J	12. D	22. C	32. H	42. G
3. F	13. A	23. C	33. C	43. D
4. G	14. G	24. D	34. J	44. F
5. D	15. B	25. A	35. G	45. A
6. E	16. B	26. E	36. E	46. N
7. O	17. A	27. B	37. F	47. M
8. A	18. F	28. D	38. B	48. O
9. L	19. G	29. K	39. C	49. P
10. M	20. D	30. A	40. H	

ELEVATOR QUIZZER

1. The interlocks of an elevator are wired in series. If they were wired in parallel, the most likely result would be

   (A) failure of the cab door to close on pressing the floor button
   (B) excessive load on the motor resulting in frequent motor failure
   (C) operation of the car when the hatchway door is open
   (D) improper leveling of the elevator at the various floor levels

2. Of the operation of the governor of an elevator, it is generally correct to state that

   (A) the governor cable travels at a higher speed than the car itself
   (B) when the car travels faster or slower than a predetermined speed, the governor will bring the car to a stop
   (C) the governor will bring the car to a stop only if the car goes up at an excessive speed
   (D) when the car overspeeds, the governor causes an overspeed switch to open the main line circuit

3. Of the following, the statement that is correct with respect to proper maintenance and inspection of elevators is

   (A) carbon and copper contacts of relays on elevator control boards can be cleaned periodically with coarse canvas cloth
   (B) to avoid slippage of safety guide rail grips, guide rails should not be lubricated
   (C) wire ropes must be thoroughly lubricated at least once a month
   (D) in checking interlocks, make certain that they are wired in parallel

4. When an electric passenger elevator stops at various landings with a jerky motion, the cause is most likely to be

   (A) scored brake drums
   (B) defective governor cable
   (C) poorly lubricated wire rope
   (D) defective limit switch

5. Of the following, the one that is *not* an elevator safety device is

   (A) interlocks   (C) limit switch
   (B) governor   (D) counter weights

Answer Key

1. C 2. D 3. A 4. A 5. A

CARPENTRY QUIZZER

1. To make pilot holes for screws, it is best to use

   (A) a rad-awl
   (B) scratch-awl
   (C) a jig
   (D) a chuck

2. The metal faces of the vise should

   (A) never come in contact with the wood you are working
   (B) grip the wood firmly
   (C) mark the wood through contact
   (D) press solidly on the wood

3. In marking circles, it is best to use

   (A) dividers
   (B) compasses
   (C) micrometers
   (D) rulers

4. When a screw is driven close to an inside corner, the best tool to use is

   (A) drill-bit
   (B) ratchet screwdriver
   (C) drill-press
   (D) cut-off tool

5. The size of a chisel is determined by the

   (A) length
   (B) width
   (C) pitch
   (D) height

6. To hold a stock firmly in place it is put in a

   (A) lathe
   (B) drill-press
   (C) drill-bit
   (D) vise

7. To hold glued parts together until the glue is dry, the tool used is a

   (A) clamp
   (B) lathe
   (C) wrench
   (D) pair of hammers

8. Except for the teeth, a rip saw resembles a

   (A) hack saw
   (B) swordfish
   (C) jig saw
   (D) crosscut saw

9. The cutting edge of a tool that is turned over is

   (A) scraper
   (B) reamer
   (C) auger
   (D) cold chisel

10. Wood scrapers are sharpened by means of a

    (A) file
    (B) plane
    (C) knife
    (D) saw

11. To determine whether stock is square the tool to be used on smaller places is a

    (A) carpenter square
    (B) framing square
    (C) try square
    (D) marking gauge

12. To determine width and thickness, the tool to be used is a

    (A) micrometer
    (B) marking gauge
    (C) ruler
    (D) tape measure

13. After a board has been planed and before it is sanded, the roughness can be removed by means of a

    (A) file
    (B) scraper
    (C) chisel
    (D) flame

14. In the pounding of wood, the tool to be used is a

(A) chisel
(B) wrench
(C) mallet
(D) plane

15. For duplicating work, it is best to use

(A) a chuck
(B) a jig
(C) a drill-press
(D) a drill-bit

16. The plane-bit stands on the part of the plane that is known as the

(A) blade
(B) frog
(C) point
(D) pilaster

17. Ordinarily the most efficient drop hammer is a

(A) heavy hammer with a high fall
(B) heavy hammer with a low fall
(C) light hammer with a high fall
(D) light hammer with a low fall

18. The tool generally used by a dockbuilder to finally shape a scrap joint is

(A) a two-edged ax
(B) an adze
(C) a hammer and chisel
(D) a saw

19. To cut a 3 x 3 angle, use a hacksaw with

(A) 32 teeth per inch
(B) 24 teeth per inch
(C) 18 teeth per inch
(D) 14 teeth per inch

20. The maximum weight that can be lifted with a block and tackle consisting of two 2-sheave blocks using a force of 500 pounds is

(A) 500 pounds
(B) 1,000 pounds
(C) 1,500 pounds
(D) 2,000 pounds

21. A straightedge is used for

(A) extending a spirit level
(B) squaring corners
(C) plumbing walls
(D) handing doors

22. A circular cut is laid out with

(A) a compass saw
(B) a marking gauge
(C) dividers
(D) calipers

23. To file a crosscut hand saw

(A) the point of the file is inclined toward the saw point
(B) each gullet is filed from both sides
(C) the point of the file is inclined toward the saw handle
(D) the file is held straight across the saw

24. To turn a nut, it is *not* correct to use a

(A) monkey wrench
(B) open end wrench
(C) box wrench
(D) stillson wrench

25. A paring chisel should be driven

(A) by hand only
(B) with a hammer
(C) with a mallet
(D) across the grain only

26. The roughing cut in a wood lathe is made with a

(A) cut-off tool
(B) "V" gouge
(C) skew chisel
(D) round gouge

27. The tool most frequently used to lay out a 45° angle on a piece of lumber is a

(A) combination square
(B) try square
(C) marking gauge
(D) divider

28. A spur center is used on a

   (A) jigsaw
   (B) drill press
   (C) lathe
   (D) disc sander

29. A tool used in hanging doors is a

   (A) butt gauge
   (B) reamer
   (C) C-clamp
   (D) trammel

30. Of the following oils, the one that is commonly used for oilstones is

   (A) penetrating
   (B) SAE No. 5
   (C) vinsol
   (D) pike

31. A scale on which the inch graduations are divided into 12 subdivisions, each $1/12$ of an inch in length, is usually found on a

   (A) try square
   (B) combination square
   (C) rafter square
   (D) T-square

32. The tool that would be used to cut out a circular disc is a

   (A) circular saw
   (B) shaper
   (C) planer
   (D) band saw

33. When sharpening a hand saw, the first operation is to file the teeth so that they are all the same height. This is known as

   (A) shaping
   (B) setting
   (C) jointing
   (D) leveling

34. The one of the following planes that is usually used with one hand is the

   (A) smoothing
   (B) block
   (C) jack
   (D) fore

35. An expansive bit should be sharpened with

   (A) an auger bit file
   (B) a mill file
   (C) a half round file
   (D) a grinding wheel

36. The abrasive grit on "open coat" paper for use on a power sander for woodwork is usually

   (A) tripoli
   (B) emery
   (C) aluminum oxide
   (D) carborundum

37. The one of the following power tools that is *not* frequently built with a slot for a miter gauge is a

   (A) shaper
   (B) band saw
   (C) disc sander
   (D) radial saw

38. A jointer may also be used for

   (A) mortising
   (B) routing
   (C) planing
   (D) shaping

39. The diameter of the arbor of a 12 inch circular saw is most likely to be

   (A) $3/8$ inch
   (B) $1/2$ inch
   (C) $5/8$ inch
   (D) $3/4$ inch

40. Of the following types of saw blades, the one that is *not* commonly used on a circular saw is a

   (A) dado
   (B) ply-tooth
   (C) novelty
   (D) tyler

41. A cap is found on a

   (A) hammer
   (B) plane
   (C) power saw
   (D) lathe

42. A tool used to plane concave edges of furniture is a

(A) rabbet plane
(B) wood scraper
(C) utility knife
(D) spoke shave

43. Beeswax would be most frequently used on a (an)

(A) auger bit
(B) scraper
(C) hand saw
(D) draw knife

44. The size of the drill that would be used to drill a body hole for a No. 7 wood screw is

(A) $3/32$ inch
(B) $5/32$ inch
(C) $7/32$ inch
(D) $9/32$ inch

45. A rectangular form can be checked for squareness without the use of a square by

(A) measuring to see that each side of the form is the same length as the opposite side
(B) measuring to see that the diagonals are the same length
(C) checking to see that the square of the length of either diagonal is equal to the sum of the squares of the lengths of either pair of adjacent sides
(D) measuring to see that each side of the form is the same length as the opposite side, and the diagonals are equal to each other in length

46. When sharpening a rip saw the usual angle between the file and the blade of the saw is

(A) 30°
(B) 45°
(C) 60°
(D) 90°

47. A function of the back on a back saw is to

(A) permit use of a thicker saw blade for wider cuts
(B) prevent the saw from buckling
(C) be able to saw in either direction
(D) increase the depth to which the saw will cut

48. To rough out a square block on a lathe the tool commonly used is a

(A) gouge
(B) file
(C) skew chisel
(D) parting tool

49. The proper bit to be used with a brace to make the holes for a $3/8$ inch wood dowel is

(A) $11/32$ inch wood twist bit
(B) $3/8$ inch auger bit
(C) $13/32$ inch wood twist bit
(D) $7/16$ inch auger bit

50. The two planes which make up the most useful combination for general carpentry work are the

(A) jack plane and the block plane
(B) jack plane and the jointer plane
(C) smooth plane and the block plane
(D) fore plane and the jointer plane

51. Splitting of wood can be reduced by using nails with points that are

(A) long and sharp
(B) blunt
(C) spirally grooved
(D) common

52. Galvanized nails would most probably be used in nailing

(A) shingles
(B) finished flooring
(C) joists
(D) interior trim

53. The length of a 10-penny nail is

(A) 3 inches
(B) $3 1/4$ inches
(C) $3 1/2$ inches
(D) $3 3/4$ inches

54. The length of a certain screw is measured from the top of the head to the point. The type of screw that this is most likely to be is a

(A) round head
(B) flat head
(C) oval head
(D) lag

55. For ease in driving, screws are frequently coated with

(A) casco
(B) oil
(C) soap
(D) urea resins

56. Of the following types of bolts, the one that would be used to anchor a shelf bracket to a plywood partition is a

(A) carriage
(B) expansion
(C) drift
(D) toggle

57. Split ring connectors are commonly used to

(A) anchor joists to girders
(B) join members of a truss
(C) anchor veneer to framework
(D) connect wood girders to steel columns

58. To drive a screw into hard wood it is necessary to

(A) start it with a hammer
(B) drill a hole first
(C) countersink the head
(D) drill and tap the wood

59. Studs must be spaced at 16 inches when

(A) the joists are spaced at 16 inches
(B) wood lathing is used
(C) bridging is required
(D) diagonal sheathing is used

60. An expansion bolt is used to

(A) enlarge a hole
(B) fasten into hollow tile
(C) fasten into solid masonry
(D) allow for expansion and contraction

61. The length of a flat head screw is defined as the length

(A) of the threaded portion
(B) of the shank plus the threaded portion
(C) of the complete screw
(D) between the bottom of the head and the point

62. A number 10 wood screw is

(A) thicker than a number 6
(B) longer than a number 6
(C) shorter than a number 6
(D) thinner than a number 6

63. Wood screws properly used as compared to nails properly used

(A) are easier to install
(B) hold better generally
(C) are easier to drive flush with surface
(D) are more likely to split the wood

64. Lag screws should be driven with a

(A) hammer
(B) screw driver
(C) monkey wrench
(D) brace and screwdriver bit

65. A brad is similar in shape to a

(A) box nail
(B) common nail
(C) finishing nail
(D) tack

66. Nails are galvanized

(A) for neater appearance
(B) for greater strength
(C) to make them smoother and drive easer
(D) to prevent corrosion

67. 4-, 6-, 8-, or 10-penny is used in identifying

(A) lumber
(B) nails
(C) screws
(D) files

68. To draw nails out of wood, the tool to be used is a

(A) claw hammer
(B) chisel
(C) wrench
(D) monkey wrench

69. To purchase screws, it is necessary to know

(A) the manufacturer
(B) the number and length
(C) width
(D) size of the screw holes

70. To prevent screws from splitting the wood when being driven

    (A) soap the screws
    (B) drive them with the grain of the wood
    (C) drive them slowly
    (D) use a drill first

71. Of the following sets of nails, the set arranged in order of the head's size beginning with the nail having the largest head

    (A) roofing, cut, common, finishing
    (B) finishing, common, cut, roofing
    (C) roofing, common, cut, finishing
    (D) common, roofing, finishing, cut

72. Nails are most likely to split the wood if

    (A) the nail point is blunt
    (B) driven across the grain
    (C) driven with the grain
    (D) they are too long

73. A requisition for nails was worded as follows: "100 lbs. 10d, 3", common wire nails—galvanized." The unnecessary information in this requisition is

    (A) 100 lbs.
    (B) common
    (C) 3"
    (D) galvanized

74. The nails holding a wooden board to a supporting piece can be most easily pulled out if the supporting piece is

    (A) white oak with wire nails driven into it across its grain
    (B) white pine with cut nails driven into its end grain
    (C) douglas fir with cut nails driven into it across its grain
    (D) yellow pine with wire nails driven into its end grain

75. Nails are sometimes coated with cement to

    (A) prevent rust
    (B) increase holding power
    (C) prevent electrolysis
    (D) increase electrolysis

76. The length of an 8-penny nail is

    (A) 2½"
    (B) 4"
    (C) 2"
    (D) 3"

77. The length of a 2-penny nail is

    (A) 1"
    (B) 1½"
    (C) 2"
    (D) 3"

78. A wood screw with a square or hexagon head for wrench tightening is a

    (A) set screw
    (B) fillister head screw
    (C) cap screw
    (D) lag screw

79. A strip of wood whose purpose is to assist the plasterers to make a straight wall is called a

    (A) casing
    (B) ground
    (C) belt course
    (D) gauge

80. A hip rafter is framed between

    (A) plate and ridge
    (B) plate and valley
    (C) valley and ridge
    (D) valley and overhang

81. A vertical member separating two windows is called a

    (A) muntin
    (B) mullion
    (C) stile
    (D) casing

82. Nosing would most probably be found in

    (A) window frames
    (B) stairs
    (C) saddles
    (D) scarves

83. A collar beam is used to tie

    (A) floor joists
    (B) laminated girders
    (C) roof rafters
    (D) columns

84. The side support for steps or stairs is called a

(A) ledger board
(B) pitch board
(C) riser
(D) stringer

85. The purpose of a water table is to

(A) prevent water from entering at the top of a foundation wall
(B) distribute water from a downspout directly on the ground
(C) prevent water from entering a cellar through the cellar floor
(D) prevent water from leaking through a roof at the chimney

86. The type of joint most frequently used where baseboards meet at the corner of a room is a

(A) miter
(B) mortise and tenon
(C) spline
(D) butt

87. A strike plate would be attached to a

(A) sill
(B) fascia
(C) jamb
(D) saddle

88. A pipe column filled with concrete is called a

(A) pintle
(B) buttress
(C) pilaster
(D) lally

89. If you were required to build forms for spandrels, the location of these forms would be at

(A) footing level between piers
(B) floor level between columns
(C) roof level between girders
(D) footing level over the grillage

90. The one of the following that is commonly used as a vapor barrier is

(A) asphalt roll roofing
(B) kraft paper
(C) plywood
(D) gypsum board

91. A valley is made watertight by means of a

(A) cornice
(B) flashing
(C) drip sill
(D) furring

92. Horizontal beams used to reinforce concrete forms and sheet piling are known as

(A) stirrups
(B) walers
(C) sheathing
(D) braces

93. The abrasive grit on "sandpaper" is usually

(A) pumice
(B) boron
(C) flint
(D) talc

94. The ends of joists are frequently supported on

(A) hanger bolts
(B) tie plates
(C) bridle irons
(D) gusset plates

95. The temporary support used in arch construction is called the

(A) formwork
(B) centering
(C) soffit
(D) falsework

96. The projecting base of a building is the

(A) arris
(B) quoin
(C) plinth
(D) corbel

97. A flat vertical column which is a part of or attached to the face of a wall is a

(A) pillar
(B) buttress
(C) pier
(D) pilaster

98. A vertical wood framing member used in making a wall for a building is called

(A) a furring
(B) a tread
(C) a stud
(D) a header

99. A joist supported at one end by a girder and at the other end by a header is called a

(A) trimmer
(B) tail joist
(C) cripple
(D) bridge joist

Answer Key

1. A	14. C	27. A	40. D	53. A	65. C	77. A	89. C
2. A	15. B	28. C	41. B	54. B	66. D	78. D	90. A
3. A	16. B	29. A	42. D	55. C	67. B	79. B	91. B
4. B	17. B	30. D	43. C	56. D	68. A	80. A	92. B
5. B	18. B	31. C	44. B	57. B	69. B	81. B	93. C
6. A	19. D	32. D	45. D	58. B	70. D	82. B	94. C
7. A	20. D	33. C	46. D	59. B	71. C	83. C	95. B
8. D	21. A	34. B	47. B	60. C	72. C	84. D	96. C
9. A	22. C	35. A	48. A	61. C	73. C	85. A	97. D
10. A	23. C	36. C	49. B	62. A	74. B	86. D	98. C
11. C	24. D	37. D	50. A	63. B	75. B	87. C	99. B
12. B	25. A	38. C	51. B	64. C	76. A	88. D	
13. B	26. D	39. D	52. A				

TOOL QUIZZER

1. Glazier's points are used to

   (A) hold glass in wooden window sash
   (B) scratch glass so that it can be broken to size
   (C) force putty into narrow spaces between glass and sash
   (D) remove broken glass from a pane

2. Of the following, the best tool to use to make a hole in a coping stone is a

   (A) star drill
   (B) coping saw
   (C) pneumatic grinder
   (D) diamond wheel dresser

3. Of the following tools, the one which is least like the others is

   (A) brace and bit   (C) plane
   (B) draw-knife   (D) spoke shave

4. A squeegee is a tool which is used in

   (A) drying windows after washing
   (B) cleaning inside boiler surfaces
   (C) the central vacuum cleaning system
   (D) clearing stoppages in waste lines

5. For sweeping under radiators and other inaccessible places, the most appropriate tool is the

   (A) dry mop   (C) counter brush
   (B) feather duster   (D) floor brush

6. To install an expansion shield in a concrete wall, of the following, the proper tool to use is a

   (A) bull nose chisel
   (B) star drill
   (C) chrome vanadium alloy cold chisel
   (D) rock wedge

7. When sanding wood by hand, best results are usually obtained in finishing the surface when the sanding block is worked

   (A) across the grain
   (B) in a diagonal to the grain
   (C) in a circular motion
   (D) with the grain

8. Of the following tools, the one that is used primarily for hanging wood doors is a

   (A) butt gauge
   (B) carpenter's plumb bob
   (C) fore plane
   (D) hardwood level

9. A screw is broken off in a tapped hole. The proper tools to use in removing the broken screw from the hole are

   (A) hammer and cold chisel
   (B) drill and EZY-out
   (C) acetylene and oxygen torch
   (D) screw driver and pliers

10. The plane to use in shaping a curved edge on wood is known as

    (A) jack   (C) spoke shave
    (B) smooth   (D) rabbet

11. The saw that is never hand filed is a

    (A) rip saw   (C) circular saw
    (B) coping saw   (D) band saw

12. The recess for a butt hinge should be made with a

    (A) brace and bit   (C) router plane
    (B) chisel   (D) rabbet plane

13. A 6-point saw is one which

    (A) weighs 6 ounces per foot
    (B) is made of no. 6 gauge steel
    (C) has 6 teeth per inch
    (D) has 6 styles of teeth for universal work

14. The set in the teeth of a hand saw primarily

    (A) prevent the saw from binding
    (B) make the saw cut true
    (C) give the saw a sharper edge
    (D) remove the sawdust

15. The proper tools for making a keyhole in a wooden door are a

(A) keyhole saw and a chisel
(B) keyhole chisel and a brace and bit
(C) keyhole back saw and a brace and bit
(D) keyhole saw and a brace and bit

16. A jointer plane is

(A) used for making close fits
(B) used for heavy rough work
(C) usually less than 12 inches long
(D) used for treaching

Questions 17-20 are true-or-false questions. If the statement is correct, write (A); if incorrect, write (B).

17. A sharp nail in the end of a long handle is a useful tool for picking up paper litter from lawns.

18. When using a knife to cut something, the user should cut in a direction away from himself.

19. Shears are a scissor-like tool used for cutting.

20. A good screw driver should be used for opening cans of paint or cleaning supplies.

21. The length of a 10-penny nail is, in inches

(A) 2½   (C) 3½
(B) 3   (D) 4

22. A wood screw which can be tightened by a wrench is known as a

(A) lag screw   (C) carriage screw
(B) Phillips screw (D) monkey screw

23. The reason that a lubricant prevents rubbing surfaces from becoming hot is that the oil

(A) forms a smooth layer between the two surfaces, preventing their coming into contact
(B) is cold and cools off the rubbing metal surfaces
(C) is sticky, preventing the surfaces from moving over each other too rapidly
(D) makes the surfaces smooth so that they move easily over each other

24. A good lubricant for locks is

(A) graphite   (C) grease
(B) mineral oil (D) motor oil

25. The liquid used in a liquid-operated door check is

(A) water   (C) grease
(B) oil   (D) alcohol

26. A wood frame/cork bulletin board is to be attached to a plaster and hollow tile wall. The proper installation would use

(A) self tapping screws
(B) miracle glue
(C) wire cut nails
(D) expansion shields and screws

27. When replacing a broken pane of glass in a wood sash, the fasteners used are called

(A) brads   (C) glazing points
(B) wire clips (D) finishing nails

28. An expansion bolt is used to

(A) enlarge a hole
(B) fasten into hollow tile
(C) fasten into solid masonry
(D) allow for expansion and contraction

29. The frequency of oiling and greasing of bearings and other moving parts of machinery depends mainly on the

(A) size of the parts requiring lubrication
(B) speed at which the parts move
(C) ability of the operator
(D) amount of use of the equipment

30. Of the following procedures, the one that is most likely to be a hazardous or unsafe practice is

(A) pulling on a wrench to loosen a tight nut
(B) using a cold chisel whose head is mushroomed
(C) leaning one's weight toward the ladder while using it
(D) carrying a scraper in one's pocket with the blade down

31. "If you are carrying a scraper in your pocket, have the blade down, not up." The chief reason for this regulation is to

(A) prevent injury to yourself or other employees
(B) keep the scraper clean
(C) protect the clothing of the man who is carrying the scraper
(D) prevent the blade from becoming dull

32. Oil is used on honing stones so that

(A) steel particles will not clog the stone
(B) the tool will slide easily
(C) rusting of the tool is prevented
(D) less heat due to friction will be generated

33. To reduce waste in the use of cleaning tools and equipment, the most effective of the following methods is to

(A) require each porter to return a worn broom or brush before a new one is issued
(B) insist that all cleaning tools be used for a specified period of time
(C) have the head porter make sure that tools are used properly
(D) order the storeroom clerk to issue new equipment only when his examination shows the old ones to be useless

34. To make certain that tools are not mislaid, lost, or stolen, a supervisor should follow the procedure of

(A) questioning each employee as he leaves for the day
(B) making a monthly check of tools in the storeroom
(C) deducting from the employees' salaries the cost of the tools lost
(D) keeping a daily record of tools given out and returned

35. The proper use or care of a mop does *not* include

(A) rinsing immediately after use and hanging up to dry
(B) wringing out the mop by hand while cleaning a floor
(C) trimming the strands to avoid unnecessary splashing
(D) dividing the floor to be mopped into equal work areas

Questions 36-38 are true-or-false questions. If you think the statement is correct, write (A); if incorrect, write (B).

36. A rake should not be left on the grass with the prongs up.

37. The blade of a folding pocket knife is safe to use instead of a screw driver to tighten a screw.

38. It is safe to use a tool with a broken handle if the tool is small.

Answer Key

1. A	7. D	13. C	19. A	25. B	31. A	37. B
2. A	8. A	14. A	20. B	26. D	32. A	38. B
3. A	9. B	15. D	21. B	27. C	33. C	
4. A	10. C	16. A	22. A	28. C	34. D	
5. C	11. B	17. A	23. A	29. D	35. B	
6. B	12. B	18. A	24. A	30. B	36. A	

PAINTING QUIZZER

1. When painting, nail holes and cracks should be

   (A) filled with putty before starting
   (B) filled with putty after the priming coat is applied
   (C) filled with paint by careful working
   (D) ignored

2. Paint is "thinned" with

   (A) linseed oil   (C) varnish
   (B) turpentine   (D) gasoline

3. The process of pouring paint from one container to another in order to mix it, is known as

   (A) bleeding   (C) cutting
   (B) boxing   (D) stirring

4. When painting wood, puttying of nail holes and cracks is done

   (A) before any painting is started
   (B) after the priming coat is applied
   (C) after the finish coat is applied
   (D) at any stage in the painting

5. The most common cause of blistering of paint surfaces is

   (A) too rapid drying of paint work
   (B) failure to fill in uneven areas of surface before painting
   (C) presence of moisture behind paint film
   (D) use of improper paint mixture

6. Suppose that you noticed the sagging and running of paint on some walls after a paint job has been completed. This is most probably due to the

   (A) application of too much paint
   (B) application of too little paint
   (C) improper sealing of wall prior to painting
   (D) bleeding of oil out of the paint surface

7. Red lead is used in painting mainly to

   (A) prevent rusting of metal surfaces
   (B) prevent pinholes and air bubbles in the finish coat
   (C) waterproof metal surfaces
   (D) prevent checking of finish coat

8. The material which is usually put on knots and sappy places before painting wood is

   (A) white lead   (C) turpentine
   (B) putty   (D) shellac

9. The most desirable preservative to apply to several new wood exterior benches several days in advance of painting is

   (A) creosote oil   (C) kerosene oil
   (B) raw linseed oil   (D) Japan dryer

10. Of the following, the best method of cleaning a calcimine brush is to wash it with

    (A) water   (C) alcohol
    (B) turpentine   (D) gasoline

11. When painting, turpentine is added to the paint mainly to

    (A) enable it to dry more rapidly
    (B) dissolve the pigment
    (C) add corrosion-resisting properties
    (D) thin it out

12. The solvent which should be used to clean a brush immediately after it was used to apply rubber base paint to cinderblock is

    (A) turpentine   (C) mineral oil
    (B) alcohol   (D) warm water

Answer Key

1. B	5. C	9. B
2. B	6. A	10. A
3. B	7. A	11. D
4. B	8. D	12. D

GROUNDSKEEPING QUIZZER

1. The speed of a power lawn mower engine is regulated by a

   (A) hand throttle   (C) brake
   (B) "foot feed"   (D) choker

2. The best way of keeping a lawn mower in good operating condition is to

   (A) clear the lawn of sticks, stones, and debris before mowing
   (B) attach a grass catcher to the mower to reduce strain on the blades
   (C) make certain that the rotating blade is tight against the bedknife
   (D) keep the blades adjusted so that the cut leaves no more than one inch of grass

3. Of the following, the first thing to check if the power lawn mower failed to start is the

   (A) lubrication   (C) sparkplug
   (B) magneto   (D) loose ignition wires

4. Of the following, the substance commonly used to kill rodents is

   (A) red squill
   (B) 2-4 D
   (C) sodium fluoride powder
   (D) carbon tetrachloride

5. Of the following, the substance which is *not* used as an insecticide is

   (A) carbon tetrachloride
   (B) sodium fluoride
   (C) chlordane
   (D) DDT

6. Material applied to lawns which has the composition "5-10-5" is used mainly as

   (A) an insecticide
   (B) a fertilizer
   (C) a weed control chemical
   (D) a soil softener

7. Generally, it is better to seed a lawn in the fall than in the spring. Of the following, the best reason for this gardening rule is

   (A) the ground is drier in the spring than in the fall
   (B) tree shading is at a minimum in the fall
   (C) pedestrian traffic over a lawn is at a minimum in the fall
   (D) weed growth is less in the fall than in the spring

8. The type of tree that is considered *least* desirable for street or housing project planting is

   (A) pin oak   (C) Norway maple
   (B) sycamore   (D) Carolina poplar

9. Of the following, the most effective way to reduce or eliminate crab grass growth is to

   (A) spray lawn areas with large amounts of DDT and pyrethrum
   (B) cut grass short in the summer months to prevent the crab grass from going to seed
   (C) pull crab grass plants in the fall just before lawn reseeding is under way
   (D) increase soil alkalinity by adding generous amounts of chloride of lime to the soil

10. The most desirable of the following practices with respect to the watering of established lawns in the summertime is

    (A) lawn areas should be watered heavily once or twice a week
    (B) daily shallow watering is preferred for established lawns
    (C) watering of lawns is best done in the late morning or noon to prevent excessive evaporation
    (D) watering should be done only when the soil appears excessively dry and powdery

11. Established lawns are watered

    (A) satisfactorily by thunderstorms

    (B) frequently and lightly

    (C) at regular intervals with sufficient water
        to penetrate to the subsoil

    (D) whenever they begin to show patches of
        yellow or brown

12. Prior to reseeding a patch of burned out grass, the ground is turned over down to subsoil preferably with a

    (A) spade   (C) hoe

    (B) fork   (D) cultivator

Answer Key

1. A	4. A	7. D	10. A
2. A	5. A	8. D	11. C
3. D	6. B	9. B	12. B

CUSTODIAL CARE QUIZZER

Questions 1-12 are true-or-false questions. If you think the statement is correct, write (A); if incorrect, write (B).

1. A little ammonia in the water is good for cleaning enamel surfaces.

2. When a caretaker is told to dampen a cloth he should wet it until it is soaking.

3. Cleaning away dirt from the glass globes of ceiling light fixtures will help to let more light through.

4. Wire guards around light bulbs in building hallways help to protect the bulbs from being broken.

5. Varnish is a soft floor wax.

6. Rock salt is used for making suds in water.

7. Waxing a floor makes the floor look good but does not make the floor easier to sweep.

8. After a mop is used it should be rinsed out and hung up to dry.

9. Oil, grease, or water on floors should be wiped up immediately so that no one will slip.

10. A wet mop may be used to wash a floor that is still dirty after sweeping.

11. A caretaker should try to mop a large hall with only one pail of water in order to save water for the city.

12. Before a floor is mopped with a wet mop, it should be swept clean of loose dirt.

13. In cleaning enamel-painted woodwork, the tenant should be advised to wash the surfaces with

    (A) ammonia water
    (B) mild soap and water solution
    (C) plain warm water
    (D) strong soda solution

14. Ventilation of public rooms without windows is accomplished by

    (A) the normal opening and closing of the entrance door
    (B) the heating and cooling of the room air by the radiators
    (C) forced mechanical circulation of fresh air and exhaust air through ducts
    (D) the use of air deodorizers

15. Considerable debris has accumulated along the bottom of a chain link fence. To properly dispose of this debris

    (A) burn it with gasoline
    (B) rake it away from the fence and put it out with the garbage
    (C) pick it up by hand and put it out with the garbage
    (D) dig it under with a round point shovel

16. After a chamois skin has been used to dry windows or other glass surfaces, it should be washed in

    (A) hot water containing a small amount of soap
    (B) warm water alone
    (C) a weak solution of trisodium phosphate
    (D) a weak warm solution of ammonia in water

17. Porters should not wring out a mop by hand mainly because

    (A) the cleaning solutions used will be extremely harmful to the skin
    (B) too much water will remain in the mop resulting in additional work
    (C) pins, nails or splinters may have been picked up in the mop
    (D) it tends to be time consuming and makes it difficult for the porter to stick to his time schedule

18. Paste wax is desirable for waxing all of the following surfaces *except*

    (A) wood furniture   (C) metal lockers
    (B) hardwood trim   (D) asphalt tile

19. Chrome plated hardware should be cleaned periodically to remove dirt with

(A) a mild scouring powder
(B) fine steel wool
(C) mild soap solution
(D) an abrasive metal polish

20. Lighting fixtures in halls of housing projects should be dusted

(A) daily   (C) yearly
(B) weekly   (D) annually

DIRECTIONS: Items 21 to 24 inclusive in Column I are cleaning jobs. Column II lists cleaning agents. For each job in Column I, select the proper cleaning agent from Column II. Then PRINT the letter of that cleaning agent next to the number of the cleaning job.

COLUMN I

21. Added to water for window washing
22. Spread on concrete pavements to melt snow or ice
23. Added to water to wash terrazzo floors
24. Remove ink stains from wood

COLUMN II

(A) Benzol
(B) Bicarbonate of soda
(C) Trisodium phosphate
(D) Rock salt
(E) Oxalic acid
(F) Carbon tetrachloride
(G) Vinegar and water
(H) Soft soap

25. Corn brooms should be wet with warm water once or twice a week in order to

(A) keep the fibers flexible
(B) keep the fibers clean
(C) prevent the fibers from rotting
(D) maintain the stiffness of the fibers

26. Painted cement floors should not be mopped with a strong trisodium phosphate solution because it

(A) will tend to decompose the cement surface
(B) may dissolve the paint surface
(C) will not remove stains and dirt from this type of floor surface
(D) tends to rot the fibers of the mop

27. The cleaning tool which is used for sweeping window sills and under radiators is a

(A) hopper brush   (C) deck brush
(B) 10 inch floor   (D) counter brush
    brush

28. The accepted procedure in wall washing is to start at the bottom of the wall and work toward the top. The reason for this procedure is

(A) the wall is less likely to show streaks after the job has been completed
(B) there is less effort required when the process is started at the bottom
(C) rinsing of the wall after use of cleaning solution is reduced to a minimum
(D) the amount of time the wall remains wet is reduced by this method

29. If the gas flame in an apartment gas range is yellow, the adjustment that should be made is to

(A) reduce the gas pressure to the burner
(B) decrease the amount of air to the burner
(C) increase the amount of air to the burner
(D) increase the gas pressure to the burner

30. A practice which should *not* be followed in the cleaning of hall windows is

(A) use of warm water containing a very small amount of trisodium phosphate
(B) use of a mild soap solution as the cleaning agent
(C) use of a sponge to apply water to the glass surface
(D) use of a chamois skin to wipe the glass dry

31. Of the following, the best spot remover for marks made with wax crayons on brick or cement walls is

(A) neutral soap solution
(B) trisodium phosphate and ammonia water
(C) Clorox and soap chips
(D) warm water alone

32. Suppose that the walls of some buildings of a housing project have been defaced by white chalk marks. To remove those marks it is generally best to use a deck or scrubbing brush and

(A) water containing a light oil solvent for the chalk
(B) warm water containing an acid solvent to dissolve the chalk
(C) warm water containing lye to dissolve the chalk
(D) warm water alone

33. Chewing gum is best removed from asphalt tile floors with

(A) kerosene
(B) hot water and scrub brush
(C) a putty knife
(D) a steel wool pad

34. Linoleum and rubber tile floors are preferably washed with

(A) large quantities of hot water
(B) small quantities of hot water and Ajax
(C) large quantities of warm water and kerosene
(D) small quantities of warm water and soap

35. The use of concentrated acid on terrazzo toilet room floors is

(A) recommended for removing stains
(B) recommended for removing odors
(C) not recommended because of harmful fumes
(D) not recommended because it pits the surface

36. Tarnishing of chromium plated valves, faucets, hinges, and door knobs of toilet rooms can be prevented by

(A) monthly wax polishings
(B) semi-annual cleaning with abrasive and solvent
(C) daily wiping with cloth dampened with cold water
(D) daily wiping with cloth dampened with kerosene

37. Floor sealer may be used on

(A) wood but not on cork
(B) cork but not on wood
(C) neither cork nor wood
(D) both cork and wood

38. A cleaner complains to you that he has been unable to clean a cement floor because there is so much oil and grease on it. You should advise the cleaner to

(A) do the best he can since he cannot expect to get the floor clean anyway
(B) use kerosene oil but no water
(C) use kerosene oil and then scrub the floor with a soap solution and scouring compound
(D) use lye to dissolve the grease and oil and then flush thoroughly with water

39. Floors that are usually *not* waxed are those made of

(A) rubber tile   (C) pine wood
(B) terrazzo   (D) mastic tile

40. In the daily cleaning of an office, the *first* thing the cleaner usually does is to

(A) sweep the floors
(B) open the windows
(C) dust the furniture
(D) empty waste paper baskets

41. A 5 foot × 5 foot slab of concrete sidewalk in front of the building is broken and creating a hazard to the public. The proper mix of materials and water to replace this slab is

(A) 1 part cement, 2 parts sand
(B) 1 part cement, 4 parts sand
(C) 1 part cement, 1 part sand, 1 part gravel
(D) 1 part cement, 3 parts sand, 4 parts gravel

42. A tenant asks you for instructions in the waxing of new mastic tile and linoleum surfaces. A proper instruction in the waxing of such surfaces with a water emulsion wax is

   (A) always use a new mop for applying wax
   (B) when two coats are required the second coat of wax should be applied parallel to the first coat
   (C) wax should be poured on the floor in small amounts before being spread with the mop
   (D) if the wax is too thick, it should be thinned with alcohol

43. Cleaning agents containing oil or kerosene should not be used in mopping mastic tile floors mainly because

   (A) they tend to give a shine to the surface
   (B) the tile surface will become slippery
   (C) use of such cleaners will tend to dissolve the tile
   (D) dust will collect more rapidly on a surface cleaned with an agent containing oil or kerosene

44. You notice one of the maintenance men lifting a heavy carton from the floor by bending over it, grasping the lower edges with both hands, and keeping both legs and arms as straight as possible as he lifts the carton. This method of lifting is

   (A) undesirable; he should bend his arms to achieve greater lifting power
   (B) undesirable; he should bend his knees and keep his back straight
   (C) desirable; it is the easiest and least tiring method
   (D) desirable; keeping the legs and arms straight provides the needed leverage

45. When a building superintendent reports corroded flashings resulting in leakage, the part of the building he is referring to is the

   (A) basement piping
   (B) boiler room
   (C) pavement adjoining building
   (D) roof

46. Although rock salt is commonly used on the walks of the project when they are iced or heavily packed with snow, the chief disadvantage of its use is that it

   (A) creates a very slushy condition
   (B) generally causes deterioration of concrete walks
   (C) increases cleaning costs if used intensively
   (D) is harmful to adjacent trees and shrubs

47. The average temperature of a household electric refrigerator should be maintained at about

   (A) 15°F   (C) 32°F
   (B) 25°F   (D) 40°F

48. When the flame of a gas range burner pops or flashes back, it is most likely caused by

   (A) too much air
   (B) clogged gas orifice
   (C) excessive gas pressure
   (D) too little air

49. It is specified that a concrete pavement be laid over a base of cinders. The best reason for this is that the

   (A) cinders provide stronger bearing surface than the soil
   (B) cinders act as a binder between the soil and the concrete
   (C) cinders provide for subsurface drainage
   (D) use of cinders reduces the amount of cement needed

50. Of the following, the one that is most important to include in the *daily* schedule of a porter is

   (A) mopping all stair halls
   (B) clean entrance doors to assigned buildings
   (C) clean incinerators
   (D) light up incinerators

Answer Key

1. A	6. B	11. B	16. B	21. C	26. B	31. B	36. D	41. D	46. D
2. B	7. B	12. A	17. C	22. D	27. D	32. D	37. D	42. C	47. D
3. A	8. A	13. B	18. D	23. C	28. A	33. C	38. C	43. C	48. A
4. A	9. A	14. C	19. C	24. E	29. C	34. D	39. B	44. B	49. C
5. B	10. A	15. B	20. B	25. A	30. B	35. D	40. D	45. D	50. D

PRINCIPLES OF SUPERVISION

1. One of the men in your crew complains about having to do a hard job. The best thing for you to do is to

   (A) ignore him
   (B) explain to him that all men must do their fair share of the hard jobs
   (C) tell him that his next job will be an easy one
   (D) take him off his job

   Answer: **(B)** It usually works out well to have the undesirable tasks rotated among all workers of equal rank. All tasks cannot be desirable, but all have to be performed.

2. Workers will respect their supervisor most if he or she

   (A) acts sternly with them
   (B) does not show favoritism
   (C) is quick to criticize their errors
   (D) does not enforce all the rules and regulations

   Answer: **(B)** A supervisor is most likely to gain the respect of subordinates by impartial treatment. A strict supervisor will not always gain subordinates' respect; on the other hand, a lenient supervisor is even less likely to be respected. Criticism of subordinates' errors should always be handled with the greatest discretion.

3. The best supervisor is usually the

   (A) best mechanic
   (B) fastest worker
   (C) man in service the longest
   (D) ablest leader

   Answer: **(D)** The successful supervisor must be a good leader. He or she must be able to gain workers' support in fulfilling the functions he is charged with. A good worker does not necessarily make a good supervisor.

The same can be said of a fast worker. A person who has worked at one job for a long time does not necessarily acquire leadership ability.

4. One of your workers offers a suggestion to improve the method of doing a job. The best thing to do is to tell the worker

   (A) that the job has always been done the same way and therefore it must be the best way
   (B) that you will check the suggestion to see if it really is a better way of doing the job
   (C) to make the suggestion to the chief engineer
   (D) to discuss it with the other workers, and if they agree with him you will try the suggested method

   Answer: **(B)** Some of the most useful suggestions come from those closest to the actual work. All suggestions should be carefully evaluated by the supervisor. Even if the entire suggestion is not valid, it may have its good points. Besides, the supervisor will do much to maintain the morale of the group if he encourages suggestions.

5. Of the following, the statement that is correct is that

   (A) every worker can do the same amount of work
   (B) the person with the most seniority will work the fastest
   (C) the strongest person will do the most work
   (D) the amount of work a person does can be increased by improving morale

   Answer: **(D)** Production and employee morale are directly related. When morale is high, production will be high; when morale is low, production will be poor.

6. Of the following, the best way for a supervisor to get the workers to follow his or her orders and directives willingly is to

    (A) ask for volunteers
    (B) explain the reasons behind the orders and directives
    (C) issue them in the form of a request or in a mild tone of voice
    (D) take part in carrying them out

    Answer: **(B)** A worker will be more likely to perform well when he knows why he is carrying out a particular task.

7. Inefficient scheduling of work should be suspected when one notes that there are several workers

    (A) absent from work
    (B) in the rest room
    (C) loading a truck
    (D) waiting to use equipment

    Answer: **(D)** The fact that equipment is not available when necessary is usually indicative of poor scheduling of work. Workers who must wait around for equipment are losing valuable time.

8. Whenever you give an assignment to one of your experienced workers, he asks you a great many question about it although he has successfully performed similar assignments in the past. The time you spend in answering many questions about minor details takes you away from more important work. Under these circumstances, you should probably *first*

    (A) answer his questions in such a way that he will be discouraged from asking further questions
    (B) ask the worker to ask his question of one of his fellow employees
    (C) assure the worker of your confidence in his ability to carry out the assignment properly and suggest that he proceed with his assignment
    (D) tell the worker that if the assignment is too difficult you will give it to someone who does not raise so many questions

    Answer: **(C)** This worker is needlessly wasting the time of his supervisor. Apparently he lacks confidence in himself. The supervisor should attempt to instill self-confidence in this worker through encouragement and praise whenever justified.

9. A supervisor should think of herself primarily as a

    (A) boss of her crew
    (B) part of the top management team
    (C) skilled maintenance and repair person in various fields
    (D) mechanic first and as a boss second

    Answer: **(A)** A supervisor is paid to supervise. Her aim should be to achieve maximum production from the workers assigned to her and the attainment of her unit's objectives

10. If, after you have been a supervisor for several years, you find that your workers never complain to you about working conditions or assignments, this is most probably a sign that

    (A) there is poor communication between you and your workers
    (B) the workers are interested mainly in their rate of pay
    (C) the workers have nothing to complain about
    (D) you are a very good supervisor

    Answer: **(A)** It is perfectly normal for workers to have some complaints. If a supervisor never receives any, the reason is probably that her manner does not encourage them. Her attitude should be such as will make it easy for her workers to come to her with work problems.

11. "The number of subordinates directly reporting to a superior should not be greater than he can supervise competently." This could be an acceptable definition of

    (A) chain of command
    (B) span of control
    (C) specialized functions
    (D) unity of command

    Answer: **(B)** The concept of span of control relates to the number of subordinates any supervisor can effectively handle. This number may increase or decrease, depending on the type of work being performed, how effectively the subordinates are trained, the conditions they perform the work under, etc.

12. A characteristic which a supervisor should consider most desirable in a worker is

(A) willingness to work as much overtime as possible
(B) keeping aloof from his co-workers
(C) the ability to carry out assignments properly
(D) the readiness to report gang gossip back to the foreman

Answer: **(C)** A worker is most valuable to the organization if he performs his duties with the greatest possible efficiency. How valuable can a worker make himself solely on his willingness to work overtime if he does not perform his regular duties well? Personality traits are not important unless they tend to interfere with work performance.

13. If a supervisor's crew continues to work effectively when she is out sick for a day or two, it would most probably indicate that

(A) she has their full cooperation
(B) the supervisor apparently serves no useful function with this crew
(C) the workers are trying to curry favor
(D) the job is not too difficult

Answer: **(A)** When a crew functions as well in the absence of the supervisor as when she is present, it is an indication that a high degree of morale exists. The workers are well trained and cooperative and fully behind their supervisor in attainment of unit objectives.

14. A supervisor would be personally to blame for inefficiency resulting from

(A) improper planning of work assignments
(B) unforeseen delays in delivery of material
(C) departmental policy of job rotation
(D) frequent labor turnover

Answer: **(A)** Poor planning causes delays in work through idle labor, lack of needed supplies, and improper staffing.

15. A supervisor is most likely to be held in high regard by her workers if she makes it a practice to

(A) exchange advice with them on personal problems
(B) be outspoken when pointing out their faults
(C) expect them all to carry out any job she gives them with equal proficiency
(D) observe the same rules of conduct that she expects them to observe

Answer: **(D)** A supervisor will be respected by her subordinates if she observes the same rules of conduct that she expects them to follow. The exchange of advice on personal problems is a practice fraught with danger. If the advice does not have good results, it is bound to cause friction. An effective supervisor will use discretion while criticizing his subordinates. Criticism should do good, not harm.

16. A supervisory practice which is most likely to lead to confusion and inefficiency is for the supervisor to

(A) issue orders only in writing
(B) relay orders to the workers through co-workers
(C) follow up orders after issuing them
(D) give orders verbally directly to the worker assigned to the job

Answer: **(B)** Aside from the chance that a verbal order will not be relayed accurately, there is also the risk that some workers will resent being given an order by a fellow worker.

17. Several of the workers in your crew start a discussion during working hours of rumored changes in working conditions. This discussion can best be stopped by telling the workers that

(A) existing conditions are satisfactory
(B) you will check on the rumor
(C) working conditions do not concern them
(D) they should wait and see if the working conditions are changed

Answer: **(B)** Uncertainty based on rumors of change can be demoralizing. As supervisor, you should assure the workers that you will find out if the rumor is valid and report back to them.

TRAINING AND RATING SUBORDINATES

1. You find that one of the workers in your crew constantly consults with her fellow workers on how to do the work to which she has been assigned. As her supervisor it would be best for you to

   (A) commend her for securing the cooperation of fellow workers
   (B) tell the workers to let workers learn by her mistakes
   (C) give this worker a job which is easy to do
   (D) see to it that the worker learns her job

   Answer: **(D)** This worker is either insufficiently trained or she is unsure of herself. Training not only will prepare her to carry out her duties with greater efficiency, but it will also serve to give her the confidence she seems to be lacking.

2. After you have given a newly-appointed subordinate complete instructions on how to use a piece of equipment, you should usually

   (A) assign him to work with another subordinate
   (B) go over the instructions once more
   (C) let him use the equipment while you watch him
   (D) tell him about the importance of the work

   Answer: **(C)** One of the best methods for training people is to let them perform a job under close supervision until they have mastered it. Then let them proceed on their own.

3. You assign a worker to take inventory of a certain item. The man gives you a figure which seems too high. Of the following, the best course of action for you to take is to

   (A) accept the figure given to you by the worker if he is willing to initial it
   (B) accompany the worker while he takes inventory again
   (C) ask the worker to take inventory again and tell him why
   (D) take inventory yourself

   Answer: **(C)** This choice will not only give you a double-checked figure but will also give the worker valuable training.

4. Upon being assigned to an important job on which she will work alone, a worker insists that she knows exactly how to proceed and that no instructions or explanations by the supervisor are necessary. The best way for the supervisor to handle this situation is to

   (A) let the worker proceed without instructions
   (B) report the worker to your superior for not listening to instructions
   (C) remain present while the worker does the job
   (D) question the worker briefly as to his intended procedure

   Answer: **(D)** This situation is not uncommon. The worker could have had previous experience at this job or at a similar job. However, since the supervisor will retain the ultimate responsibility for seeing that the job is performed correctly, he should question the worker briefly on the assignment before it is begun, and should follow this up with a check from time to time to see how the work is progressing.

5. The most logical reason for a supervisor to rotate job assignments among the men in his crew would be to

   (A) improve maintenance procedures
   (B) make sure that absences do not slow up the work too much
   (C) determine which of his men are not readily adaptable
   (D) reduce absenteeism

   Answer: **(B)** Note that there was no mention of the type of job assignments which were to be rotated. Assuming that there is a variety of different jobs, rotation will give the workers a degree of skill in handling any of them. If one worker were to be absent on any given day, there would be another available to fill in without prior training. Therefore you would have a flexible unit in which one worker could fill in for another whenever necessary.

6. Assume that one of your subordinates made an error. It was found and corrected, but your subordinate seems rather depressed about the matter. Of the followimg, the most advisable course of action for you to take is to

   (A) ignore the entire situation unless it happens again
   (B) praise her
   (C) reprimand her mildly
   (D) show her how she can avoid such a mistake in the future

Answer: **(D)** Everybody is likely to make errors at one time or another. Of the four courses of action depicted in the choices, the only sensible one would be to show the subordinate how she can avoid similar errors in the future.

7. A training program for workers assigned to the information section should include actual practice in simulated interviews under simulated conditions. Of the following educational principles, the chief justification for this statement is that

(A) the workers will remember what they see better and longer than what they read or hear
(B) the workers will learn more effectively by actually doing the act themselves than they would learn from watching others do it
(C) the conduct of simulated interviews once or twice will enable them to cope with the real situation with little difficulty
(D) a training program must employ methods of a practical nature if the workers are to find anything of lasting value in it

Answer: **(B)** The best way of teaching a new task is to permit the trainee to perform it under close supervision, correct his errors, and when he masters it permit him to work on his own.

8. At a training session involving the use of a new piece of equipment, the supervisor, after demonstrating one of the uses of the equipment, calls upon a subordinate to operate it. The subordinate makes several mistakes, but the supervisor says nothing to him until the operation is completed. Then the supervisor points out the mistakes and once again demonstrates the correct method of operation. The supervisor's method of teaching was

(A) good, mainly because the subordinate was permitted to complete the operation without frequent interruptions
(B) bad, mainly because the subordinate's errors were not corrected immediately
(C) good, mainly because the supervisor demonstrated thorough knowledge of the equipment
(D) bad, mainly because the supervisor did not call upon other subordinates to correct the errors and demonstrate the correct method of operation

Answer: **(B)** For best and most lasting results all errors made by workers should be corrected immediately, especially during the training process. The actions of the supervisor in this training session were indeed faulty.

9. For a worker to carry out an order most effectively, it is important that she

(A) be aware of the reasons for the order and understand her own exact role in the department's organization structure
(B) know what the order is about and be convinced in her own mind of the necessity for the order
(C) respect the superior's authority and have confidence in the superior's ability
(D) understand the order thoroughly and have the necessary skills to carry it out

Answer: **(D)** Every worker must thoroughly understand all orders that are given to her. Unless she does, she cannot perform her tasks effectively.

10. In conducting a meeting to pass along information to subordinates, a supervisor may talk to those subordinates without giving them the opportunity to interrupt him. This method is called one-way communication. On the other hand, the supervisor may talk to subordinates and give them the opportunity to ask questions or make comments while he is speaking. This method is called two-way communication. It would be more desirable for the supervisor to use two-way communication rather than one-way communication at a meeting when his primary purpose is to

(A) avoid, during the meeting, open criticism of any mistake he may make
(B) conduct the meeting in an orderly fashion
(C) pass along information quickly
(D) transmit information which must be clearly understood

Answer: **(D)** The supervisor must permit his subordinates to ask questions on material that is transmitted to them and which must be thoroughly understood. In the absence of this opportunity, subordinates could not be held responsible for work performance because they were not afforded the opportunity to clear up any questionable matter. This could be used as an excuse for poor work performance.

11. In breaking in a group of new workers placed under your supervision, it is important to keep in mind that they will probably learn most by

(A) attending well-prepared lectures
(B) studying printed instructions
(C) seeing training films
(D) doing the work under close supervision

Answer: **(D)** There is no better way to teach a new task than to have the workers perform the task under direct supervision until they have learned it well enough to perform it on their own.

12. A four-step method of training is widely used to train unskilled people on new jobs quickly. The proper order in which to use the various four steps for training unskilled workers is

(A) 1. Tell the man how 2. Show the man how 3. Let the man try the job 4. Check the man's work

(B) 1. Check the man's work 2. Tell the man how 3. Show the man how 4. Let the man try the job

(C) 1. Let the man try the job 2. Tell the man how 3. Show the man how 4. Check the man's work

(D) 1. Show the man how 2. Tell the man how 3. Let the man try the job 4. Check the man's work

Answer: **(A)** These four steps constitute the ideal method for training unskilled workers in job performance. Previous experience is not taken into consideration here.

13. Of the following methods of instructing workers in the discharge of their duties, the one which a supervisor would find *least* valuable is to

(A) construct a hypothetical case which might possibly occur and then discuss the solution with his workers

(B) discuss the weaknesses of each worker at unit meetings

(C) observe the errors each worker makes in his handling of work and then discuss them with each worker individually

(D) refer them to the proper procedure or section of the manual when it appears that its application might be required

Answer: **(B)** It is never a good training procedure to have an individual's mistakes pointed out and corrected before a group. This should be done on an individual basis and never before an audience. This question requires the *least* valuable; choices (C) and (D) illustrate very good training procedures, and choice (A) contains an acceptable but inadequate training procedure.

14. After having given a subordinate an assignment, a supervisor returns and notices that the subordinate has not done the work according to instructions. The *first* thing that the supervisor should try to discover is whether the subordinate

(A) dislikes this type of assignment

(B) had ever done anything similar before

(C) had understood the instructions given

(D) is a willing worker, but often incompetent

Answer: **(C)** Perhaps the reason for the subordinate using a different method than the one ordered by the supervisor was that he had misunderstood instructions. This in itself would require no action other than a session of retraining. If the reason for the poor work performance was other than a misunderstanding, more stringent disciplinary action might be called for.

15. A member of your crew was absent on a day when you instructed the crew in the use of a new piece of motorized equipment which can be dangerous if improperly operated. To acquaint this worker with the use of the machine, it would be most desirable for you as a supervisor to

(A) give him the manufacturer's instruction booklet to study and then let him use the equipment

(B) have him observe other crew members using this equipment and then let him operate it

(C) advise him to observe special caution in using the machine

(D) teach him about the machine the next time it is used

Answer: **(D)** The key to the answer to this question is that a dangerous situation may be created if the equipment is not properly used. Therefore this worker must be instructed in its proper use as soon as possible, which will probably be the next time it is put in operation.

SAFETY AT WORK

The majority of accidents can be avoided. They usually fall into one of two categories: those which may be attributed to carelessness either on the part of the injured or some other worker, or those which are caused by unsafe working conditions. A desk drawer or file drawer which is left open for another worker to trip over would be an example of the first type. An unsafe working condition may or may not be recognized by the employer, but even if it is safety precautions are often not taken either because of the expense involved or because speed of performance may have to be sacrificed for safety. Some employers hope that the expense of installing a safety device or control can be avoided. However, once an accident has occurred the employer soon realizes that he has acted foolishly because the cost of one accident is usually much greater than many safety devices which could have been installed to protect many workers.

Besides being expensive, accidents have an adverse affect on employee morale. Since employee morale, organizational efficiency, and production are directly related, one can readily see why progressive organizations, small and large alike, have seen fit to safeguard their workers while they are performing their duties.

When workers see accidents occurring around them, they are likely to grow apprehensive. They will worry that they may fall victim to the next one. In an effort at self-protection they may slow down their working pace. Sad to say, however, overly cautious workers who perform their duties under unsafe conditions are not immune to accidents.

Modern personnel administration today recognizes that workers must perform their functions in an atmosphere permeated with safety precautions and that is the responsibility of every employer to see that they do. Every organization should have a safety program to insure that accidents occurring on its premises will be kept to a minimum. The size of the program would depend upon the type of work that is being performed and the size of the organization. But even in the smallest organizations one individual should be given the responsibility for looking after the safety of the workers. It would be his or her function to see to it that the safety aspects of all of the jobs are looked into and that sufficient safety guards are installed wherever a hazardous condition exists. The safety program should not be limited to locations where physical work is performed because a large number of accidents occur in offfices, where one might think them highly unlikely.

It is believed by most experts in the field that there is a definite relationship between a worker's mental alertness and physical well-being and his involvement in accidents. A worker who permits his mind to wander to matters other than the work being performed is more likely to become involved in an accident than a worker who gives his work his full concentration. A worker who is bothered by a physical ailment or who is not feeling up to par while performing his duties is also prone to accident involvement. Mentally alert workers seldom fall victim to industrial accidents. Their minds are fully occupied by the work they are doing. They are naturally careful and attentive to their surroundings.

It is impossible to implement a successful safety program without the cooperation and understanding of the workers. Signs can be posted throughout the plant attesting to the importance of the program, but if the workers are not convinced it is to their benefit to be alert and careful, they will not comply. Therefore it is imperative that every safety program, before it is implemented, have as one of its initial steps the indoctrination of the workers with the knowledge that work performance in a safe atmosphere will be of benefit to them. They must be shown how an accident is likely to cause them grief, economic hardship, and may even interfere with their careers. It is important that they understand the safety program is intended to protect their interests as well as those of the organization. A good method of getting them to accept a safety program is to permit a representative group of workers to have a say in its formation.

The responsibility for the formation of a safety program in an organization is one task that may be successfully delegated to a subordinate by the head of the agency. The individual who is chosen to conduct the safety program should be familar with the intricacies of the various working units, and should be allotted sufficient time and help to carry out a carefully planned program. Funds should be provided for the purchase of safety devices wherever necessary, and maintenance help should be provided to eliminate dangerous situations. Loose desk lamp wires, faulty file drawers, and overloaded top drawers of standing files are examples of dangerous situations which can be easily and quickly corrected.

The actual safety program should begin with a collection of all available data concerning accidents that have occurred in the past. This data should be carefully categorized and then analyzed. Much can be learned from this information which will aid in the prevention of similar accidents in the future. Enough time should be taken for this study so that definite conclusions may be reached as to the causes of the previous accidents. The safety officer must have some "meat" with which to begin his own program. The next step should be a concentrated effort to gain the cooperation and support of all of the workers in the program. The safety officer should also consult with the various supervisors and workers throughout the organization because much can be learned from those closest to the actual work.

One of the most important aspects of a safety program is its reporting system. A report must be filled out whenever an accident occurs no matter how insignificant it may be. These reports will provide the basis for the elimination of hazardous conditions. One individual in each unit should be held responsible for completion of such reports, and should be adequately trained to do so properly. The workers must be convinced that the sole purpose of accident reports is to bring to light hazardous conditions which may be eliminated; otherwise they may attempt to cover up small accidents which then may lead to bigger ones at some later date. The report form should be designed with simplicity in mind, but it should call for enough information so that when completed, it will reflect the cause of the accident. The safety officer may find it necessary to conduct an investigation on his own in some instances, but most accident reports, if properly filled out, will form the basis for pinpointing the cause of an accident.

A safety program should be designed to bring to light hazardous conditions before accidents occur, but in the event an accident does occur the program should move swiftly to eliminate the cause of the accident so that it does not happen once more.

Attractive posters designed to alert workers to avoid dangerous situations are an integral part of a safety progam. They should be placed in work locations, locker rooms, and areas where workers spend their breaks and eat their meals. The workers must constantly be reminded of the importance of safety. For example, posters depicting the proper way to lift heavy objects should be placed in strategic areas because incorrect methods of lifting are the cause of many industrial accidents.

The final part of a safety program is the follow-up. It is the safety officer's job to see that his or her recommendations are implemented. This can prove to be quite a task. Supervisors have the job of producing maximum return from the labor and material afforded them. They may be reluctant to sacrifice speed for safety. Some supervisors may feel that "it can't happen here." The safety officer must therefore be extended sufficient authority to put the recommendations into effect. He or she should not resort to force, however, until absolutely necessary. The safety program will be much more beneficial if the supervisors and workers alike are convinced of its value and are willing to cooperate with the safety officer in putting his findings to work. Therefore the safety officer's job may involve some selling, too. A safety program is bound to be successful if the supervisors, workers, and safety officer all pull in the same direction.

The Accident-Prone Worker

Are individuals actually accident-prone? Are certain people more liable to involvement in accidents than others? Authorities are divided on the question. However, it is certain that some people become involved in a continuous stream of accidents while others avoid them almost entirely during their life span. Surely there are other factors besides lack of attentiveness and mental alertness while performing work that contribute to one's becoming involved in accidents. Some people avoid accidents by simply avoiding hazardous work situations. However, if a worker has a knack for becoming involved in accidents, how should he or she be treated? Should that worker be excused from work situations which involve any danger or treated as all of the other workers are? The latest thinking on this subject places special emphasis on instructing workers who have multiple accident records. They should be taught how to work safely and to be safety conscious. An organization could not function properly if assignment of personnel were determined solely by the individual's accident record. A worker must perform at the job that will best suit the organization.

If a worker continues to become involved in accidents after sufficient training and indoctrination in safe work procedures, consideration should be given to discharging him. Most workers can avoid accidents if they put their minds to it. Special assignments for workers should only be made at the convenience of the organization.

Although abstinence from accidents is reward in itself for a working unit, most safety programs will also issue formal awards to accident-free groups in an organization. These awards are usually made in certificate form so that they can be displayed within the working area of a unit.

These awards are more accurately certificates of recognition. They serve to indicate that a working unit has recognized the value of safe working procedures to itself and to the organization alike. These units have seen fit to comply with the rules of safety in order to promote organizational efficiency and to rid the workers of an evil to which they do not have to fall victim.

These certificates of recognition tend to take on added importance in time. For a working unit not to possess a safety certificate may symbolize more than a poor safety record. It will indicate a lack of desire on the unit's part to do what has been deemed best for both itself and the organization. The certificates will then become something that every unit will strive to attain to show that it wants to "join the team." The competition for acquisition of safety certificates will indirectly achieve the result that the entire safety program was intended for: an accident-free organization with increased efficiency.

Practice Questions

1. If a new employee becomes involved in an accident he should be

   (A) given additional training in safe working methods
   (B) discharged immediately
   (C) held strictly responsible for the accident
   (D) no longer assigned to tasks where there is any danger involved

2. One of the workers under your supervision asks to be excused from performing a task on a particular day because it involves the use of a 12-foot ladder. She has performed this job before on numerous occasions, but she says she is not feeling just right today. You should

   (A) insist that she perform the function
   (B) tell her to find another worker who is willing to change places with her
   (C) assign the task to another employee this time
   (D) report her to your superior

3. If a worker continues to perform a job in an unsafe manner after he has been trained by his supervisor to perform it in the proper manner, he should be

   (A) permitted to perform the job in his own way because it is easier for him to do so
   (B) disciplined
   (C) praised because he has not yet become involved in an accident
   (D) once again retrained by his supervisor

4. A supervisor who observes one of her subordinates performing his duties in an unsafe manner should

   (A) wait until the next staff meeting to correct him so that the whole staff will benefit
   (B) say nothing at the time, but wait until he observes him doing something else wrong to bring it up
   (C) have another subordinate correct him at the first opportunity
   (D) correct him at once

5. A report of an accident should be made as soon after the occurrence as practical chiefly because

   (A) the witnesses may change their stories before the report is written
   (B) the reporter should strive to rid himself of the chore so he can devote himself to more important work
   (C) the details of the accident will still be fresh in the reporter's mind
   (D) reports should be submitted promptly even if they do not contain all of the facts

6. If one of your subordinates approaches you, a supervisor, with the information that one of the functions he is performing may cause an accident, you should tell him

   (A) you are the supervisor and it is your function to determine work procedures
   (B) to put his information in writing
   (C) to refer the information to the safety officer
   (D) that you will investigate the matter at once

7. If you, as a supervisor, observe a worker not under your jurisdiction performing her duties in an unsafe manner you should

   (A) immediately instruct her in the proper method of work performance
   (B) ignore her because the worker is not under your jurisdiction
   (C) seek out her supervisor and inform her of her subordinate's action
   (D) report the worker to the safety officer

8. If you observe what seems to be a serious accident to a worker in your unit, your first course of action should be to

   (A) seek out the supervisor
   (B) fill out an accident report
   (C) notify the injured worker's family
   (D) render any possible first aid to the victim

9. It is a poor practice to fill the top drawer of a file cabinet entirely before using the drawers beneath it chiefly because

   (A) some file clerks may be shorter than others
   (B) the cabinet will topple forward when the top drawer is opened entirely
   (C) the file is not being used to its utmost capacity
   (D) material should be distributed equally throughout the file

10. In order to avoid injuries it is proper to lift heavy objects

    (A) with the knees bent and the back held stiff
    (B) with both the knees and the back held stiff
    (C) using the arms only
    (D) in the manner best suited to the individual doing the lifting

11. If a worker who is to perform a job in a hurry notices that a piece of equipment she is to use is defective she should

    (A) hold off completing the job until the equipment is either replaced or repaired

    (B) go ahead with the job because it must be completed in a hurry
    (C) consult with another subordinate
    (D) be cautious while using the defective equipment

12. A worker notices a piece of equipment which he believes can aid him in performing his work. The equipment is somewhat complicated, and he has never received any instruction as to its operation, although other employees have. He should

    (A) use the equipment because he will be able to do his work faster
    (B) put off doing his work until he has received adequate instruction in the use of the equipment
    (C) ask another worker to teach him to use the equipment
    (D) not use the equipment until he has received adequate instruction in its operation

13. If after completing an accident report you discover an additional piece of information which may influence the conclusions drawn from the report you should

    (A) ignore the information because the report has already been completed
    (B) rewrite the report including the additional information you have discovered
    (C) submit the original report and wait to see if the additional information is pertinent
    (D) ask the injured worker if he thinks it should be included in the accident report

14. When a veteran worker with a clean safety record suddenly becomes involved in a series of work accidents it would be wise for the supervisor to *first*

    (A) retrain the employee in safety procedures
    (B) discipline the employee
    (C) try to discover the cause of the accidents
    (D) transfer the employee to another unit

Answer Key

1. A	4. D	7. C	10. A	13. B
2. C	5. C	8. D	11. A	14. C
3. B	6. D	9. B	12. D	

Explanatory Answers

1. **(A)** The new worker has demonstrated that he may not yet be familiar with all of the safety aspects of his duties. This is the time to give him additional training and observe how he responds.

2. **(C)** There is nothing in the question to make one believe this worker is a malingerer. It is reasonable for the supervisor to grant her request.

3. **(B)** This employee is disregarding specific instructions given to him by his supervisor. He should be disciplined immediately before he becomes involved in an accident. Once he has, it will be too late.

4. **(D)** There is no point in delaying the correction of a subordinate who is performing his duties in an unsafe manner. He may fall victim to an accident in the meantime. The worker should be corrected immediately.

5. **(C)** Accident reports should be prepared promptly because the facts will still be fresh in the mind of the reporter and he will be less likely to omit important items.

6. **(D)** Often those closest to the actual work will see things in a job the supervisor will overlook. The supervisor should always keep an open mind to suggestions from her subordinates.

7. **(C)** It would be proper for you to talk to her supervisor first. Both the worker and the supervisor may resent any direct contact you may have with the worker because she is not actually responsible to you.

8. **(D)** In this situation all formalities should be abandoned. Your first action would be to render any immediate help to the victim that you can.

9. **(B)** If a file cabinet is loaded from the top down, it will topple forward when the top drawer is opened all the way. This is a common cause of office accidents.

10. **(A)** When this method is used, the stress is equally distributed between the back and the legs.

11. **(A)** The use of defective equipment is the cause of many an accident. Unfortunately, caution will not always prevent accidents if dangerous equipment is utilized.

12. **(D)** It is wrong for a worker to use any piece of equipment on which she has not been adequately trained. If the supervisor had wanted her to use the equipment in question, he would have seen that she was trained in its use.

13. **(B)** An incomplete report may become a harmful instrument.

14. **(C)** This veteran employee has demonstrated through long service without accidents that he knows how to work safely. Obviously something is bothering him; it is the supervisor's job to discover what it is.